THE RACE

THE RACE

The inside track on the ruthless world of elite athletics

DAVID GILLICK

WITH CATHAL DENNEHY

Gill Books

Gill Books
Hume Avenue
Park West
Dublin 12
www.gillbooks.ie

Gill Books is an imprint of M.H. Gill and Co.

© David Gillick 2025

978 18045 8418 7

Designed origination by Typo•glyphix, Burton-on-Trent DE14 3HE
Edited by Noel O Regan
Proofread by Jessica Spencer
Printed and bound in the UK using 100% renewable electricity at
CPI Group (UK) Ltd
This book is typeset in Minion Pro by
Palimpsest Book Production Ltd, Falkirk, Stirlingshire

*The paper used in this book comes from the wood pulp
of sustainably managed forests.*

All rights reserved.
No part of this publication may be copied, reproduced or transmitted in
any form or by any means, without written permission of the publishers.

*To the best of our knowledge, this book complies in full with the requirements
of the General Product Safety Regulation (GPSR). For further information
and help with any safety queries, please contact us at productsafety@gill.ie.*

A CIP catalogue record for this book is available from the British Library.

5 4 3 2 1

For Charlotte, Oscar, Olivia and Louis

'A goal without a plan is just a wish.'
Antoine de Saint-Exupéry

CONTENTS

Prologue — 1

Chapter 1	On Your Marks	9
Chapter 2	Cool Runnings	29
Chapter 3	Changing the Numbers	37
Chapter 4	'Ireland? Where's That?'	46
Chapter 5	The Chicken on the Plate	61
Chapter 6	Mind Games	78
Chapter 7	Going Pro	99
Chapter 8	Climbing the Ladder	119
Chapter 9	The Toothpaste Incident	137
Chapter 10	'Just Fucking Run'	163
Chapter 11	Unsportsmanlike Behaviour	185
Chapter 12	The Burger Incident	203
Chapter 13	Lost in Translation	221
Chapter 14	The Mattress Incident	244
Chapter 15	Into the Void	267
Chapter 16	The Aftermath	284
Chapter 17	Behind the Lens	296

Acknowledgements — 310

PROLOGUE

It can be lethal, the silence.

It's there when you finish your career and step into that vacant, terrifying void. It's there when you get injured and suddenly no one seems to care. But it's also there on the biggest stage in athletics, minutes before you walk out into a packed stadium.

Welcome to the call room, where it's just you and your rivals, cramped together like caged animals. No race is ever won in a call room but, trust me, many of them are lost there, with time to think – or overthink – all that's about to unfold. There are no phones allowed in the call room, no music, nothing to distract you from the hundreds of thoughts fizzing through your anxious mind. There are no coaches or team managers or support staff. It's just you and your rivals, sitting around, avoiding eye contact. Waiting.

The minutes tick by in slow motion. You hear the occasional roar from outside, an eruption from tens of thousands of fans as a high jumper or pole-vaulter either clears or knocks the bar. Success or failure. Soon, that would be me, with a strict, objective line dividing everything I wanted and everything I feared. The most important 44 seconds of my career were just minutes away: the 2009 world 400 metres final in Berlin.

In truth, there are two call rooms at major championships. The first is at the edge of the warm-up track. As you go through your drills, stretches and strides, you hear the summoning calls blast over the PA.

'Men's 400 metres, fifteen minutes.'

'Men's 400 metres, last call.'

So you grab your stuff, say goodbye to your coach, then walk in there, alone.

The first call room is usually a large tented structure, with chairs arranged in rows. You go up to a desk and they tick your name off the list. You're still in your tracksuit and runners at that point, as you take a seat alongside your rivals. Soon an official walks over, checks your bag for electronics. Once everyone is assembled, they lead you into the stadium, sometimes in a golf cart, other times by walking in line behind an official, like kids on a school tour.

Call room two is always in the stadium, alongside the track. That's where they check your numbers, your footwear, your kit. Any oversized logos are taped over, given that there are strict rules governing the number and size of logos allowed on your kit. Then you lace up your spikes and, mentally, start to turn a corner. It's almost go-time.

PROLOGUE

But first you must sit there and wait. Maybe 10 minutes. Maybe 20. All call rooms, all championships, are slightly different. No one enjoys that time. But some hate it more than others.

Nerves can do strange things to the body. So do large amounts of caffeine or sodium bicarbonate. The toilet is always in high demand. 'Getting light', as we call it. Some athletes will sit in silence with their heads bowed. Others will grunt, slap themselves, prowling around like raging bulls, desperate for release.

Sometimes there's a small strip of track, so you can stay active. Other times there isn't, and all you can do is sit and wait and think, trying not to let your mind sabotage your body.

In Berlin, ahead of the world final, I wore sunglasses. Not to protect against the glare of the lights outside or to look cool, but so my rivals couldn't see my eyes in that call room. In a place where you can feel so nervous, so vulnerable, that was a protective visor.

As I sat there, I pictured a feather resting on my nose, a trick I'd often use to centre myself and block out all around me. Nothing else mattered but that fictitious feather and calming my breathing so I wouldn't dislodge it.

Some athletes are big talkers in the call room, trying to distract themselves. Others hate chatting. I was the latter, usually sitting in silence, closing my eyes, running the race one last time in my head.

It was so quiet in Berlin, so still, so awkward. You're getting up, sitting down, bumping into rivals. 'Oops, sorry, mate.' Ahead of my 400 metres heat, a few days earlier, the silence had been broken by one of my rivals letting rip a massive fart. It felt like I was back at school – doing that somewhere you shouldn't – so I burst out laughing. But no one else reacted, my rivals too caught up in the tension. It sounds stupid, but I knew in that moment, with that laugh, that I was in the right headspace: calm, relaxed, centred – just how you want to be.

For a long time, it hadn't been like this. But in Berlin I felt no fear, just excitement. I'd been waiting long enough to race the world final. Not just in my career, but also on the night itself.

It had been a beautiful, sunny day, but as night started to fall, an ominous cluster of thick, dark clouds loomed on the horizon. The 400 metres was the last race of the night and by the time I got to the warm-up track – usually a busy, chaotic place – we had it almost to ourselves. I was going through my warm-up when the Irish team manager, Patsy McGonagle, came over. 'They're forecasting thunder. They're going to delay everything.'

Fuck. I just want to get this out of the way.

I took shelter in the Irish tent, lay on the physio bed and tried to switch off my mind. But the race wouldn't stop running through my head. Then some doubts crept in. I looked at my watch, annoyed I was knee-deep in this process when, by this stage, it should have been all over. I went to the bathroom, sat on the toilet and spoke to myself.

David, no matter what, the world will keep spinning. Whatever happens tonight, there's people who'll get up

PROLOGUE

tomorrow and not know who the fuck you are. You're in good shape, you deserve to be here. Get over yourself, get out there and run.

An hour or so later, they set us free from the call room, out into the daunting, vast openness of the Olympic Stadium. What struck me first was the colour of the track: a rich, deep, brilliant blue. My heat had been in the morning, my semi-final in the early evening – both in daylight – so this was my first time seeing it under lights. I thought about the history of this place: the same stadium where Jesse Owens sprinted to Olympic gold in 1936, watched on by Adolf Hitler.

In 2009, I was studying sports management and one of my textbooks had a picture of this stadium, which I looked at in class every day. Now I was here, about to race a world final – something very few Irish sprinters had done.

We walked out on the track midway up the back straight. In previous rounds, we'd taken a left turn to head to the start, but this night, for some reason, they turned us right, leading us the long way around. I heard my name shouted from the stands but avoided looking up. It felt like the longest walk of my life.

When we reached the start, we had several minutes to set up our starting blocks and do some practice runs. I was drawn in lane two, with the two previous Olympic 400 metres champions – LaShawn Merritt and Jeremy Wariner – in four and six.

Both of those US stars had been quiet, subdued, in the

call room, but something changed in Merritt once he got on the track. Suddenly, he had this giant smile, flashing a big, toothy grin. He walked around, high-fiving everyone. His energy levels went through the roof. Maybe it was a tactic to get inside our heads. If so, the fact it stayed with me shows that it worked. Maybe he was subtly putting us down.

I'm so confident I'm gonna beat the shit out of you, I'm gonna walk around high-fiving you.

Or maybe that's just what he always did, flicking a switch when the time was right. It didn't feel like he was doing it in a negative way, just that he was buzzing to get going. Me? I'd never high-five my rivals before a race. It just wasn't my style.

In time, given what transpired, I'd look back differently on Merritt's behaviour. A few months after that final, my training partner called me and dropped a bombshell: 'Did you hear Merritt got done for drugs?'

I was shocked. It turned out that he had tested positive for an anabolic steroid, DHEA, which Merritt claimed he ingested through an over-the-counter penis-enlargement supplement. Yes, really. He got a 21-month doping ban but was able to keep his Olympic and world titles, given his positive test came after those races. When the news broke, I thought back to the moments before that final.

Of course he was high-fiving everyone. He knew he wouldn't get beaten.

I thought about him walking up, with his million-dollar smile, and shaking my hand. Suddenly it felt different – hollow.

PROLOGUE

You're a fucking cheat and you're prancing around, wishing everyone good luck.

At the time, of course, that didn't enter my mind. I was focused only on nailing a great performance. One of the things I had long wanted was to get an Irish vest to a sprint final, but I didn't want to get there and then trail in at the back. I wanted a medal. And I knew I could get one. Wariner and Merritt looked a cut above the field, but after that it was wide open. I told myself all the right things in those final minutes.

This is where I want to be. This is an opportunity.

I set up my blocks, did some starts, and if I spotted something in my lane, like a pebble, I'd kick it into someone else's. People might have thought I was an arsehole, but elite sport breeds a sort of selfishness.

I again heard some Irish voices raining down.

'Come on, Gillick!'

'Come on, Ireland!'

I felt good, fast, calm. Then my tranquillity was broken by an official.

'Tracksuits off!'

I handed my gear to the kid holding my kit basket and said a little prayer as I stood behind my blocks, the noise of the crowd descending into a deathly silence.

'On your marks.'

In my head, I repeated the same thing.

The dynamite is lit, the dynamite is lit.

I jumped up, then settled into the blocks. I pushed hard on each pad, making sure they were stable, then took a couple of slow, deep breaths.

THE RACE

Silence.

My mind went blank, which is how you know you're properly focused. Once the gun fired, instinct would take over and I'd press play on a process I'd rehearsed thousands of times, focusing only on my first few steps. *Run through that wall in the first five metres.* After that, the race would flash by in a frantic blur of noise, lights and adrenaline – 44 seconds which, regardless of how they went, would stay with me forever.

Through much of my career, before big races, my old coach Jim Kidd told me, 'You've got a ticket to the ball, now go and dance.' I had done everything right in 2009, and as I crouched in those blocks, waiting for that gun, I knew I was more ready than ever.

It's time to dance.

CHAPTER 1

ON YOUR MARKS

The first race I ever ran was against a car.

Growing up in Ballinteer, on the southside of Dublin, our local shop was about 500 metres from my house. The challenge was always: how fast can you run down and back? One day, as I was hurtling along the footpath, a car passed by, driven by a guy in his twenties with long hair.

So I picked up the pace, chasing it down. When I drew alongside, the driver looked over, surprised, then went a little faster. Challenge accepted. I started to sprint, all out, and drew level just before I swung a left turn into our estate – content, as I arrived home, that I hadn't been beaten.

I was a hyperactive kid. At family functions, I was the one wired on sugary drinks, buzzing around, kicking a ball against the wall. I was the fastest kid in my area, which gave me a certain street cred. When I'd win races at school sports days, or burn someone on the wing in a football match, word spread around the community: 'Gillick is a bomber.'

When I was eight, my friend told me that a boy he knew from school, Paul, was lightning quick. 'Faster than you,' he swore. So one day, Paul came up to our area in a flowery shirt and the showdown was set: me versus Paul, on the footpath on our road. I won.

Not long after, word spread that there was another kid, Micko, who had a reputation for speed and who was about to join our school. He played on the same football team as some of my classmates and he'd later become one of my best mates. Another sprint showdown was arranged outside the school, with all our classmates watching. I won that, too.

Despite these successes as a kid, I honestly never dreamed about being an athlete. It was all about soccer. I'd thrash about in the garden, firing the ball around, picturing myself in the Premier League.

My first memory of organised athletics was a schools cross-country race in Marlay Park. I started like a bat out of hell – without a notion what I was doing – and died several slow, painful deaths. Endurance was not my forte.

At Our Lady's National School in Ballinteer, my teacher Olive Horgan used to get us all out running, taking a horde of kids each spring to the Cumann na mBunscol event in Santry. That's where I ran my first track race, over 80 metres. I rocked up to the start in a Judge Dredd T-shirt and sprinted to victory. And so, for the next two years, I wore that same T-shirt for every race, convinced it was key. Those superstitious ways stayed with me into adulthood.

For years, I had to use the same pair of socks for every

race, convinced they were essential because I ran well in them the first time. I'd line up at a European or World Championships with socks riddled with holes. And it went far beyond that.

One time, as a professional, I went to a race in Belgium and arrived at my hotel late at night. The only thing available to eat was pizza. Beggars can't be choosers. The next day, I ran a personal best (PB) and so for years after that, I had to *always* have pizza the night before a race. It wasn't up for debate.

It extended to other areas, too. Like beds. Athletes typically share a twin room on the circuit, and you could be thrown in with anyone. But one big PB after sleeping in the bed nearest the door was all the evidence I needed. At every meeting, I wanted – *needed* – that bed. One time, I arrived late to the hotel and was sharing with a Japanese athlete. I walked in and he was lying down with a towel around him, properly relaxed, in the bed closest to the door. He only had a few words of English but, well, I had to try.

'Are you happy in that bed?' I asked, hoping he'd take the hint.

'Yes, sir,' he said. 'Yes, sir.'

I accepted my fate and hopped into the other bed. The next day, I ran brilliantly. And that was when I decided my superstitions were bullshit.

I was the youngest of four, with two brothers, Tony and John, and a sister, Eileen. Tony was eight years older than me, John was seven, while Eileen was five years my senior. So, it's fair to say I was an accident.

Dad worked nine to five, Monday to Friday, for a wholesale, hardware distribution company. Mum was a nurse, who often worked nights, and was always trying to help others, sometimes to the detriment of herself. That rubbed off on me. Even now, I'd class myself as a yes-man, a people pleaser, a trait that became hard to manage when I had some success in sport. I'd agree to things to the detriment of myself or those close to me. Trust me, it's not always a good thing.

Dad was hard-working, unassuming. One time we got a new car. When I saw it, I immediately hopped up to run and tell Dermot, my best friend who lived next door, but Dad stopped me. 'You don't need to tell them that.' That was Dad. There was no ego, no need to shout from the rooftops about anything you did or achieved.

We weren't well off, but we had everything we needed, my parents making sure all of us understood the value of hard work and money. Mum would save for holidays using a two-litre bottle she kept beside her bed, throwing in 20p, 50p or pound coins whenever she had them.

One day I found it and fleeced it. I went down to the local shop, buying a quarter-pound of apple drops. Later, just before our trip to France, Mum was counting it out and said aloud, 'Ah, I see someone found my stash of money!' I sat there, saying nothing. I never owned up to it (until now), but I was riddled with guilt. It was, after all, money she'd saved so we'd have something to spend on holiday.

As the youngest child, by far, I was at the bottom of the food chain. I'd try to get the seat closest to the TV to have some authority in the living room, but the moment my brothers came in, I was chucked aside. If the channel had to be changed, I was ordered up to do it.

I gravitated towards Mum, which might have been my way of getting attention. Given she worked nights, she'd often be asleep when I came home from school and there might be a note for me: *Boil the ham.* So from a young age, eleven or twelve, I had independence: doing things myself, helping out around the house.

I wasn't lonely, as such, but I was by myself a lot. In my early teens, the rest of the family would often go out and I'd be in the house alone, entertaining myself. At times, it was isolating, but I was always comfortable on my own. Still am. It doesn't faze me. As an athlete, that's a good trait because it's something you have to get used to.

Sport was always in our house. There was no escape from it: on the radio, on TV, in conversations. As the youngest, I was loaded into the back of the car at weekends, off to watch an older sibling's game. My brothers did soccer, GAA and athletics. My sister ran and played basketball. My dad did GAA and tennis. He'd take me along to games and I'd sit courtside, going through horse-racing cards with the guy who ran the courts.

Because of Mum, I grew up largely on the side of basketball courts. She played on the first Irish women's basketball team in 1973 and was recently inducted into the Basketball Ireland hall of fame. She went from player to official to referee, then set up the Dublin Ladies Basketball Board and became president of the association. Long before the term 'women in sport' became a thing, Mum was its very definition.

The first time I got on a plane was to go to the Isle of Man with Mum. She was playing in a tournament and said she'd take me along. I was buzzing. The only issue? I missed a big soccer tournament with my school team: the Snickers five-a-side. Due to my no-show, I got kicked off the team and they went on to win the All-Ireland. I was livid. They had a photograph in the school after, with all the lads in their kit and then me, edited into it in my school GAA jersey. I always looked at that with regret.

When it came to sport, my parents were supportive but never pushy. When I was 10 or 11, I played soccer for one of the two clubs in my area, Leicester Celtic.

Dad picked me up after training one day, but before we left, the manager took him aside. When we were back in the car, he broke the news to me. 'You've been cut from the team.' My world caved in. The manager had told him that I wasn't at the standard they were looking for and suggested to Dad: 'Maybe you should play football with him in the back garden.' The way Dad recounted it, I knew that had got to him.

The following year, I joined the other local team, Broadford Rovers. They played me up front, where my speed was a game-changer: a long ball over the top and I was *on it*. I went on a streak that season, scoring 28 goals, and was waiting for the day when we ran into Leicester

Celtic. I scored a hat-trick. After one of the goals, I ran to the sideline and, like a cheeky little brat, unleashed a sliding 'Klinsmann' celebration at the feet of my old manager. When we arrived home, Dad told my older brother all about it. He's never one to get too emotional, but I could see his deep sense of pride.

One of my best athletics memories was from my final year of primary school: a 4x100m relay in Santry. I was on a team with three classmates and, before the race, I sat on top of a steel shed at Morton Stadium, so nervous I felt sick. The lads on the team were also my friends; I didn't want to let them down. As for the race, I took the baton in front for the final leg, bringing us home to victory. It was brilliant: four friends from the same class beating all the other schools in Dublin.

Dundrum South Dublin (DSD) was the athletics club at the end of our road and my older siblings all ran with them, so I followed suit. It was the brainchild of Liz and Eddie McDonagh, who ran sessions in the sports hall at Ballinteer Community School.

I'd go down there early, play soccer for an hour, before Liz and Eddie showed up around 6.30 p.m. 'Put that ball away!' We paid 20p per session and would do some warm-ups before they set us off running around the area, Eddie following us in the van, leaning out the window and telling us to run faster. Then we'd return to the hall and do relays. Liz would pull out two big mats for the long jump. The variety was fantastic, plus every weekend a bus would be going to Gormanston, Tullamore or Julianstown for races.

THE RACE

I fell in love with the feeling of winning. After each race, a guy would come over and hand out cards corresponding to your finishing position. Every time I got the '1', it was like I'd won a world title. One time, the guy with the cards asked me if I liked Linford Christie, the alpha male of sprinting at the time. Something about the way I'd been striving for the line, eyeballs out, neck straining, made him spot a similarity.

The Cumann na mBunscol was my first big victory. I won it three years in a row: Under-10, Under-11 and Under-12. I also did Community Games, which was where I developed one of my first big rivalries, with Paul Howard, who ran for Blackrock. There was another kid, too – Cormac Kearns – who was my childhood nemesis. I'd turn up for races and scan the crowd, searching for their faces.

Is Paul here?

Is Cormac here?

My first national medal was at the Under-13 All-Ireland's – a bronze over 80 metres. At that age, the nationals felt like the Olympics. I'd put on my best tracksuit, have my hair slicked, knowing I'd see girls from all over the country. But for years after that, I won nothing at national level. I was a skinny little whippet, who didn't develop as fast as my peers.

Thankfully, I had great mentors who kept me in it. In fifth and sixth class, I had Mr McGonagle – Macker – who gave us responsibility, treating us like teenagers instead of kids. He'd get us to set up the sports hall, imprinting lessons about discipline that stayed with us.

One of my best mates, Micko, was a talented footballer. But, like me, he was hot-headed in sport. One day, he was messing around and Macker warned him that if he continued, he'd revoke the football team captaincy. Mick kept messing, so Macker made me captain, demoting Mick to a sub. Mick was like a caged animal on the sideline of our next game – 'Can I go on now?' – but Macker stayed firm, ensuring he learned his lesson.

I was competitive and often boiled over if things didn't go my way. There was one game in particular: I was 12 or 13, playing Gaelic football for Ballinteer St John's on a rainy day in Marlay Park. I wasn't playing well and was growing more and more frustrated when I went over the sideline with the ball. When the ref blew his whistle, I started giving him stick, claiming I hadn't crossed the line. First yellow card. A while later, I was near the ref when he ignored a clear foul on my teammate. I lost the plot.

'You've got a whistle!' I shouted at him. 'What more do you want – a foghorn? Blow the fucking thing.'

He quickly pulled out a red card: 'You're off.'

My dad was on the sideline, watching. He didn't get angry. But his look of disgust spoke volumes. We didn't speak a word on the journey home, but once we arrived, he let me have it.

'Right, you're up to your room, you're grounded. You've let yourself down, you've let your club down and you've let me down. If it was a bad tackle, I might let you away with it. But you can't walk around the pitch acting like that. You're not coming out of that bedroom for the rest of the day.'

THE RACE

That was the only time I was grounded, and I never saw him do that to my brothers or my sister. I spent the day pacing around my room, brooding.

What the fuck do I do now?

But Dad's plan worked. As I sat there, I started to connect the dots. *If I lose the head, I don't play well.*

I was always very vocal on the pitch, but at times my desire to win tipped over into something unhealthy. When we lost, I'd be holding back tears. It mattered so much. But I also loved that: the binary nature of sport, where there has to be a winner and a loser. A loss would eat away at me. It's not a bad thing, once you can control it, and I see it now with my own kids and their teammates. My eldest son, Oscar, is nine and the lads on his team get fired up, emotional. So does Oscar – he is a Gillick, after all – but I'd never try to bleach that out of him.

Sometimes a bit of petulance isn't a bad thing. In sport, you want that bit of grit. It shows something very fundamental: that it matters.

In my childhood, sport was a kind of sanctuary, a place where I felt the best about myself. I had speed, which opened doors across sports, making me an asset. Soccer and Gaelic Games had my heart in my pre-teen years, but I was also winning a rake of medals in athletics – at least up until I turned 13 or 14.

I went to secondary school at St Benildus, Kilmacud, where sport is woven into the fabric of life. I loved it there. As one of our year heads said, 'Lads, these are the times of your lives.' We groaned, but then he told us to 'go home and think how many times you smiled today.' He was right. No matter how monotonous it felt, we always had a laugh.

It was many years before I appreciated how much time and effort the teachers gave us outside of school hours, and how their efforts shaped who we became. We had one teacher, Maurice McMahon, who we called Batman because he always wore a kind of cape. He loved cross-country running and would take us to the Leinster Schools Championships. Batman gave one hell of a pep talk, the raw emotion spilling out in every word. 'Have pride in the crest!' he'd shout, shaking his fist. 'Think about the people who got you here. You're all winners, all battlers!'

In cross-country, there's always a team competition as part of the race, with the sum of the first four finishing positions of your team adding up to an overall points total. The fewer points, the better. 'No matter where you are on that team, whether you're the first or last person, you've got to keep fighting!' Batman would say. 'Whoever's in front of you, even if it's one inch in front, you find it.'

Later, a younger teacher, Oisín McKeown, took us to events and Batman would give him notes to read out before races, the kind that'd make the hairs stand on your neck. That was my first time realising athletics is not something trivial. It matters. When I saw an adult with that enthusiasm, how much he wanted it for us, it sparked something.

Oisín had been a student at our school and while I never

had him as a teacher, he became one of those rare mentors who you strive to make proud. My maths teacher, Mr Fitzgerald, was another, speaking to us on a different level: not like a teacher but a friend.

Another abiding memory was winning a Dublin senior schools' title in Gaelic football and our coach, Martin Johnson, looking around the dressing room after the game and telling us: 'Never, ever forget this winning feeling.' I didn't, and I wanted more of it.

For years, we had the same year head, Manus McGowan, who was stern. But down the line, I saw the value in his approach. After my first big international medal as a senior, he was among the first to text me. '*Comhghairdeas, táimid go léir chomh bródúil asat.*' Congratulations, we're all very proud of you.

The school had a great cross-country tradition. Alan McCormack was in my year, for example; a very good distance runner who went on to win a national senior title. I was way down the ladder, number five or six on the team, but even if I wasn't a scoring member I could still contribute, trying to beat one of the scoring athletes on a rival team, adding to their points tally.

I'd usually finish in the fifties or sixties, but our team was winning. That kept me in it, because cross-country is not for the faint of heart. It's a suffer-fest. I remember slogging around a field in Dungarvan, dying a horrible death, only to be the fifth man home for our school.

Another year, we went to Galway for the All-Ireland Schools, which was run around the racecourse in Ballybrit.

They wouldn't have let the horses out that day, given the conditions, but we didn't have much choice.

It was our first trip away as a team and we travelled there the night before, staying in a B & B. The morning of the race, a lady came into the dining room. 'OK, lads, what do you want for breakfast? A full Irish?'

I didn't hesitate in saying yes, a decision I came to regret. As I slogged three and a half kilometres around the racecourse, ankle-deep in mud, my stomach churning, all I could taste were those bacon rashers. I was retching as I was running, then puked everywhere after, having run like a sack of potatoes. As a team, however, we won bronze medals.

If I wasn't part of a team that was doing well, that rasher-induced nausea would probably have caused me to quit there and then.

In my teenage years, I was a bit lost. I was a sheep, flocking with other people, doing what they did instead of what I really wanted. Lots of teenagers get caught in that trap, lacking the confidence to be their true selves, unsure who they really are.

One time at school, our guidance counsellor, Mr Kirrane, got us to do an exercise, filling out questionnaires. One of the questions: 'Are you interested in having a girlfriend? If you had one, what would resonate more with you: going to the pub or going for a walk?' The other kids were like, 'Who the fuck would want to go for a walk?' And so, of course, I opted for the pub answer. But, in truth, I'd have much preferred the second option: the quieter aspect of being with someone you like with no one else around.

I just wanted to be one of the gang – to be popular. I was so aware of what I'd say or how I'd act for fear of people thinking I was a fool. I'd suppress myself, trying to fit in. It stemmed from not feeling confident in my own skin.

I don't know why I wasn't. I wasn't bullied. But maybe it went back to growing up as the youngest, by far, in a busy household, where sometimes you're not getting the attention you want. Success in sport is so much about having belief, but I struggled with that in school, and in life, unable to convince myself I could be any good. I was always hard on myself, always focusing on the negative, and many times I'd talk myself out of a good performance on the start line.

Any boy that was bigger. *Well, he's going to beat me.*

Any kid with fancy racing spikes. *He must be faster.*

In my teenage years, one of the star names in Irish sprinting was David McCarthy, who we called 'Big Red' due to his ginger hair. He was a tall, strong, explosive athlete from Kildare who'd later become my international teammate. When we were 14 or 15, he towered above me. It was like a man against boys. He'd grunt as he warmed up, which intimidated the hell out of me. Instead of focusing on myself, I was worrying about him.

That approach filtered into life outside sport. I was always looking at my peers, trying to mould myself into that person who'd be popular, a guy who could make people laugh, who all the girls liked, instead of just accepting that I am who I am.

Decades later, when I took part in *Celebrity Hell Week*, an RTÉ show that put contestants through a week of physical, mental and emotional turmoil, one of the Special Forces directors told me, 'Even in high-pressured situations, you're hyper-aware of your surroundings.' From their perspective, that was a great thing: a valuable tool in a conflict zone. But in athletics, it wasn't.

I'd study my rivals, looking at what spikes, shorts or even jewellery they had. Even as a professional, I'd often be in fantastic shape but turn up on the start line, look over at some guy from Jamaica, and talk myself into a defeat. *Well, he has to be good.*

Has to be.

These days, people ask if I'd like my children to grow up to be sportspeople. Of course, but the thing I want most is for them to be comfortable in their own skin, to be happy and make their own decisions based on what they want to do – to trust their gut and back themselves. Whatever route they choose is fine by me, but I'd love for them to *not* be like I was as a teenager, feeling like I was always acting, trying to play the part of someone else.

I wasn't a golden child, but I wasn't a troublemaker either. Being the youngest, there was an element of freedom and trust involved. I didn't cause problems at school so there was no reason for my parents not to give me that. They'd have liked for me to work harder, of course, but I did OK.

Despite being a decent athlete, I didn't live an ascetic life. I'd go drinking with my friends on Friday nights then show up for training the next morning. We'd wait in a laneway by an off-licence and approach adults, asking them to buy us beer: six cans of Dutch Gold for a fiver. Then we'd leg it up to a farmer's field where all the young lads and girls from the area would assemble, boozing up before we hit the teenage disco at Wesley Rugby Club.

We were always sketchy of the Guards and so we made sure to drink about 200 metres from the road, giving us an early-warning sign once they showed up. That's when my speed came in handy. At the first sight of blue, we'd leg it. I'd be gone at first sight, the lads trying to keep up.

My parents probably knew that was going on but it was harmless enough; I never got dragged home by police. One bank holiday weekend when I was around 15, I'd been out drinking cider all afternoon and landed home drunk. I disguised it well, telling my mum I was going to my room to study. I collapsed into bed, fell asleep, before coming down a few hours later for dinner.

'Were you studying away up there?' asked Mum.

'Yeah, yeah,' I said.

'Well, I popped my head in, and you were fast asleep.'

I look back at my teenage years and think it was a good thing that athletics didn't take over my life. It helped me have a long-term career. So many talented kids get caught up with early specialisation, and I see that now, following my own kids. You go to a race or a match and see parents on the sideline whose whole world revolves around their kids' achievements. You wonder if they're giving them space to have a normal, fun childhood.

In our club, we had a slew of athletes who smashed underage records, but I'd often wonder: Is that what you need to do? To me, their lives didn't look fun. Fast forward 10 years and, sure enough, most of those prodigies had nothing to do with the sport.

I was lucky. My parents were relaxed: in sport and in life. If I was out with friends, I just had to be home by 10 p.m. They were never vocal on the sidelines; they were always great taxi drivers, ferrying me everywhere I needed, and I never felt I had to do sport to keep them happy.

Up until fifth year in school, I saw athletics as something that sharpened me up for what mattered most: team sports. But then something began to shift. I was playing a lot of Gaelic football, and we had a strong team, but there was one training session when the coach came over and said, 'Jesus, the speed of you.' I'd gone through a growth spurt and, suddenly, I had so much more pace – *Gillick is a bomber* – and the fitness to run all day. Athletics started taking centre stage. I won my first national gold medal at the age of 16: the Irish Schools' intermediate boys' 400 metres hurdles title.

As I progressed, Jim Kidd, the lead sprints coach at DSD, took over my coaching. He's from Glasgow and had moved to Ireland many years before with his wife, Patricia. He had that bit of Scottish gruffness, that brilliant bluntness. For most of my teenage years, we called him Mr Kidd – not sure why, we just did – but as I got older, that became Jim.

As a former sprinter, he understood the delicate balance you need to strike as a 400 metres runner between speed and endurance. He knew I was coming from an over-distance, endurance background, but he understood how to marry that with my natural speed to get the best out of me over 400 metres.

That was hard within the club. Eddie was the head coach and believed in running lots of miles, trying to mould me into an 800 metres runner. Jim had a sprinter's mindset, however, and saw my future in the 400 metres, and so Lucy Moore worked alongside him on the technical and conditioning side.

There was tension at training. I was making inroads and Eddie wanted to have a role in my career, but his philosophy and Jim's were very different. It came to a head at the track one Wednesday evening before the track season. We'd switched from doing hills on the grass through the winter to doing speed work on the track. I was warming up, getting ready to do a session with Jim, when Eddie pulled in in his van and went berserk. He and Jim had a massive row, Eddie demanding that we go up to do our hills. Off we went to do them, against Jim's wishes. They had very different approaches but given my goals and my profile, Jim was a natural fit as my coach. I went with him.

I never made any internationals as a schoolboy, but I would look on with envy at those who did. One day, Alan McCormack rocked into training in his Irish kit and as I was admiring it, another athlete who'd made an international said he'd sell me an Irish vest. I agreed. But then someone said, 'Why would you want to buy that? You have to earn it.' He was right, but that was never on the cards for me. I just wasn't good enough.

But in my late teens, things started to change. A year after winning the Irish schools' intermediate 400 metres hurdles title, I finished second in the senior 400 metres. A year after that, in my final year, I won the senior boys' 400 metres, clocking 48.54 seconds, equalling the schools' record at the time. Still, that was over three seconds slower than the best teenagers were running elsewhere in the world.

Leaving school, I had no idea what to do with my life. During my final year, I had a meeting with a career guidance teacher who asked me if I'd consider a sports scholarship to University College Dublin (UCD). I was thinking GAA but he said, 'What about athletics?' Until then, it had never even entered my mind.

I was like many students as they reach that crossroads: lost. I liked elements of science and so, in the end, I chose to study that at UCD. They offered me a half scholarship for athletics, worth about €1500, but the catch was that I would have to leave DSD and represent UCD in all club competitions. I felt I was worth a bit more than that, given my potential, and decided to turn it down.

My parents wanted me to take it, but I didn't see why I should jump through hoops for such meagre support. I didn't even chat to Jim about it, I just walked into the office of the UCD Director of Sport, Brian Mullins, and told him I wasn't taking it. I was half-dreading his reaction, as he was a hulk of a man. He muddled around the desk for a few moments before eventually saying, 'I think you're making a big mistake.'

'We'll have to wait and see,' I told him.

From my first day at UCD, in September 2001, I was overwhelmed. It was such a vast campus and the fact that I didn't do chemistry for my Leaving Cert meant I struggled in class. There'd be hundreds in the lecture hall and, not wanting to stand out, I never put up my hand to ask for explanations.

I did one year there and failed two exams: chemistry and computer science. As I was weighing up the option of repeats in the summer, I told Mum, 'I'm not enjoying this, I'm struggling. What's the point of doing the re-sit?' I re-filled out the CAO form, switching to business at the Dublin Institute of Technology (DIT), where I was much happier. It was a cosier campus, with smaller classrooms that suited me much better.

The summer before I started at DIT, the big event was the World Junior Championships. To qualify for it, I had to run 48.00 seconds for 400 metres. I just missed out, running 48.48 just before the deadline. But there was a big silver lining: Ireland was sending a team in the men's 4x400m relay. I got a call-up, and was soon packing my bags for Kingston, Jamaica, where I'd represent Ireland for the first time and race the fastest teenagers in the world.

One of those who was also making his major championship debut there? A tall, gangly 15 year old who many experts were hyping as a potential superstar. I didn't know much about him, but he certainly had a great name for a sprinter: Usain Bolt.

CHAPTER 2

COOL RUNNINGS

The first thing that hit me was the smell. Every track has a very distinctive scent and in high summer that tartan surface seems to soak up the heat and breathe its essence right back at you. It's a slightly toxic smell – sort of like burning rubber – and it invaded my nostrils the moment I set foot on the red track at the national stadium in Kingston.

It was a vast, rickety place, with flecking paint on the walls and rusted hinges on the gates. There was no roof, no individual seating, just rows and rows of benches that would soon be thronged by tens of thousands of fans.

It's hard to overstate how much of a religion athletics is in Jamaica, specifically sprinting, where this tiny country with under three million people goes toe to toe with the biggest athletics superpower, the US, which has over a hundred times the population and infinitely better resources.

For any aspiring Olympian, the 'World Juniors' are a crucial pit stop. They take place every two years and bring together about 1500 of the world's best teenage athletes from around 160 nations. Many youngsters can coast along in their teenage years, being a big fish in a small pond, but at the World Juniors, you get tossed overboard into a huge ocean of outlying talent. Sink or swim. It's where athletes learn, via those objective numbers on the clock, just how vicious the standard is in this global sport.

For athletics, World Juniors is the great exposition of future stars. Retrace the steps of most champions to their teenage years and you'll find the majority competed there, from Mondo Duplantis to Noah Lyles, Faith Kipyegon to Jakob Ingebrigtsen. Not every one of them was a champion – Ingebrigtsen, despite being the ultimate child prodigy, only won silver and bronze – but it's where countless stars first announce their ability to the world.

As a result, it's also a huge shop window for emerging talent, with representatives from the leading professional management companies all loitering around, trying to sign up the next big thing. So too are hordes of coaches from the US collegiate system, the National Collegiate Athletic Association (NCAA), trying to lure kids to their universities with a scholarship which, when tuition, travel, accommodation and other costs are factored in, is worth around $300,000 across four years.

Some promising careers get derailed at World Juniors, with many realising just how far they are behind their international peers. Athletes learn just how difficult it'll be to earn a living from the sport or realise their childhood dream of being an Olympic champion is starting to look like delusion. But many more dreams are emboldened: the medallists earning the support they need to graduate to the next level, with most of the others inspired to believe that the dream is worth chasing, still within reach.

One of the best parts of the 2002 World Juniors occurred before I even left for Jamaica: picking up my kit. I was like a kid on Christmas when I got back to my house after the visit to Athletics Ireland's offices, laying all the Irish gear out in the front room and calling in Mum and Dad. It started to hit home then: *I'm going to represent my country.*

Our team assembled at Dublin Airport, then flew to London before boarding a plane to Kingston. We were staying in student accommodation at the local university where we all had single rooms – a rarity in athletics.

The halls in the dorms had concrete floors and, every morning, I'd hear a door swing open, with the echo of footsteps down the corridor, followed by a knock. It was Bill Cuddihy, the Irish team doctor, looking for a urine sample to check our dehydration levels. It was roasting in Kingston, humid and sweaty – far from ideal for the Irish.

At a championship, the days pass slowly, with nervous energy bubbling up a little more as your race draws near. It's a strange set-up. Suddenly you become best friends with people you'd never met, living in each other's pockets.

That Irish team had some great characters. Darragh Graham would blast 'Ireland's Call' in the dorms, over and over, while two of the chief messers were Thomas Chamney and Liam Reale. One day in the dining hall, they landed over to our table with an athlete from some small African country, whose name I've long forgotten. The chap didn't have any team tracksuit but was wearing an Ireland T-shirt from the USA '94 World Cup, the kind you'd buy in Penneys. In the eight years since that tournament, it had obviously found its way into a second-hand clothes market in Africa, and our new mate – who joined us for lunch – was putting it to use in Kingston.

Before the championships, we raced a pre-event at the stadium, a meeting put on so organisers can make sure everything is working well. I ran a 400 metres and was in rag order after it, laying on my back with my feet burning, feeling like I was suffocating as I tried to suck in some oxygen from the hot, humid air. It was like racing in a greenhouse.

Having never been to even a Schools' International, it was overwhelming to see the variety of nationalities, a kaleidoscope of colourful tracksuits. It was my first time getting a little starstruck. I sat on the bus to the stadium as all the Americans got on board, including two of the biggest names, Allyson Felix and Sanya Richards-Ross, who both went on to win Olympic titles.

The 4x400m relay wasn't until the end of the week and so we went to the stadium to watch some early action. I stood trackside as Darrel Brown, a 17-year-old Trinidadian sprinter, clocked 10.09 to win the men's 100 metres, and had to pick my jaw off the floor. I'd never seen someone run so fast in the flesh. It was so different to seeing it on TV; he'd glided so effortlessly, so gracefully, across the track.

The 4x400m was on the Sunday, but the race most

Jamaicans were waiting for was the night before: the men's 200 metres final. In the heats, Usain Bolt had set an age-15 world best of 20.58, and with so much talk about his talent, a nation expected – *demanded* – gold.

I was literally speechless the moment I walked into the stadium, which was rocking, with hordes of fans climbing over gates to find a way in. There was no real law and order. Many fans were wearing their Jamaica football jerseys from 1998, the year they qualified for the World Cup, and shortly before the men's 200 metres, before their star prodigy emerged, the fans started a rhythmic chant, swirling their flags and T-shirts in the air.

'Bolt, Bolt, Bolt, Bolt.'

It felt like the foundations of the old place were shaking.

'Bolt, Bolt, Bolt, Bolt.'

Having experienced the electricity, the chaos, I understand why Bolt later said that nothing in his career – not any of his Olympic finals – ever made him as nervous as that night. You could see it in his face as he stood behind the blocks; he was fidgety, anxious, sweating, looking the complete opposite of the smiling, chilled-out champion the world would come to adore many years later.

Despite being the youngest in the race, Bolt towered over his rivals, but when the gun fired it was clear he was still a diamond in the rough. He ran with his head back, as if someone was tugging his hair from behind, and his sprint mechanics were all over the place. He raced around the bend in third or fourth place. He was long, gangly, awkward, ragged. He didn't look like a natural sprinter, but when you see someone move that fast, with technique so poor, you know he has something special. Once he turned into the straight, he opened his giant stride and left his rivals trailing, crossing the line to win the first global title of many in 20.61 seconds.

As he slowed to a stop, Bolt looked up at the crowd and raised his hand to his forehead, giving an army salute. The crowd erupted, dancing, singing, cheering. It was deafening. We were dancing along with them, a cluster of Irish teenagers in the thick of thousands of Jamaicans, and when we returned to the dorms that night, all of us were thinking the same thing.

What have we just witnessed?

For young, impressionable athletes, experiences like that have a seismic impact. At the time, I'd been juggling Gaelic football with athletics and had yet to choose which one I wanted to pursue. But as I'd stood in that stadium, looking around at that magnificent, intoxicating madness, it became crystal clear.

I'm going home, packing in the GAA, and becoming an athlete.

In the heats of the 4x400m, I was on the first leg and would hand over to Daniel Tobin, with Liam McDermid next and then David McCarthy – Big Red – bringing it home. Before the race, I was painfully nervous. I was overthinking, overanalysing, but having the lads around helped calm me a bit. I tried to stay focused, but this unwanted voice kept barging into my thoughts.

Jesus Christ, this is massive – the biggest race I've ever run.

The environment was overwhelming. There was a cycling track on the outside of the running track, which made the stands look bigger, more ominous, as if we were fighters down on the Colosseum floor.

I gave it everything in the race, but we were nowhere near mixing it with the sprint superpowers. We finished seventh, a long way off making the final.

That night, we did what most athletes do after a season filled with discipline and denial: we went on the lash. We walked down to the reception and asked where we could buy some beer, and they said they'd call us a taxi. Two cars soon pulled up and it could just as easily have been two random people – they might well have been – but we hopped in regardless, asking them to take us to a petrol station.

My car had no suspension and I bounced around the back seat as we drove along the pot-holed streets of Kingston. We bought stacks of beer and the two drivers came drinking with us that night – a great way to say goodbye to what was, for me, a game-changing championships.

When I got home, I hung a souvenir Jamaican towel on my bedroom door, a reminder of the fork in the road I had reached in Kingston and why I was going all-in on athletics.

Jim had never tried to get me to pack in Gaelic football, but I knew – aged 18 – that the time was right. After Kingston, I had more belief in my potential, but I was still a big fish in a small pond.

One night, after nationals in Tullamore, I was out with the DSD crew when the Raheny lads were throwing some good-natured abuse at us, with Feidhlim Kelly, who'd just missed out on qualifying for Kingston over 800 metres, shouting: 'Gillick, you were only there as part of a relay!' He was right. I hadn't reached the standard as an individual. I wanted to go to major championships and line up in the 400 metres.

In Ireland, turning your back on the GAA is not an easy thing to do, but I knew it had to happen. Kingston was all the proof I needed of where athletics could take me – even if some saw it as the wrong decision. A couple of years later, I had my twenty-first birthday party at the local GAA club and Jim told me a story that summed up the insular attitude among some in Gaelic Games.

By then, I had run for Ireland at the World Championships as a senior, but that didn't matter much to one of the Gaelic football coaches, who'd asked Jim, deadly serious: 'Why is he going off and doing this running stuff? He could play for Dublin one day.'

CHAPTER 3

CHANGING THE NUMBERS

Heading into 2003, with my focus fully on athletics, I started ramping things up in training. A bit too much. Early that year, I got a stress fracture in my tibia and couldn't run for three months.

I'd never had a serious injury before, but Lucy was great, giving me things to do to keep active, like aqua-jogging. It was a setback, but I knew the bone would heal and I kept telling myself that I was a late developer, that I had only scratched the surface of my potential.

I got back racing in June and after a mediocre season opener over 400 metres, I surprised myself, clocking a huge PB of 46.80 seconds. That booked my place at the European Under-23 Championships in Bydgoszcz, Poland – my chief goal for the summer. But it also put me in contention for a spot on the Irish senior 4x400m team for a far bigger event: the World Championships in Paris.

THE RACE

I went to Poland dreaming big, believing I could make the final. But it turned into a nightmare.

In my heat, I was drawn on the outside lane, which most 400 metres athletes hate. Yes, it's a gentler curve so it's not as tricky as the inside lanes, but the issue is you're running blind, unable to gauge what your competitors are doing or how fast you're going. Meanwhile, they're using you to gauge their efforts, preparing to pick you off on the last turn.

The European Under-23s were my first championship as an individual, and I learned there's a big difference between running with a team and running alone. I bottled it. I choked. Warming up, my head wasn't in it. I had never done any work in sports psychology and it showed. I was doubting myself constantly.

Am I good enough?

Fuck, just get this over with.

Nerves can be useful at times, once they're kept in check, but this was something more: outright panic, which left me unable to focus. In the races I nailed in my career, I always had some nervous tension, but there was also a clarity about what exactly I was going to do.

Bydgoszcz was different. It was the first time nerves caused me to self-destruct. When I didn't feel present, in control, I'd develop a lethargic, heavy feeling. I'd do some block starts. *No power. The batteries are flat.* When nerves grab a hold of you like that, it's suffocating. You're helpless. It builds and it builds and reaches a point where you start to feel apathy about the race. The nerves actually disappear and you feel drained, defeated, before it even begins.

Just get it done. No one cares.

When the gun fired, I had a mediocre start and then watched, helpless, as athletes charged past me on my left. Around the last turn, I basically packed it in, trailing home eighth – and last – in an embarrassing 47.67 seconds. I was devastated. I wanted to crawl in a hole and hide. What made it worse was that, in another heat, Big Red had risen to the occasion, running a PB to make the 400 metres final, where he finished sixth. That only heightened my sense of failure.

How did Gillick do?

Oh, he shat the bed.

Thankfully, there was another, bigger event approaching to get it out of my mind. But to make the relay team for the World Championships, I had to perform at nationals, which served as a trial race. I did just that, finishing second in 47.13, and was selected for the relay – my first step on to the sport's big stage.

Going to Paris, I was like a starry-eyed child: just 20 years old and part of the Irish team alongside Sonia O'Sullivan and a slew of other Olympians.

Paul McKee was the big name on our relay team, having won world indoor bronze in the 400 metres earlier that year. I'd never met him but got to know him after arriving in the French capital. One day, I went into his room and saw his gear bag open and he had a sticker with his name on its inside panel – the sticker given to athletes to wear on their tracksuit for medal ceremonies. I was in awe when I saw it.

This guy is a world medallist.

Thankfully, he was also sound, good craic and down to earth.

We stayed in student dorms and I was sharing a room with Paul Opperman, an Olympian in Sydney 2000 and an ideal man to be around in a high-pressured environment: he was laid back, funny and a clubmate of mine at DSD. He took me under his wing, introducing me to everyone, telling me how it all worked at major events. Walking around in our Irish gear, people would stop us and ask us if Sonia was running – the one Irish athlete known to everyone in athletics.

I'd never met Sonia and I hoped to do so in Paris, but she didn't stay with the team – one of my earliest indications that there are very different levels to this sport. She had won world titles, set world records and could afford for no expense to be spared when it came to ensuring that her preparation was on point for major events. Her fame was also on a level where she'd likely be hounded for autographs by other athletes if she was staying among a couple of thousand less accomplished athletes.

On the track and off it, she was in a different sphere to the rest of us.

The training track in Paris was in Stade Charléty. In my first session there, I looked around at stars who I'd only ever seen on TV and felt like a rabbit in headlights. I was timid, fitting around others, nervously asking permission to use a lane. *Should I even be here?* But Big Red, who was the same age as me, showed me the way forward. He did a time trial and strutted out on to the track, not caring who was around. He owned the space, walking tall, head up, chest out.

Before our race, there was an awful lot of downtime. We'd sit around in the food hall or chill out in the games room, chatting for hours. In one of those moments, I came to understand just how important your personal best was in athletics.

That PB number – your fastest time – is worn like identification, gauging your social currency. If it's 47 seconds, people don't pay much attention. They won't care how you train or what you eat or how you warm up. But if it's 43 seconds, it's very different. For guys like that, every rep at the warm-up track will have eyes watching, stopwatches clicking. Every opinion they offer on training or racing is listened to attentively.

One day, a group of us were hanging out in the common area and among them was Irish sprinter Karen Shinkins and her then boyfriend, now husband, Paul Doyle – an American who's one of the sport's top agents. Someone came in who I didn't know but Doyle did, and he went around introducing the Irish athletes to them: first the name, then the number.

'This is David McCarthy, a 46.6 man indoors.'

Meanwhile, I was sitting there, thinking, *I'm nowhere*

near that. I'm irrelevant. It didn't really matter what your name was; what mattered was how *fast* you were. If I wanted status, then I had to change those all-important numbers.

I got on great with the Irish team. Karen and Derval O'Rourke used to take the piss out of my diet, calling me 'The Carb King', as I'd load up my plate with pasta at every meal. I hadn't a clue about nutrition at the time.

Given our race was at at the end of the championships – and athletes have free access to a section of the stadium every night – I went to watch the men's 100 metres final, seeing Kim Collins upset the favourites to win from lane one. Looking around a packed Stade de France, I got a vicious jolt of anxiety.

Fuck, I've to race here soon.

On the day of the race, I was shitting it. As I warmed up, I kept looking over at the huge stadium and thinking, *I have to perform.* McKee was leading us off, handing the baton to Gary Ryan, then it was Big Red, then me. I had run with the lads earlier in the summer at the Europa Cup and they gave me some constructive criticism after. 'You got out like an 800 metres runner,' they said, referring to my sluggish start. I listened to every nugget of advice, assured them it wouldn't happen again.

During our warm-up, Paul could see I was nervous and he came over: 'You've had a great season, you deserve to be here.' Coming from him, that meant the world.

I do deserve to be here.

Before we walked out on track, there was plenty of grunting, slapping, psyching each other up, but there was a certain calmness too. The call room was bigger in Paris than I'd ever experienced – with more TVs, more officials – and when I walked out, the Stade de France looked even more colossal than it had from the stands. But it didn't feel daunting, just inspiring.

I didn't want to let anyone down and those first three legs, as I stood waiting for the baton, seemed to last an eternity. At last, Big Red came thundering up the home straight and I was standing, waiting. Part of you wants the baton and another part is like: *Fuck off, give it to somebody else.*

Once I got it, adrenaline took over. I went hell for leather around the bend, all out, and trained my sights on the Russian athlete up ahead. It was only a morning session, but there was such noise ringing around the stadium. I emptied the tank, gave it everything, but couldn't catch the Russian. We finished fifth in 3:04.31, two seconds away from making the final, which is close to 20 metres on the track.

It was a solid run and a positive first experience of the sport's top level. But I was also made aware that there was an awful lot of work to do. I needed to find a few seconds, not just fractions.

At the time, I looked to the professional athletes with envy, wondering how I could join them. When I got selected for Paris, part of me thought I was on the pathway to getting funding, sponsorship – a professional deal with a major brand. But I soon realised that wasn't the case. Not even close.

In Paris, I went for a burger with Joe Rafferty, an Irishman who worked in sports marketing for Nike at the time. Part of his job was to sign athletes to professional deals, deciding how much they were worth. We chatted about various topics and after a while, I plucked up the courage to ask.

'So, is there any chance of a contract?'

'I'd love to,' he said. 'But Dave, you're just not running fast enough. You're only here as part of a relay.'

It was a necessary jolt of reality: just because you're representing your country doesn't mean you'll get sponsored.

By hitting the qualifying standard for the European Under-23s, I got my first bit of support from Athletics Ireland, earning a €4,600 grant for the year, which was paid in quarterly instalments. At the time, you had to expense everything, so at the end of each year I'd be scouring for receipts for physios, flights, shoes or gear, needing to justify every cent.

My 400 metres PB was 46.80, over two seconds down on the world's best. As much as there had been some euphoria in Paris, with friends patting me on the back for making a senior team, I was nowhere near where I needed to be to earn a living from the sport, never mind winning medals.

Gillian O'Sullivan had won Ireland's sole medal in Paris – silver in the 20km race walk – and after the race she landed into the dining hall with it. She probably had no idea who I was, but I sat there in awe of her, trying not to stare at that cherished prize which she had resting on the table.

I wanted one of those, and even though I was a long, long way from getting one, I was ready to start the journey and do whatever it took to give myself a chance.

CHAPTER 4

'IRELAND? WHERE'S THAT?'

To reach the elite level in the 400 metres is to enter a committed, long-term relationship with pain. There's no way around it: you will suffer and suffer greatly.

When Usain Bolt first broke through at senior level, it was over 200 metres, but given his build and his stride length, he was often told that his greatest potential was in the 400 metres. 'A lot of people want me to, but I don't want to,' he said. When asked what put him off, he had a simple response: 'Training. It's very hard.'

Heading into 2004, I understood what he meant. Jim and Lucy began to move the dial in training, seeing what I could take. I started running five or six days a week and hitting the gym a lot more, trekking across the city to do weights under an Australian coach at Dublin City University. Most of our running sessions were in UCD, which had no floodlights on the track, just a dim glow off the lights on the N11, which ran parallel to the back straight.

Lucy would arrive in her little red Ford Fiesta, which was essentially a mobile gym packed with medicine balls, mats and weights. We'd set up on the track and do circuit training no matter how horrible the weather. There was no glamour to it but, really, these were all the facilities we needed. It was rough and ready, and I loved it. Lying on your back, suffering through med-ball exercises on a freezing winter night instils character. It *makes* you as an athlete.

On the track, Jim was also pushing me harder. I'd be dizzy after the last rep of each session, collapsing on the track, retching and writhing around in agony. My nose would tingle, my head splitting, and I'd struggle to stand for several minutes. Across the track were the lads from Dublin City Harriers, who had a load of stars at the time. Their presence spurred me on to work harder, to get better. And I did.

There was a three-mile loop I used to run from my house in Ballinteer down to Dundrum, up to Goatstown and back around through the area. I never used a watch at the time but would just go by feel, glancing up at the clock in the kitchen as I left and again the moment I returned. One day, I looked up and the progress was clear.

Fuck, that's pretty quick.

My first 400 metres of the 2004 indoor season was the AAA Championships in Sheffield, otherwise known as the British indoor nationals, which were also open to competitors from abroad.

THE RACE

The logistics of getting to Sheffield weren't conducive to optimal performance: a late Friday flight, followed by a bus to central Sheffield and then a taxi to the hotel just before midnight. My then girlfriend came along with me.

I ran an indoor PB in my heat, 48.53, but got tripped in my semi-final and stumbled. I was spiked: slashed by the steel pins on the bottom of a rival's shoes. I finished fourth in 48.68, missing out on the final, and had to watch from the stands as my DSD clubmate, Rob Daly, led an Irish one-two, clocking 46.68 ahead of Big Red. Rob threw his arms out in celebration and I was delighted for him, if a little envious. There was great prestige to the 'triple-As'. I wanted to come back and do what he'd done.

The following weekend, I lowered my indoor PB to 47.44 at Irish nationals – changing those numbers – and earned a spot on the Irish men's 4x400m team for the World Indoor Championships in Budapest. It was a similar team to Paris, with Rob Daly competing instead of Paul McKee, alongside Big Red, Gary Ryan and me.

In our heat, only the first two teams would automatically make the final along with two 'fastest losers' – the third- or fourth-placers with the overall quickest times. We ran well, finishing fourth in an Irish record of 3:08.83, then had a nervous wait to see if it was enough. It was.

The final was later that day and we were up against USA, Russia, Jamaica, Bahamas and Switzerland. There was no expectation, no pressure. We were seeded fifth, but the medals looked well out of reach. We thought we could realistically target fourth, and you just never know after that.

The indoor 4x400m, after all, is chaotic, with collisions almost guaranteed as athletes pass the baton, bunched together, with the outgoing runners forced to weave through others who have just handed over. The indoor 400 metres is similar: a true contact sport. With the tight, banked turns on an indoor track, you need your elbows engaged and a kill-or-be-killed mentality.

In the final, I was running the third leg and took the baton from Gary well adrift of the top three: USA, Jamaica and Russia. I passed the Swiss guy, who was probably not very good, and handed over to Big Red in fourth place. But soon disaster struck for the US, their third-leg runner Joe Mendel dropping the baton at the end of his leg. It was picked up by his teammate, Godfrey Herring. They still finished third despite that, with Big Red bringing us home fourth in 3:10.44.

Immediately, people started telling us, 'The Americans will be disqualified.' In relays, the rule is that if someone drops the baton, they must also be the person to retrieve it. The Americans hadn't done that. The incident replayed again and again on the big screen and while it was a clear infraction, we didn't want to tempt fate and start celebrating. USA were soon disqualified but quickly lodged an appeal. Meanwhile, we walked through to the warm-up area and waited, pacing around anxiously, waiting for the final decision.

In athletics, there's no greater difference in finishing positions than the gap between third and fourth. It's the chasm between having your face splashed on the front of newspapers and the whole thing being largely forgotten. It's the difference between having dozens of interview requests and zero. A medal opens doors to funding, sponsorships, endorsements. A fourth-place finish, despite being almost as good, does very little of that. It's also not something you can carry around, showing off in schools or clubs.

Here, take a picture with the … fourth-place finish.

After an hour or more of waiting, the Irish team manager Michael Quinlan came down to us with a verdict: the US had lost the appeal. We were world bronze medallists. 'Fucking yes,' I roared, which drew a few annoyed glances given there was another medal presentation happening at the time.

Soon after, it was our turn to step on the medal podium. We were handed a sticker for our tracksuits – that same one I'd admired in Paul's bag in Paris – and walked behind the rostrum alongside the Jamaican and Russian teams. As bronze medallists, we were called out first and as I stepped up on the podium, I heard one of the Jamaicans say to his teammate: 'Ireland? Where's that?'

I laughed and didn't bother explaining. But it was an indication of just how unknown we were, how against the odds it was for an Irish team to win a medal at a global championships.

The major nations? They didn't respect us: four white guys from a small nation without much sprint history. But in the years that followed, I got used to that, often being the only white guy in the race.

At the time, there was a widespread belief that 'white

'IRELAND? WHERE'S THAT?'

people can't sprint', but Jeremy Wariner helped change that in 2004, the Texan winning the Olympic 400 metres title in Athens. Whatever about the 100 metres or 200 metres, I always thought the 400 metres was an event where Irish athletes – regardless of skin colour or their background – *can* compete. It's one of the few events you'll see most corners of the globe represented in finals, from Africa to Latin America, Europe to Australia.

At the end of the day, athletics is a sport where, if you have a fast time, your nationality or your race doesn't matter. If you have the right number, the fast PB, *that's* what counts. *That's* what earns respect.

But by getting on that podium, we had at least shown lots of young athletes back home that it was possible, that Ireland could compete with big nations. I was thrilled. We all were, scarcely able to believe we'd snatched a world medal despite what was, being honest, a very mediocre time in the final.

'We'll be bound forever by this,' Gary Ryan said, and he was right.

That night, we didn't hold back on the celebrations, heading to the athletes' after-party and enjoying every minute of it. But as we were chatting, laughing, drinking, we spotted Joe Mendel, the American who'd dropped the baton, staring at us.

He looked especially pissed off and kept eyeballing us. I tried not to look back, but I could sense his anger. I felt for him. The poor guy was probably number ten or twelve in the US over 400 metres, given their depth, and then he got a call-up for this – meaning a huge chance at a gold medal – and he drops the baton. He was moping around all night, looking at us with a face of thunder as we celebrated. The lads were convinced it was about to kick off at any moment and tried not to add fuel to the flames, but thankfully it never did.

Back home, the medal got lots of headlines and there was a guy on the radio the next day talking about the significance of an Irish team getting a world medal. That was the moment it hit home – what we'd achieved.

I hoped the exposure might lead to some financial backing, but athletics wasn't consistently part of the news cycle, so that proved a hard leap to make. However, Jim had a contact in the corporate world and made him aware I was on the lookout for opportunities. A while later, he reached out to Jim to see if I'd do a photocall. Jim told me he'd asked for €500, which sounded good to me. But the guy came back, unimpressed. 'Five hundred euro? I can get a GAA player for that.' Jim told him where to go: 'Then go and get a GAA player.'

It was indicative of how athletics was viewed: a fringe sport, where even global medallists were less well known than intercounty GAA players. As a result, nothing really changed after the medal. I did some interviews with the national newspapers, trying to put myself out there, and dropped the hint on TV that I was looking for sponsorship. But nothing came. In truth, no one looked at athletics as an attractive sport to sell. It wasn't rugby, soccer or the

'IRELAND? WHERE'S THAT?'

GAA. Unless you won an Olympic medal, no one was trying to hop on board.

I got back to work, placing that podium sticker on my wall as a reminder of what I was striving towards. It was an Olympic year, but the Athens Games weren't really on my radar. I wasn't running fast enough to qualify for the 400 metres – the qualifying standard was 45.55, over a second quicker than my PB.

Looking back, I ask myself *why* it wasn't on my radar. I wasn't a million miles away from the standard but there was something I lacked: belief in my ability to make that jump. I saw the Olympics as above me when, in reality, they were almost within reach.

There also seemed to be no realistic plan in place to qualify a relay team – though we were scheduled to at least try. To qualify for the relay, we'd have to post two fast times that averaged among the top 16 nations in the world ahead of the qualification deadline, which was just under six weeks before the Olympics began.

Prior to this, I put the head down, looking to the outdoor season. I had a decent start, lowering my PB to 46.57 in Namur, Belgium, in early July. The next day, I flew to Shannon and hopped in a car to go to Cork, where we were making our last attempt at relay qualification for Athens.

But the set-up was amateur, with no proper planning by Athletics Ireland to have us all firing on the day. I had bought beers at the airport in Belgium to bring home – which says a lot about my mindset – and ended up forgetting them on the plane.

As we assembled at the Cork City Sports, we met Dermot Henihan, the Chef de Mission (team manager) for the Irish in Athens. He had a brown envelope that he held aloft. 'I have the papers here, lads. Get this time and you'll be on the flight to Athens.' We did not get the time; it wasn't even close. I watched the Athens Olympics from afar.

For the Irish, it was a dire Olympics, mired in scandal. The only medal we won, by Cian O'Connor in show-jumping, had to be handed back after his horse tested positive for a banned substance. And shortly before the Games began, Irish athletics had a huge doping scandal of its own. I was flying to a race in Hungary when I found out. Derval O'Rourke was also on the plane and, after we landed, she got a text message from someone in the association saying an Irish athlete had failed a drugs test. 'If anyone rings looking for comment, please don't say anything,' they told her.

Derval had no idea who the athlete was, and so we started guessing, with everyone's name getting thrown around. Soon enough, the news broke. It was Cathal Lombard, a distance runner from Cork, who'd tested positive for EPO, a banned blood-boosting drug.

He'd been on the Irish team in Paris but I didn't get to know him there. I knew he'd taken a major step forward in the year or two before but didn't know enough about his background or his event to be suspicious.

Lombard came clean straight away. 'Hands up, I did it,'

'IRELAND? WHERE'S THAT?'

he told the *Irish Examiner*. 'I didn't set out to try and win medals or to make money. I just wanted to be as competitive as I could and have an equal chance.'

I thought back to a media day a few months before at the University of Limerick, where the Olympic federation had brought in a reporter from TV3 to give athletes guidance on interviews. The reporter picked an athlete at random to bring up for a mock interview, and who did he choose? Lombard.

He started off with the usual post-race questions, then threw in a curveball, asking Lombard how he coped with the presence of performance-enhancing drugs in his sport. Lombard nailed the response, saying that all he could do was to focus on himself, that he didn't get caught up in what others might be doing. When the interviewer pressed him with more questions, he had all the right answers. I was sitting beside Rob Daly, who nudged me and whispered, 'Jesus, he's fucking brilliant.' The guy from TV3 was also impressed. 'Excellent answers,' he said.

When Lombard got busted, I thought back to that moment. *That fucker had it all planned.* He knew his day of reckoning was coming. He had stood before us, his teammates, and was so confident, so polished, so articulate. He had the answers clear in his head long before that moment so that if he was ever challenged about his improvement, he'd be ready.

I had heard some people in Irish distance running whispering about Lombard here and there, but the news still shocked me.

We're not like that. We don't cheat.

For some reason, I thought Irish athletes had a better moral compass. But of course, every nation is just as susceptible to doping. He wasn't the first Irish doper and he wouldn't be the last. But he did succeed in fooling a lot of people.

When Lombard was quizzed about his progression – which took a sharp upward turn at the age of 27 or 28 – he put a lot of it down to plyometrics: drills that improve power and efficiency. They are standard practice for sprinters and field eventers, but were rarely done by distance runners, where the benefits are not as obvious.

One time, I ran into Eugene O'Neill at the track, a good steeplechaser, and saw him diligently doing a series of drills. When I asked him why, he said, 'Don't know, but Cathal Lombard does it and he's running fast so I'm gonna do it too.'

That's athletics in a nutshell: if the fastest guy was brushing his teeth 10 times a day, then rest assured the others would soon follow suit. But Eugene wasn't the only one to buy into what Lombard had been selling. Still, when the news broke about his positive test, it was Eugene that I thought back to, diligently doing his plyometrics in UCD.

It's not the drills, mate.

Not long before the Athens Olympics got under way, I ran a big PB of 46.29, shy of the qualifying 'B' standard I needed of 45.95. My last race of the season was in Ljubljana, Slovenia, and I took a train there from Hungary with a couple of Irish athletes: Paul Hession and Darren Haugh. The scenery was stunning as we weaved through the countryside. 'Lads, this is the life,' said Darren.

It was a moment where we stopped and appreciated how lucky we were, realising what athletics made possible – the places you see that few others do. I ran terribly in the race, however, going off far too slow and clocking a slow 34.99 for 300 metres. I needed a break.

'You're improving,' Jim told me in our end-of-season review. 'But there's still a lot more work to do.'

Heading back to the hard graft of winter training, I stepped it up another notch. Consistency became a given. I didn't miss sessions. By then I was settled in my course at DIT, had good friends and was 21 years old, with no shortage of potential distractions. But I stopped going out as much, skipping a lot of Friday nights in town, keeping myself fresh for Saturday mornings. I got stronger. We added extra sets in sessions, added extra weight in the gym.

I'd do 'back-to-backs' once a week on the track: walking 10 metres, hammering 60 metres, then turning around and repeating it. I'd do six sets of six – thirty-six sprints in total – then collapse in a heap.

When it came to the 400 metres, I wasn't an out-and-out speed guy. My speed endurance – the ability to maintain your speed – was my strength. I built that up off the back of long, gruelling sessions, and I didn't have many interruptions that winter. Things just started to flow.

As the indoor season grew closer, I began to look at

results elsewhere. *Where's he racing? How fast is he running?* In previous years, I didn't really care, but I was becoming aware I could actually do something.

I had never done a proper indoor season, always seeing it as just a way to tune up for outdoors, but Jim saw something in me and my training. He knew I needed to be exposed to better competition and race faster people.

I went to the Scottish Indoors in Glasgow and won in an indoor PB of 47.28. I went to Birmingham Indoor Games and won in another PB: 47.14. Two weeks later, I headed to Sheffield for the AAAs to face the best in Britain. Jim came along, as he did for all my races that year, paying his own way and leaving his wife and kids at home.

I was a better athlete when he was around. Jim had a calm presence. He wasn't someone who'd rant and rave on the side of the track. He'd know not to talk to you about athletics at certain times, but then he also knew when to switch it on.

He saw huge potential in me, but knew I had to be pushed: that I needed a plan and a structure. When I'd brought my girlfriend to the AAAs in Birmingham the year before, he didn't object but he also didn't exactly approve, seeing it as a potential distraction. When I hopped into the taxi to the stadium, Jim turned to me: 'Right, the holiday's over. You've got a fucking job to do today.' He wasn't afraid to dish out some tough love, but that was because he knew I had a talent. He didn't want to see it wasted.

In the warm-up area in Sheffield, ahead of the British indoor 400 metres final, we looked around at the big names, with Linford Christie, who was now a coach, among them. I was nervous, knowing I was about to go through a world of hurt.

Fucking 400 metres. Why didn't I become a long jumper? It'd be easy.

Jim could see me getting wound up so he sat beside me and started talking about something unrelated to athletics. He was generally calm and quiet in those pressure moments but as I warmed up, he'd slowly dial up the intensity.

I had won my semi-final in a big PB of 46.43, which made me the man to beat in the final. Before I walked into the call room, Jim gave me a pep talk, hitting me with a gentle punch to the chest. 'You need to fucking get stuck into this.' There was bite in his words. Conviction. 'You can win this. Don't worry about times and all that bollocks. Focus on the process of the race. Get out, impose yourself. Be big, be strong, and let them try chase you.'

I walked into the call room filled with belief. In the race, I led the whole way, never really seeing my rivals, and I hit the line first in 46.45, copying the celebration I'd seen from Rob Daly the year before.

The European Indoor Championships were a few weeks away and, having gone into the season as a nobody, suddenly I was ranked in the top five: a contender. The weekend before I left for Madrid, I went to a mate's birthday party in Dublin and because the AAAs had been on the BBC, a few people asked me about the win and about my plans.

One of those was my friend's mother, a lovely woman

who used to babysit me as a kid. She congratulated me on the win in Sheffield and after I told her there was a far bigger event coming up, her answer stayed with me.

'Oh,' she said. 'You're going to do well.'

CHAPTER 5

THE CHICKEN ON THE PLATE

The nerves began a few days before I left for Madrid, the races running themselves in my head. Every time my mind pressed play on that vision, a swell of anxiety rose up inside, growing a little bigger, a little stronger, each day.

I was flying out on a Wednesday afternoon, and shortly before I left for the airport I sat at the kitchen table, my mum serving me a plate of pasta. I looked down at it with a knot in my stomach. *I can't eat this.* Food is fuel, though, so I shovelled some of it in before I departed.

On the plane, I was sitting next to Ciara Sheehy, a sprinter on the Irish team, who was full of chat and energy. Meanwhile, I was the worst conversationalist on earth, responding with one-word answers. She was unfortunate to get stuck alongside me, as I just wanted to get to my hotel room and hide.

That always happened before big events. As the body and mind started to ramp up into fight-or-flight mode, I'd grow withdrawn, unsociable, narky with those around me. I could feel the race approaching in my stomach and my chest. My mind would start racing, with efforts to distract myself only temporary, usually futile, before the race would again intrude into my consciousness.

Once I reached the sanctuary of my hotel room in Madrid, I didn't venture out much. That would require energy – and acting. I just wanted to be alone. I was rooming with Paul Hession, a model professional who was always easy company. The following day, I checked out the stadium, did some training, getting used to the banked turns and leaning into them just as I would in the race.

The night before my first race, Rob Daly came down to our room and we sat around, watching *School of Rock*, a weapon of mass distraction in keeping my mind off the race. But that was never going to last. The following morning, as I waited around, resting up and killing time, I was ridiculously nervous.

At major championships, athletes are seeded based on their fastest times of the season, so the top contenders are typically drawn in different heats, only clashing in the final. Thanks to my time in Sheffield, I had a great lane draw: on the outside. That's huge in the indoor 400 metres, where the track is half the size. Not only are the bends not as tight, lessening the braking effect, but the track is also banked, with lane six a metre or so higher on the bends. As a result, the athletes in the outside lanes benefit from running downhill over the first lap. The advantage is so great that they no longer run 200 metres indoors at major championships, given it's virtually impossible to win from the inside lanes.

But no matter where you're drawn, getting out fast is a must indoors: the first lap of the 400 metres is run in lanes and once you turn into the straight, just before halfway, it's open season and an all-out war to get to the next bend in front. Get stuck behind other athletes there and, with the tight turns and short straights, it's very difficult to get past.

And so, when the gun fired in my 400m heat, I exploded from the blocks like a scalded cat, getting to the lead at halfway and never looking back. I hit the line well in front, smashing my indoor PB with 46.17 seconds. The next heat was won by the gold medal favourite, David Canal of Spain, in a comfortable 46.72, with Russia's Dmitriy Forshev winning the third heat in 46.60. These were my two big danger men.

Initially, there was euphoria. *I made the European final!* But that was soon washed away by a tsunami of fatigue. As I wandered through the mixed zone, the vicious levels of acidosis in my muscles made their presence felt. My nose started tingling, my head pounding. My muscles were burning, stomach churning. I lay down with a growing nausea in my stomach. Then I puked. I was unable to stand, and started crawling around, waiting for the pain to subside.

How the fuck am I going to run tomorrow?

When I finally got to the warm-up area, Lucy was there

and she led me to a wheelie bin filled with ice water, which I hopped into and stood, delirious, for several minutes. I slowly started to come around.

The elation about my time had lifted the nerves, at least, and so back at the hotel, I was able to eat dinner without any issues, feeling relaxed for the first time since getting to Madrid.

I didn't bomb. I didn't shit the bed.

A few of my friends had made the trip over, and I sat with them and a few members of the team in the lobby. It was close to midnight when Paddy Fay, an Irish team manager, came over. 'Right, it's time to go to bed,' he told me. I knew well what time it was but I didn't want to because I knew what was waiting once back in the room. I'd kickstart the next phase: looking to the final. Sure enough, once I got there and was alone with my thoughts, the knot returned to my stomach, with hours of nervous contemplation following.

Most sprinters take caffeine before races – which helps reaction times – and that, coupled with the adrenaline of the heat and the thoughts about the final, made it impossible to sleep for many hours. I stared into space, my mind flip-flopping between pride about my run and panic about what was ahead.

Great run, brilliant.
Now you have to do better.

The butterflies were fluttering around my stomach all night, but eventually I drifted off. When I woke, it took a few seconds to realise where I was and what day it was.

THE CHICKEN ON THE PLATE

Fuck, I'm racing tonight.

I didn't want to get out of bed. I rolled down to breakfast late, shovelled some food into me, then went straight back to bed, trying to kill time, which always passed at a glacial rate on the day of big events.

Jim eventually came up and, sensing my cabin fever, brought me out to lunch. I didn't want to go but I was doing myself no good in the room. We went to a nearby restaurant and Jim tried his best to distract me. But my mind was fixated on the race. The final was several hours away, but I was already sweating. I ordered some food and when it arrived – a flat piece of grilled chicken – I sat there, motionless, looking at it. My stomach was in knots. I cut a few pieces and forced one down with the help of some water. But I had zero appetite. It may as well have been covered in fungus, given how revolting it seemed.

It was impossible. I left the chicken sitting on the plate.

Then, all of a sudden, I had to get up and leave the restaurant, my heart racing, my chest feeling like it was about to explode. I crouched on the path outside, hands on my knees, taking short, sharp breaths. I didn't know it at the time, but it was a panic attack. All I wanted was to get back to the hotel, to be alone, and for all this to be over.

A few hours later, I arrived at the arena. After I hopped off the bus, an old Irish man wearing a big green hat came over, shook my hand and wished me all the best. I'd never had that before, but it was a reminder that this was different. In Ireland, 99 per cent of the people who watch athletics go because they know someone competing, so to be at an event that people had paid good coin to see, not knowing the athletes personally, was a novelty.

In the warm-up area, I went to the exact same spot as the day before, lying down and looking up at the same light, passing those painfully slow minutes, taking some deep breaths. That was the only time all day where I felt a little relaxed. The internal dialogue began to switch, with some confidence returning.

You've run really well here. You're in the form of your life.

Jim and Lucy were there and we were near David Canal, the Spaniard who'd been at the centre of a media scrum in the days before. Jim, as ever, knew the right thing to say in that moment. 'All the pressure is on him. He *has* to perform. If he doesn't win, it's a failure.' That brought some calmness.

Who gives a shit about me? As much as I'm nervous, what the fuck is Canal feeling?

The warm-up went well – I felt fast, explosive – and after enduring the purgatory of the call room, which was underneath the track, we were led up into the arena via a flight of stairs.

Before a race, steps mess with your mind. They're one last, little test of your legs and even the tiny effort of climbing a few can bring on some fatigue. I wasn't letting that happen.

Power in the step, power in the step. Fucking bound up these.

The arena was loud, and it was a vertical sound, the stands rising far more steeply than any arena I'd encountered.

The Spanish had long earmarked the men's 400 metres for a gold medal. As I set up my blocks, I spotted a few Irish flags draped over the railings and heard some people shouting my name. I was in lane five, with Canal to my left in four and Forshev outside me in six.

I had broken the race down into 50-metre sections, hatching a plan for what I'd do in each of them. I'd get out hard, be in the top two – or at worst top three – at halfway. If I was only third, then I needed to be up the arse of the guy in second. If you're not in touching distance at that point, then you can kiss goodbye to gold.

As we were called to our marks, the constant chatter and cheering began to dissipate into that familiar sound: silence. I crouched into the blocks, waiting for the starter to say '*listo*' (ready), then all that was left was for that gun to release us.

But when it arrived, it was followed by another loud bang – the recall gun. False start. At the time, athletes were allowed to have one false start without being disqualified, a rule which authorities eventually got rid of because so many sprinters used to chance their arm to get a flyer. The rules state you can't react faster than one tenth of a second and someone – not me – had done so. I went through the same process again, trying to silence my mind as I waited for the gun, primed to move on the B of the bang.

I got out fast the second time around, or thought I did, but Canal soon came powering by me on the inside, blasting to the front as we came off the second bend and broke from lanes. Forshev was also ahead of me, cutting across from the outside, and so I slotted into third, right behind both of them.

Get close, get close.

Forshev stayed wide into the back straight but then he started to fade, leaving the door open on the inside. As I darted past him and up to second entering the final turn, he threw his left arm out, trying to block me. But I swung my right arm right back at him, protecting my space, and entered the final bend just one metre down on Canal.

The noise was deafening, the crowd urging Canal towards a gold medal. I'd been trying to close on him for the previous 100 metres but had made no inroads. The gap stayed fixed – one metre – but then suddenly, as we hit the straight, he started tensing up, a rigidity appearing in his stride. I knew that feeling, as does every 400 metres runner. His shoulders tensed up, constricting towards his ears.

I have him. I fucking have him.

I switched into lane two off the bend, went for broke, and as I drew alongside him I threw a little glance to my left because that's what Eamonn Coghlan did on his way to winning the world 5000 metres title in 1983 – a moment that lives forever in Irish sporting lore.

There was nothing Canal could do, and I knew it. He was running through honey, with no gears left to call upon. I looked ahead again and saw the most beautiful sight: clear track between me and the finish. When I crossed the line, I threw my arms wide, then kept them in the air until I had slowed to a stop.

Amid the ecstasy, I didn't know what to do. *Wave? Blow*

kisses? I'd never won something like this. An official came over, told me to do a lap of honour, and someone ran down from the stands with an Irish flag, which I held up behind me for photographers, not realising I had it the wrong way around. (In my defence, it was my first win.)

My parents were up in the stands, as well as my mates, who came dressed as leprechauns. I looked up and saw one of them, Mick, fast asleep. *Why the fuck is Mick asleep?* As it turned out, they'd been out drinking all day, sitting around in a Madrid square with a bag of cans. They had also been knocking back beers at the arena. Mick had been in great form an hour earlier, downing a can in one go as a horde of Spaniards cheered him on, unaware that it was actually non-alcoholic beer. But shortly before the 400 metres final, the day finally caught up with him and he nodded off. Around the time I was finishing my lap of honour, he awoke to a Spanish guy whacking him in the head with one of those cardboard cutouts they give to fans to make noise.

'Your friend!' the man told him. 'Your friend won!'

I was interviewed by the stadium host, who asked what it meant, and gave a too-long spiel that the poor chap then had to translate for the crowd. Then I ventured off into the mixed zone, meeting the Irish press pack: Tom and Ian O'Riordan, Greg Allen, Brendan Mooney, Cliona Foley. They were all true athletics people and I could feel how delighted they were to have an Irish gold, with Alistair Cragg winning another one soon after over 3000 metres.

That night, people started showing me the medal table,

laughing that Ireland was ahead of Britain. I had to answer a barrage of questions from international journalists, who had no idea who I was. *How have you got here? What have you changed?* I didn't know what to say. It was a whirlwind. As much as I knew I was in great shape, I never considered how I'd act following a victory. It's much easier to plan for what happens when it *doesn't* go well.

Back in the warm-up area, I met Jim and Lucy and thanked them for all they'd done. Then I met Mum and Dad, who are usually calm, reserved people, but there was so much emotion as we embraced. This was before social media and smartphones, but my phone was lighting up with text messages, many of which came from people I hadn't spoken to for years. That night, a huge crew gathered for a celebration at an Irish pub – where else? – and I saw the impact of a gold medal, the joy it brings to people far beyond your inner circle. That made it so much sweeter.

Whether you succeed or fail, it's only the following morning when it really sinks in: that moment when you wake up, take stock of where you are and realise that whatever happened was real, that it would be lasting. When you don't run well, a sadness loiters overhead like a dark cloud. But in Madrid, I woke up and was infused with an immediate jolt of joy: that *did* really happen.

Sport can be so fickle, with fractions of a second separating screaming success from abject failure. The difference in how they're received is stark. Win a medal and, suddenly, the media are all over you. Fall short and it's a lonely, anonymous walk off into the night. That Sunday morning in Madrid, I was suddenly in high demand, my first appointment being to meet one of the Irish photographers who took me to a spot in the city to pose with the gold.

While waiting in the hotel lobby, people from various nations came over to offer their congratulations. Then there was the buzz of flying home. That was the most surreal part. I had flown to Madrid as a complete unknown to most in Ireland. But the win made national headlines.

When our plane landed in Dublin, I was ushered to the front and asked to wait for several minutes before they opened the doors. As they did, I saw a horde of people waiting and a guy playing bagpipes. Alistair Cragg hadn't flown back with us so it was just me up there, following Mr Bagpipes as we walked through the airport, with heads turning all around and me cringing with embarrassment. I went to pick up my bag and was told not to worry about it, and at the arrivals hall there was another crowd gathered, with many clubmates, friends and relatives. One of my mates had a big placard: *Gillick, will you marry me?*

In the weeks after, I heard countless stories about the thrill that race had given people. Friends of friends would tell me how they were on their feet, roaring at the TV. That was always what I'd do when watching Irish athletes or teams. It was strange, surreal, to hear others say they had done it for me.

At home, our landline was inundated with calls, my mum sifting through the messages. Letters were dropped into the house, with various people in the area offering congrats.

But when I took a step back, and had a few moments to contemplate, there was a question awaiting: what do I do now?

I arrived back on a Monday and went to a reception in the local pub that night. But on Tuesday morning at 9 a.m., I was back in a lecture at DIT. That was exactly how I wanted it – for normal life to resume as fast as possible. But that was easier said than done. I hopped on the Luas tram to head to the city centre but, immediately, I could sense that something had changed. People were looking at me, noticing me. I sat beside a guy who was reading the *Metro*, a free newspaper, and in the corner of my eye I saw that he was reading a story about me. A while later, he looked up, then across.

'Are you ....'

'Yeah,' I said awkwardly.

'Ah, Jesus! Fair play to ya.'

At college, one of our lecturers announced my win to the class, though most of them already knew about it. For days, weeks, months, there were reminders that things were now different – not in terms of how I felt or acted, but in how others perceived me.

Three days after arriving home, for example, my mates and I went on a night out to Copper Face Jacks, Dublin's most famous nightclub. As we stood in the queue, one of the bouncers recognised me and gave me a nod, ushering us all up to the front and giving us VIP access.

I had a girlfriend at the time, so I wasn't going out looking to meet anyone, but I could sense the increased attention. People would come up to chat throughout the night or look over from afar, wondering why others were doing that. *Who's your man?* I'd walk around Dundrum Shopping Centre and notice heads turning, with whispers between friends. It made me uncomfortable. Before I'd leave the house, I started to worry about what I was wearing, how I presented myself.

I was only 21, an immature student, and while part of me wanted to go on nights out, to be the guy having my ego stroked, a much bigger part just wanted anonymity, normality.

The gold medal, as great as it was, also affected my relationship. After Madrid, I started putting more of a priority on athletics. Before I wanted to perform, but now I *needed* to. The training began to absorb so much time and energy that there were many weeks where I didn't see enough of my girlfriend, which created conflict. We came from different backgrounds – I was embedded in sport, she wasn't – and it was hard to have understanding and empathy for the other's view. For most people our age, weekends are all about nights out, and it was hard to be with someone who, suddenly, had little interest in that.

'Why won't you go out on Saturday?'

'Because I've got 6x300 metres on Sunday morning.'

The victory in Madrid heightened the need to be professional, to prioritise athletics over everything – even those close to me. My girlfriend and I broke up later that year and while the change in attitude after the gold wasn't the only reason, it was definitely among them.

For some people, fame is a goal, a dream, but for me the novelty of it quickly wore off. It felt exhausting. One day I was sitting at home, hungry, and thinking about going to the shop to get a roll. But I stopped myself. Why? I had a fear of bumping into someone who'd ask me about athletics. It seems stupid, a real first-world problem, but it had become a constant occurrence and started to wear on me. I just wanted things to be normal. But they weren't.

When I got back training, there was an influx of new athletes in the group. People were saying, 'This is great, they're all here because of you!' Meanwhile, I thought: *What about me? I still have a season to do. Why are things changing?*

There was a weight that came with being well known, one that felt like a burden.

I was dreading the outdoor season. Suddenly there was pressure, expectation. This wasn't just a hobby anymore. My neighbour came in one day and while she meant well, she voiced what many thought: 'We knew you were good, but we didn't think you were *that* good.' I had come from nowhere to win a European title and sometimes people assumed I was loaded as a result, that people were knocking on the door to give me cheques. The reality was so different.

I didn't have a shoe or kit sponsor and had bought the spikes I wore in Madrid myself. The only funding I had was the €4,600 grant and there was zero prize money for winning the Europeans. I hoped it might bring in sponsorship but I didn't have a manager and had no clue how to get it. Pierce O'Callaghan, a former international race walker, was working for a company called Platinum One which operated in that area. He rang me one day and said he'd love to help me out, arranging a meeting with Fintan Drury. I soon realised money wasn't going to fall out of a tree, with the value of athletes so far below that of team sports. As Fintan told me: 'The hard thing about athletics is if Donncha O'Callaghan walks down Grafton Street, people are gonna go, "There's Donncha O'Callaghan." If you walk down Grafton Street, they don't know who you are.'

How could I argue with that?

Madrid had been something I never expected. But when I came home and things settled down and I had time to think, my old insecurities reared their ugly heads. The imposter syndrome got stronger.

Did I just get lucky? Did the stars align because everyone else ran shit on the day?

That golden moment had been magical, as were the celebrations with friends, family, teammates and fans. But when I thought back on the build-up to that final, the only time I felt calm was when I started my warm-up. Every moment before, I was hating life, just wanting it to be over.

I needed to do something about that because I couldn't face into that at every championship, having panic attacks and feeling nothing but dread before the gun fired.

You might think a big win would instil confidence, banish some doubts. But for me it just added to them. I struggled more in the aftermath of Madrid because, suddenly, people had an interest.

'When are you racing again? Are you gonna go to the Olympics? Will you win gold?'

Before, no one really cared, but now I could feel the eyes, the attention.

Nothing changed in my routine, but people's expectations of me did. Suddenly, a lot of people wanted me to do stuff for free. It's not a bad thing, turning up at events, presenting medals or saying a few words, and it's only right to give something back to the sport. But Mum is a nice person and, at times, she was too nice. She'd come home and be like, 'David, there's this woman I know who's a teacher and they'd love you to go down to the school and give a talk.' It was hard to say no, especially given the requests often came from people I knew. But it meant I got dragged left, right and centre, with training sessions also becoming a social engagement where I'd be asked to show off the medal.

Two weeks ago, no one gave a shit and I could train in peace.

I'd try to oblige people because that's the kind of person I am, a people pleaser, but elite athletics requires a level of selfishness and it's hard – very hard – to know where to draw the line. But if you don't, you become very busy doing things that aren't necessarily helping your career or rewarding you financially, solely out of fear of saying no. You're damned if you do, damned if you don't.

Going to Madrid, I'd lacked self-confidence in believing I could win a medal but when it happened, I was dazed. I heard what everyone was saying and I began to internalise it.

You're going to make a world final. You'll win an Olympic medal.

These things, which hadn't been in my head before, moved front and centre. When a month or two passed without any sponsorship offers, it was clear a European indoor title was not enough to earn a solid living from the sport. Not even close. I thought of that quote from Nelson Mandela: 'After climbing a great hill, one only finds that there are many more hills to climb.' The outdoor track season was looming, ominously, on the horizon, and I hadn't even paused to enjoy my achievement. All I could think of, and obsess about, was what came next.

Shit, now I've got to back this up.

CHAPTER 6

MIND GAMES

There's a theory in athletics that whatever time you run for 400 metres indoors, you'll run one second faster outdoors: partly due to the bigger track, partly due to the summer being the time when everyone peaks.

People would be flippant about that, telling me how my 46.1 would mean a 45.1 outdoors, maybe even 44.9: entering true world-class territory.

And so, as I got back to work, those numbers became etched in my mind. The only issue? I was emotionally drained, physically fatigued. The outdoor season hadn't even begun and I felt an invisible weight: the burden of expectation.

I had a catch-up with Elaine Fitzgerald, the High Performance Director with Athletics Ireland, who told me she felt burnt out after the indoor season and had to take a holiday. All I could think?

I need a holiday too. I need to get away from all this.

But I couldn't. There was a big summer ahead: with the

European Under-23 Championships, the World University Games and the World Championships. My first race was in Turin at the start of June, and I went there wracked with nerves. But I ran well, a PB of 45.93: a decent way to blow off the cobwebs. Two weeks later, at the European Cup in Portugal, I won but wasn't any faster, running 45.96.

My next race was in Bangor: the North Down International Games. It wasn't the kind of place you'd go to run fast, the weather too unpredictable, but Andy Norman – a no-nonsense British agent and meeting organiser – didn't so much ask me to run as order me to: 'You Irish need to run in Ireland.'

He was bringing over a South African, Marcus la Grange, and as I sat on the phone to Andy in the box room at home, I scribbled that name down, then swiftly went into research mode, again worrying about others. I won the race in a slow 46.72, then queued up outside a hotel room with other athletes to get my prize money: a couple of hundred quid, paid in cash.

My summer goal was to win gold at the European Under-23s, but one Saturday morning while walking out of a café in Enniskerry, that ambition took a dent. I got a text that made my stomach drop. Robert Tobin, one of my British rivals, had run a blazing 45.01 in Geneva. I felt a rush of nerves, a sense of dread. But I didn't tell anyone how I felt and just did the usual: lock it all inside. I knew something wasn't right with my mental state, but didn't know what to do.

Stress does strange things to the body, the increase in

cortisol levels wreaking havoc with your sleep and ability to recover from hard training. It wasn't long before that manifested in my Achilles tendon. I started to feel a burning sensation every time I hit top speed.

The European Under-23s were in Erfurt, Germany, and the Achilles issue meant my training was severely limited in the final few weeks. Despite that, the championships got off to a solid start. I ran 46.25 to finish second in my heat. But in the semi-final the next day, I had to absolutely bury myself to finish only fourth, sneaking into the final as the last qualifier. This wasn't how it was supposed to be. I tried to get my head in the right place before the final, but I felt red-hot pain every time I planted my left foot into the track. In the warm-up area, Jim was watching my every step.

'This isn't right,' I told him. 'I can't put pressure through the Achilles.'

'Right, I'm calling it,' he said. 'You're not running.'

An Achilles injury is not one to mess with. Tear that tendon and you could be dealing with pain for the rest of your career. Rupture it and your career might be over. It was the right decision, I knew, but that didn't lessen my devastation. I broke down in tears, then stood and watched the 400 metres final through gritted teeth, with Tobin winning gold in 46.81. The mediocre winning time only heaped on more misery. If I was healthy, that would have been well within reach.

I rehabbed the Achilles in the weeks that followed and, because I'd run the qualifying B standard for the World

Championships, I was selected on the Irish team to go to Helsinki. This was in the days of Aertel, the teletext service on RTÉ, and as I was scrolling the news I saw my name listed on the team. I felt like a fraud. I wasn't remotely fit enough to take on the world's best, and knew what would happen if I did. I had a chat with Jim and, again, he took the decision out of my hands.

'There's no point,' he told me. 'You're not going.'

A few days later, I was back scrolling Aertel and saw the headline: 'David Gillick pulls out of World Championships'.

The season wasn't over, though. My Achilles started to feel a little better and I got back doing a few sessions. There was still the World University Games in Izmir, Turkey, an event that's a big step down from the World Championships. Given my fitness, it was a more appropriate place to run. Maybe I could salvage something from the season.

But there are no such things as miracles in this sport. If you haven't done the work, hit the necessary times in training, then all the willpower in the world won't magic up a great performance on the big day. I travelled to Izmir knowing I wasn't right physically, which made things worse mentally.

Maybe it's all in the head? Maybe I'm a one-hit wonder? Before too long, people will hear my name and be like, 'Whatever happened to him?'

My brother called me and I was honest about how I felt. 'It'd be good for you to just get out and run,' he said.

I thought so too. I needed to get back on the horse and

put Erfurt behind me. I also knew that, if I didn't run, the negative voice would grow exponentially louder in the off-season, that I'd become that person who talks themselves out of racing if things weren't perfect. But still, if you take a knife to a gunfight, the inevitable result is a swift death. I finished second in my heat, clocking a pathetic 50.09, feeling as if I was running on one leg. I went to the stadium the next day for the semi-final but felt pain again on my warm-up. I pulled the plug. My mind was in a dark place soon after when I got a call from my girlfriend, who'd gathered with a crew at the local GAA clubhouse to watch the race.

'What happened?' she asked. 'We're all sitting, waiting to watch you, and suddenly you don't appear.'

I lost the rag, shouting down the phone. 'You don't have a fucking clue what I'm dealing with.'

Once again, I just wanted to hide from the world. I felt like a total failure. There was only one thing for it: a proper break.

I went to Thailand with my girlfriend for a month, trying my best to forget about athletics. But that's easier said than done. We went to the Full Moon Party in Koh Phangan, spent four or five days sleeping in a shack on the beach. We went out most nights, knocking back countless buckets: a concoction of Red Bull, vodka and orange juice. We met other Irish people there and socialised with them most evenings.

There was one guy in the group who fancied himself as a sprinter. Every night, as the alcohol was flowing, he'd start up. 'C'mon Gillick, I'll race you.' I had no interest in doing so, but he wouldn't let it go. Night after night, as we knocked back drinks, he kept at me. Eventually, I cracked.

'Right, fuck you. Let's go.'

We went down to the beach, lined out a track of about 80 metres on the hard sand near the shore, with the rest of the group watching. I was polluted drunk, and when we set off, I didn't manage anything close to a straight line. It was *Wolf of Wall Street* stuff, the two of us wobbling towards the finish. But he beat me, fair and square, and I didn't hear the end of it that week. 'I beat David Gillick!' he told everyone who'd listen.

The trip proved a great line in the sand, a chance to recover physically and refresh myself mentally. The summer had been horrendous, but as 2005 ended, I had learned something crucial: how racing the 400 metres to a high level indoors can impact your outdoor season.

On reflection, I realised I should have factored in a decent break after Madrid and then started my outdoor season later, putting in a six-to-eight week training block to prepare. But I'd rushed that process, burnt the candle at both ends and pushed my body too much, too soon. It didn't help that I was also in a chronically stressed state, so of course the wheels had fallen off. What else did I expect?

It all ended with me in Turkey, shouting down the phone at my girlfriend who, a few weeks later, had to stand and watch as I came up short in one last race – against a drunk guy on a beach.

*

Looking to 2006, I decided two things.

One, I wasn't going to do a big indoor season, focusing instead on a long, steady build-up for outdoors. Two, I was going all-in on athletics. I had been due to enter the final year of my degree at DIT but decided to take time out, asking Paul O'Reilly, the head of the course, if I could defer. 'This will always be here for you,' he told me, and with that, I was a full-time athlete.

That lasted a whole two weeks.

The thing I didn't consider? My training group and coaches had other stuff going on in their lives and we trained in the evenings, which left me waiting around, twiddling my thumbs, all day. I was bored out of my tree. I went back to Paul: 'Can I come back?' Thankfully, he had no issue with it.

The World Indoor Championships were in Moscow the following March but I decided to skip them. The decision was based on something I'd read years before from Roger Black, an Olympic silver medallist in the 400 metres. 'The best athletes don't run indoors,' he said, and while there were exceptions, by and large it was true. It's much the same today. For every Femke Bol who does usually race indoors, there's a Sydney McLaughlin-Levrone or a Shelly-Ann Fraser-Pryce who won't go near an indoor championship, preferring to build their base for what matters most.

After the summer I had in 2005, carrying the emotional and physical fatigue of Madrid, I knew there was something in Black's comments. Indoor success is all well and good, but everyone knows what counts most, the races that go down in history. If I wanted to be taken seriously, I had to do it outdoors.

Training went well through the winter and I did enter a few indoor races, purely to work on improving my speed over 200 metres. In February, I went to Jacksonville, Florida, for a training camp and spent time alongside Peter Coghlan, a world-class sprint hurdler from Ireland, and his brother John, who was making waves as a top coach.

Being around them gave me a brilliant insight into elite-level training, seeing how true pros operate. After one session of 300-metre reps went well, Peter said to me, 'Why don't you just go and do World Indoors?' I had qualified from the previous year and figured I had nothing to lose by giving it a lash.

And so, a few weeks later, I was on a plane to Moscow, abandoning my original plans. Bad idea. I ran like an anaesthetised mule, finishing second last in my heat in 47.61. It was the championship every athlete dreads: one and done.

But it wasn't a completely wasted trip. In Moscow, I was rooming with James Nolan, a great character who had vast experience and we had great chats as we whiled away the hours in our room. I learned lots from him. It had been a decent championships for the Irish, with James finishing sixth in the 1500 metres, Alistair Cragg fourth over 3000 metres and Derval O'Rourke winning gold in the 60 metres hurdles. I sat in the stands watching Derval get her medal and thought: *What am I even doing here? I didn't prepare for this.* Ultimately, my ego got in the way, convincing myself I could do well without proper preparation and without proper speed in my legs given I was focusing on endurance work. Again, I had taken a knife to a gunfight.

Derval came up and sat beside me after her ceremony, with the gold medal in one hand and a Big Mac in the other. I was delighted for her: she'd worked hard for that medal and fully deserved it. But her win only heightened my sense of failure. I felt like I was back at the bottom of the pile, the gulf to the world's best now wider than ever.

When we arrived home in Dublin, I felt the polar opposite of the previous year and the welcome back from Mr Bagpipes. When championships go well, everyone wants to be around you. When you fail, it's like you don't exist. You might as well be coming back from a lads' trip to Newcastle. The doors open at the arrival hall and you feel embarrassed.

Get me the fuck out of here.

As Derval walked into the hall to an eruption of cheers, with various cameras rolling and photographers snapping, I put the head down, several metres behind, trying not to be in the background of shots in case people remembered I went to Moscow.

'Oh, there's your man. How'd he get on?'
'Shit.'

I took an immediate turn after going through the doors, walking as fast as I could away from the crowd.

My first race of the outdoor season was in Zaragoza, Spain. I travelled over with Jim and, again, I was stupidly nervous, doubting myself, asking if I was good enough. That voice just wouldn't leave me alone.

There was a tall Polish athlete in the race, dressed head to toe in the adidas pro kit, which of course wreaked havoc with my mind.

This lad looks like the shit. He MUST be good.

I finished second in 47.03, spending more time thinking about the Pole than my own performance. I only really started racing with 50 metres to go and he pipped me on the line. I felt like I was dying after the race, and couldn't stand up a full 40 minutes later. Jim came over. 'Are you sure you're alright?' My head was pounding, I had my legs up on the wall, trying to flush the lactic acid out. I just couldn't get up. And I had run slow. That night, I didn't sleep a wink, staring at the ceiling, trying to sift through the wreckage of another bad race.

Was it the pressure of last year? The flop indoors?

It wasn't like I'd been everywhere in the media. Yet, I was putting so much pressure on myself, expecting everything to be perfect. But in this sport, it just never is.

I ran better the following week in Geneva, setting a PB of 45.80, but that was followed by three more bad races, none of which saw me crack 46. *So much for 45.1.* At the nationals in Santry, I pulled out a decent run, winning in a PB of 45.67, which restored some confidence ahead of the summer's big event: the European Championships in Gothenburg.

I was touted as one of the best Irish chances, a potential medallist. But the week was a nightmare from start to finish.

THE RACE

The team hotel was central, close to the stadium, so journalists and fans and friends and family would all hang around the lobby. It was no disrespect to any of them, but I preferred to be cut off from all that before a big race, tucked away in my own little world.

'You need to get out of the hotel,' Mum told me. 'You can't be sitting in your room all day.'

But I didn't listen. That was where I felt comfortable, secure.

I ran OK in my heat – second in 46.16 – but the semifinal was one of the worst races of my life. I bottled it. When the gun fired, I completely froze and from there, I was just never in the race. My body wouldn't shift. There was no power, no speed. I was cut adrift halfway through the race and turned into the home straight only to be greeted with the sight of six lycra-clad arses moving away from me. My morale sank lower, I slowed even more. I needed to finish in the top four to make the final but came home seventh in a pedestrian 46.84. As I slowed to a stop, I had one thought.

Get me the fuck out of here.

But that's not how it works. When you walk off the track at major championships, you pass through the long, snaking path of the mixed zone: first to the TV folk, then to the radio, print and internet journalists. Within a minute or two of crossing the line, before you've got your breath back, there's a camera in your face and a microphone put in front of you. You're asked questions for which you don't remotely have an answer.

'You won a European Indoors last year, came here with a bit of expectation,' said one journalist. 'What happened?'
I don't know what happened. You tell me. You watched it.
'Was there any moment where it went wrong?'
Any moment? The WHOLE FUCKING THING was a disaster.

But I didn't say that out loud, of course, instead going down the road of, 'There's no reason we can't perform at this level' ... blah blah blah.

I was so embarrassed. I wanted to run and hide. In those moments, it's close to impossible to contextualise a failure. You're in a state of shock, sadness, anger, frustration. I told the journalists a cover story, putting on a brave face for 60 seconds so I could give them what they wanted and get the hell out of there. I did that a lot when things went wrong, the alternative being to have a meltdown live on air, go viral and draw more attention to my failure.

When things don't go well, the mixed zone is a lonely place. Hardly anyone wants to talk to you, bar the few Irish journalists. You zig and zag through that maze and journalists avert their eyes, pretending you're not there: the opposite of what they do when you run well.

I don't think I ever blanked anyone in a mixed zone, but some athletes do when they underperform, marching right past the media and ignoring all requests for a chat. I was usually level-headed on the surface, hiding the turmoil within. It was easier that way.

Many years later, those experiences helped when it was

my turn to stand behind the camera, being the one asking athletes about their races.

Interviewing Rhasidat Adeleke after she finished fourth in the Olympic final in Paris, I thought back to Gothenburg. You're asking the question, as you must, but you know the athlete doesn't remotely have the answer. It could take days, weeks, months, to reflect on it with clarity and identify exactly what happened. In ways, it's madness to put people in front of the camera during some of the most crushing moments of their lives. Given how you feel, you could say anything. It's a surprise more don't.

I always had a good relationship with the media, though I'd avoid any coverage before or during an event, knowing there was zero upside to consuming it – and potentially a big downside. Sometimes Mum would tell me over the phone, 'They were all really nice about you on the telly.' But that was as much as I'd hear. Some Irish athletes would go looking for coverage. They'd be sitting at the team hotel, wondering who was in the RTÉ studio and what was being said, or asking teammates who'd already competed which journalists were in the mixed zone. Some would have opinions on certain journalists, but I tried not to go down that road. I never felt they were out to get me.

For me, the hardest part of dealing with the media was doing interviews before the race. I'd try to avoid those, feeling that if I talked about it ahead of time, I'd only heap more pressure on myself.

'What does success look like for you?'
Eh, obviously if I win the fucking thing.

But, of course, I didn't say that either, even if sometimes I was tempted.

At the end of that summer, I had an honest conversation with myself, which went something like this.

What the fuck are you doing? You have a talent, that's great, but are you going to use it? You've pricked around the last couple of years, had some success, with people patting you on the back, recognising you in nightclubs. Well done, hunky-dory. So what are you going to do now?

Gothenburg was the biggest schoolday I'd ever had and it made it very clear that I was allowing my mind to sabotage my body. There was no good reason I should have been so flat, so devoid of power and speed, in that semi-final. But I had let the nerves win, allowing them to drain my strength before I reached the start line.

It was time to start fighting back.

The first time I met Enda McNulty was in the gym at Dublin City University. He was a well-known Gaelic footballer who was in the latter years of his career with Armagh and had started to make a name for himself in sports psychology. He told me he'd love to go for a coffee. So we did. During that meeting, he asked about my goals and when I told him about the Beijing Olympics, still two years away, he said: 'How are you going to do that?'

I said the usual. 'Train hard.'

'I *know* you train hard,' he said. 'I can see that. But *how* are you going to do it? Who's going to help you?'

I realised I had no proper plan, no detailed blueprint

for how I was going to become a 44-second 400 metres athlete and make an Olympic final. But I knew one area I had to address was my mindset, and Enda seemed like a man who could help. We started to meet up more often in an informal way and Enda, who was looking to build a career in sports performance, agreed to help, without ever looking for payment.

I opened up to him about the doubts: that self-made diss track, loaded with negativity, which played on a constant loop in my mind.

'Right, what are you going to do with those doubts?' asked Enda.

His idea was to write them all down on paper before I'd go to a race, then take them out into the garden and burn them. So that's what I did, writing down every anxious thought that crossed my mind.

I'm not good enough. I'm gonna come last. What if I don't perform? What will happen to my grant? I'm Irish: we can't compete with the world's best. Have I done enough work? Am I ready?

Then I'd look at them all on the page, take it into the garden and set it ablaze. After that, I'd write positive things about myself on a new page, trying to instil confidence.

I also started to keep a training diary detailing every session and, before races, I'd look back at all the work I'd done. When I took a step back and looked at it rationally, these were all things that *actually happened*, whereas so much of the irrational stuff had never happened; they were just fears about the future.

In later years, I'd go on YouTube, downloading videos of my best races, then put a highlights clip together, overlaying a song that stirred positive emotions: 'Hoppipolla' by Sigur Ros. I'd watch that before going into the call room, a timely reminder that I did have the ability to perform.

I started doing a debrief with Enda after each race, writing down three areas of improvement and three areas that worked well. I spoke to him at length about the emotions of performance, how to deal with pressure and setbacks and even how to handle success, not wanting the mistakes of Madrid to be repeated. Before, I had kept all this stuff bottled.

Enda coached me on how to deal with the media before big events. 'In the world of performance, you're gonna get these interviews because they're interested in you,' he said. 'It's not a bad thing. They're giving you the opportunity to tell your story. So roll with it. Don't push it away. If someone wants a piece of you, do it. But dictate the answers.'

If a journalist asked me what success looked like, for example, I'd refuse to go down the road of talking times or medals. I'd just say it was to 'reach my potential, whatever that might be.' That reflected my change in mindset. My perception of success shifted. It wasn't just about a medal or a final – a goal that was dependent on external factors. It was *how* I performed.

Before races, I'd call down to Enda's house and practise visualisation in his living room. He'd get me to stand up and start running in place with my eyes closed, talking through each phase of the race: 'What are you feeling now?'

We did breathing techniques to keep a lid on nerves, practising the routine I'd use – two deep breaths – before getting into the blocks. We worked on my posture, how I carried myself on the track or in the call room. We worked on slowing my heart rate and keeping adrenaline under control when I'd hear the roar of the crowd, trying not to block that noise out but invite it in – accepting it and rolling with it.

Before big races, I'd sit in the call room and imagine myself running around Marlay Park as a child, remembering why I took up this sport: because it was fun, free-flowing. I'd visualise that feather on my nose, breathing in and out slowly, gently, trying to keep it in place.

One day, Enda handed me an axe sharpener and told me to put it in my car. Why? 'As Abraham Lincoln would say: "if he'd six hours to chop down a tree, he'd spend the first four sharpening the axe," he said. 'Every time you see that, what does it signify? You're fucking sharpening the axe every day.'

The mental techniques extended to training sessions, knowing that if I could ingrain them there, they'd be second nature on race day. If I had a horrible session like 6x300m and was getting wound up about how much I'd suffer, I'd flick an elastic band on my wrist: a trick to break up that thought pattern and get myself centred.

I'd draw a little dot on my fist and every time I saw it, it was a reminder to bring my thoughts back to the here and now, to stop worrying about the future – something I did far, far too much.

Midway through the summer of 2006, not long after I handed in my thesis, I was sitting on the couch in the living room when my mother, who was ironing clothes, asked me an uncomfortable question.

'So, what are you going to do now, David?'

'What do you mean?'

'You're finished college. What are you going to do?'

'I don't know. Probably get a job or something.'

'Would you not give athletics a go?'

'What do you mean?'

'Would you not give it a solid effort, and see what happens?'

'I tried that before and ….'

'No, I don't mean here. Would you not go abroad?'

That was the first time the seed was planted. *Maybe I should give this a go – somewhere else.* In the weeks after, I began to look at opportunities abroad, environments that could help me reach the next level. I started by researching who was running well in the 400 metres and where they were based.

Two of the best British athletes at the time were Tim Benjamin and Martyn Rooney. Benjamin trained in Windsor under coach Tony Lester, while Rooney trained at the University of Loughborough under Nick Dakin. I visited both groups, and both coaches were keen to have me join. I was still weighing up the decision when, one day, Tony called me, explaining that because he was employed by British Athletics, his contract didn't allow him to coach an Irish athlete.

That made up my mind: I was going to Loughborough.

It meant breaking the news to Jim, a conversation I dreaded. I arranged to meet him in the Orchard Pub in Stillorgan and, on the drive there, I was a nervous wreck. *How am I gonna say this?* I went in, we got the niceties out of the way and I just blurted it out: 'Jim, I've decided to move to Loughborough.'

I was in floods of tears. But Jim was brilliant. 'Look, I am disappointed,' he said. 'I'd love to work with you up to Beijing, but if I was you I'd be doing exactly the same. You've got an opportunity, you've got talent, you have to do these things. Always know you have a safety net here with me. If it doesn't work out, I'll be more than happy to work with you again.'

I had my plan in place. But the one thing I needed? Money. At the time, my main source of funding was my grant from the Irish Sports Council, which had risen to €20,000 a year due to my European indoor gold. I got wind that there was extra money available through what we know now as the Institute of Sport. I just needed to convince them I was worth the investment. I arranged a meeting with Patsy McGonagle of Athletics Ireland and Paul McDermott and Finbarr Kirwan of the Irish Sports Council, meeting them in the bar at the Red Cow Moran Hotel in Dublin.

Enda helped me prepare. 'Go in there with a suit on,' he

said. 'Blow them away; show you're professional and the way you approach your sport is professional.'

So that's what I did, walking in looking like a banking executive and flipping open a laptop to take them through a PowerPoint presentation. It detailed my two-year build-up to the Beijing Olympics, marking out all the milestones I'd hit along the way: why I chose Loughborough; who Nick was and his coaching credentials; who was in the group; why it was the best environment for me; what I needed to improve to make a world or Olympic final. I broke down everything it would cost between my rent, food, coaching fees and training camps. I didn't want to go into the meeting with my hand out, begging for charity. I wanted to show them I was an investment worth making and explain how extra funding would benefit my performance.

It worked. I got an extra €10,000. About six months later, Finbarr got in touch and asked if I could send him that presentation, telling me it was the benchmark of what they wanted their athletes to be like. He didn't mention anything about the suit.

It was time to spread my wings. On 14 October 2006, I said goodbye to my girlfriend of three years, packed up my little Toyota Yaris and drove to Dún Laoghaire with my mum. We ferried across the Irish Sea and then drove to Loughborough, a university town that's under an hour's drive from Birmingham. We stayed in a hotel the first night before I drove her to the airport. As she walked away from the car, she looked back and I gave her a wave.

We're not the kind to share our inner thoughts or get overly sentimental, but I knew we both felt the significance of that moment. There was sadness and trepidation as we went our separate ways. On the drive back to Loughborough, I got emotional. I was excited about what was ahead, but also a little daunted, about to head into the great unknown.

You've left the nest now, David. It's shit or bust.

CHAPTER 7

GOING PRO

The reason I went to England was simple: to run fast. I did enrol in a master's degree in sports management, but decided to spread that out over three years, allowing me the time and freedom to live and train like a professional – even though I wasn't one just yet.

From the start, I felt at home in Loughborough, surrounded by like-minded people: athletes shooting for the sport's highest level. What's more, it offered a clean break, a blank canvas. Leaving home meant I didn't have to be a people pleaser and could throw everything I had into athletics, not worrying what people would think if I turned down invites to birthdays or weddings or nights out. It was a quieter, simpler life, where it was easier to focus.

Nick's group was loaded with world-class talent. Chief among them was Martyn Rooney, a bright young star of British athletics. He was just 19 and coming off a big year when he'd run a British Under-20 400 metres record of

45.35 – which made him faster than me – and a bronze medal at the World Juniors.

Knowing I'd be training with him was a big reason I chose Loughborough, along with knowing I'd be coached by Nick, who had brought the likes of Chris Rawlinson and Kemel Thompson to world finals in the 400 metres hurdles. *That's* where I wanted to be, and Nick was the man to get me there.

To do so, I needed to train with faster athletes. It was no disrespect to those I trained with in Dublin, but if I had a good day on the track there, I'd be 10 metres ahead. A bad day meant I was five metres ahead. But over in Loughborough, a bad day meant I got my arse handed to me.

We trained six days a week, often twice a day. I clicked with Rooney from the start: both in training and away from it. Both of his parents are Irish so there was a level of understanding of who I was, the culture I came from. He and Nick had a discussion before I joined and I was worried they might turn me down, not wanting a challenger, a rival, in his daily environment. But Rooney gave me the thumbs up. The fact we were of different nationalities put a welcome space between us as we weren't competing for national titles or for places on teams. We both knew we could help the other to the next level.

Training for the 400 metres is gruelling, and it lightens the load significantly if there's someone beside you of a similar standard so you can alternate who leads the reps, encouraging each other to gut it out. Nick was great at managing our competitive nature, ensuring sessions didn't turn into races. There were always target times. If we wanted to drive on and blow the session to pieces, we could, but he was always very clear: 'This is what I want you to run.'

Occasionally, he'd put 'AQAP' beside a rep on our training programme: as quick as possible. You knew then it was time to blast it. On some of those, if I finished ahead of Rooney, it gave me a huge lift because I knew just how good he was. It was like tennis, and while the standard was a shock to the system at the start, it wasn't long before I was returning his serve in training.

Rooney had an amazing engine. He was an athletic freak: six-foot-six with a long, raking stride that seemed to cover ground with zero effort. I knew I had to be ready for every session or he'd destroy me. I started paying more attention to rest and recovery, knowing I had to be *on it* every day.

Graham Hedman was also in the group, a 45.8-second 400 metres runner. We called him 'Kamikaze Graham' as he'd go off like a lunatic in the last rep of each session, then usually blow a gasket, with Rooney and I pacing things more evenly and then storming past.

Our training week revolved around three key sessions: on Tuesdays, Thursdays and Saturdays. On Monday mornings, we did speed drills and a technique session, working on our sprint mechanics alongside the true speed merchants, guys like James Dasaolu (a 9.91-second 100 metres man) and Harry Aikines-Aryeetey (who ran 10.00). In the evening, the entire group, from Nick's elites to his college athletes, did circuit training together.

Tuesday morning was the hardest session of the week:

the one we dreaded. Ahead of the track season, it'd be something like two sets of 3x300m, with three minutes' rest between reps and six minutes between sets. It left us all in rag order, with bodies strewn across the track, resembling a warzone. That afternoon, we'd hit the gym for core stability work. On Wednesdays, we did weights and recovery running. On Thursdays, we did a grass endurance session through the winter, which would be replaced by another stomach-churning track session in spring and summer. Fridays were the same as Wednesdays: weights and a recovery session.

Then the big, ball-breaking finish to the week was on Saturday morning: a *fartlek*.

That's a Swedish word meaning 'speed play', and it involves running at various paces and distances for a set amount of time overall, whether it be twenty minutes or sixty. It was a great way to develop conditioning, but few elite sprinters did that type of training. It's torture for speed or power athletes, and every *fartlek* became a war of attrition: survival of the fittest.

The first one of the training block might be 25 minutes and that would build up to 45 minutes across the winter. But that only counted the time spent running, and with recoveries included, you might be out there, suffering, for an hour and a half. It was all done on grass, with various markers on the landscape – a row of hedges or a tree – denoting the start and finish of each rep. Given the underfoot conditions were usually mucky, we'd wear cross country spikes and, no matter the weather, we'd soldier through. I loved that. As the rain pelted down and the wind cut through me, my feet slipping in the mud, I'd think, *the Americans and Jamaicans aren't doing this shit.*

Nick broke the *fartlek* into different units. We'd do a series of 'short hedge rows' (50 metres fast, with a jog back recovery) and 'long hedge rows' (100 metres fast with a jog back recovery). That would be followed by short hill reps up a steep 40–50-metre incline. On some of those, we'd run up the hill backwards, which burned the hell out of your glutes and hamstrings: a great way to develop strength in the posterior muscle chain. Then we'd do shuttle runs before moving back to the side of the rugby pitches for the grand finale: upslopes. They were done along a grass bank that was 170 metres long, the incline growing steeper with each step. The finish line was a fire hydrant that we ran towards as if our lives depended on it.

We always finished with four upslopes, and everyone in the group kept something in reserve for them, knowing they'd drain whatever life was left in us. It was always carnage at the end, with bodies dropping like bowling pins. But there was elation amid the exhaustion, with high fives all around once the pain subsided. Nick oversaw various groups, from Olympians to club athletes, but everyone did the *fartlek* together, running and suffering as one. There were no egos, no elitism, with everyone feeling the same pain and encouraging others to get through it.

At training, Nick wasn't overly vocal, but he'd give clear and concise cues as we ran past him. 'Controlled. Smooth. Shoulders.'

If you didn't know Nick, you probably wouldn't warm to him, but once you're in his circle, he's helpful, accommodating, approachable. He understood the type of athlete I was: obsessive. I'd wreck his head at times, banging on the door of his office for a chat. 'Nick, how are we gonna do this?' But he liked that, seeing how deeply I applied myself. As Chris Rawlinson told me in those early months, 'You'll do well because you're committed to this.'

If you weren't applying yourself as Nick wanted, he'd let you know. One time we were on a training camp in Los Angeles and went to an NBA game. We were all relaxed, enjoying the break from the daily grind, when Nick turned around and spotted my tub of popcorn.

'What the fuck are you eating that shit for?'

Oh, OK.

In Loughborough, I started paying much closer attention to my diet, learning how to fuel properly. *RIP to The Carb King*. Rooney had a more relaxed approach and he had one hell of a sweet tooth. In LA, we were sharing an apartment with Nick. Rooney went out one day and bought a tub of Sun-Maid raisins. He came back in, dumped all the raisins in the bin, then filled the tub with Skittles. Then he'd walk around, eating his 'raisins', with Nick none the wiser.

A few times a year, our group would do a skinfold callipers test to measure body fat. On the male side, it wasn't a big deal, but on the female side, it created pandemonium. There'd be tears on the day of the tests. Some people were very sensitive about it. Two decades on, times have changed in this department; now, it's often considered taboo for a coach to discuss athletes' weight or body fat.

But the reality is that as a performance coach, Nick was simply looking at every angle he could to help his athletes improve. While it can be a hard conversation, there are times where it's necessary. It's obviously not something that needs to be done at every level, and it has to be handled responsibly, without encouraging destructive habits. But when dealing with elite athletes, weight has to be talked about on occasion.

Genetically, I was lucky in that department, but I'd always review my results and take them on board. At the end of the day, my goal was to run as fast as possible and I wanted to be cheetah-lean to achieve that, not carrying excess weight or muscle, but the *optimal* amount.

In sprinting, a hugely important metric is your power-to-weight ratio. In the gym, it was all about building power, but there's a reason the strongest men in the world don't run very fast, and it comes down to the weight part of the equation. Nutrition was a key part in managing that.

For a 400 metres athlete, I had always been a skinny whippet, but in those first few months at Loughborough I went through a hypertrophy phase, doing a lot of work in the gym, my weight rising from 78kg to 82kg. When I went home a few months later, that didn't go unnoticed. I was sitting in a bar in Dublin with friends when one of them said, 'Fucking hell, Gillick, what are you doing over there?' A few months after that, I came home again and another guy, who I didn't know as well, thought it was too good to be true.

'C'mon, David, look at you,' he said. 'You must be fucking taking something.'

'What do you mean?' I asked, indignant.

'You must be taking some sort of drugs. You're ripped, lean, you're strong.'

I nearly threw the pint over his head. I knew just how much work it had taken to put on that muscle, naturally, and here was this guy, sitting in a pub, telling everyone it wasn't possible without drugs.

'Fuck you,' I told him.

Heading into 2007, I was reluctant about racing indoors, the wounds from the aftermath of Moscow and Madrid yet to heal. But there was no denying I was fitter, stronger, faster, in every department.

My endurance was on a different level thanks to the *fartleks* and I was lifting heavier in the gym. My mindset was also better, the doubts subsiding, my confidence rising. Still, I wanted to keep building for the summer and skip the indoor season.

'Nick, I moved over here to try be the best I can be *outdoors*,' I said.

But the European indoors were being staged just down the road in Birmingham. Nick didn't want me to pass up a medal opportunity. 'I'll tell you what we'll do,' he said. 'We'll map everything out for the summer, but we might look at one race, see how you go, early in the indoor season.'

That race was in Düsseldorf, where I came up against a

strong German: Bastian Swillims. By that point, I was living with Rooney and, as I left the apartment, he gave me a good-luck handshake. 'You're gonna surprise yourself,' he said. He was right: I smashed the Irish indoor 400 metres record, running 45.91 to edge victory over Swillims. It was the fastest time in Europe that season, and the Europeans were just four weeks later. Given the form I was in, I had to go and defend my title.

Still, our eyes remained focused on further down the line. Two days after the race, Nick threw me into another hard session with Rooney. 'Look, you need to get through these. It's the summer we're thinking about. The plan is still the plan.'

To perform at their peak, athletes need to taper off their training for several days, sometimes weeks. But do that too often and you lose your conditioning, meaning the eventual highpoint – which I was shooting for in the summer – might be lower. The decision was made: I would go to Birmingham, try to defend my title, but I wasn't easing off the gas on the way there.

The run in Düsseldorf turned heads. A few days later, Charles van Commenee, the UK Athletics Head Coach, came over at training. 'Well done, great record,' he said. That meant a lot, given compliments weren't easily won from the Dutchman, who had a reputation for being blunt and occasionally brutal. He once implemented a no-excuse policy at the World Championships, telling them that athletes complaining of injuries were seen by the public as 'pussies and wankers'.

Van Commenee had come to the track to watch Rooney's session but also took an interest in me, seeing me for what I was: a useful person to help Rooney reach the top.

Being at Loughborough, and seeing champions like Jessica Ennis rock in behind me at the gym, cranked up my professionalism several notches. As I looked to the European indoors, I was adamant that I'd be the model professional, deciding to take a taxi to Birmingham the day before to minimise disruption and conserve maximum energy.

By this point, I had bought fully into visualisation. I had raced in Birmingham a lot over the years and it was easy to close my eyes and picture the arena, the crowds, with me at the centre in my Irish vest. The 400 metres heats and semi-finals were on Friday, and every day up until Thursday, I visualised all that could happen. The result was always the same: me crossing the line first, arms outstretched.

The weekend before, Rooney and a few of our training group went to a pub to watch Ireland play England in the Six Nations. That was the year it was in Croke Park and, while I wasn't drinking, Rooney had a pint or two as he wasn't racing the European indoors. Guinness had a special offer: buy a pint, get a free hat. It was a green and white jester hat and Rooney returned to the table with a proposition. 'If you win gold next weekend, you have to wear that on your lap of honour.' We had a deal.

I coasted to victory in my heat in Birmingham, then was back on track that evening for the semi-final, drawn alongside my old rival Robert Tobin. It was a bumpy race, in which I just about got the better of Tobin in the home straight, edging victory in 46.16. The three hundredths of a second between us making a huge difference: it gave me a better lane for the final. Before that semi-final, I stood trackside watching Swillims win in a much quicker time, 45.92.

Fuck, he looks good.

I knew I'd have to be at my very best to beat him. There was just one hundredth of a second between our personal bests. One tiny mistake and the gold was his.

The team hotel was near the arena and, as I was walking back to it after the semi-final, I got a text informing me of the lane draw for the final: I was in five, with Swillims in six.

I have it. I fucking have it.

I could see how the race would unfold: Swillims was a fast starter and, drawn on the outside, he was certain to go off fast and take the lead as we broke from lanes. But I was confident I could get in pole position behind him and, just as it had been in Madrid, be the hunter and not the hunted on the second lap. My plan was hatched, and it was a very simple one.

I'm gonna track him all the way, and then kick like a fucking mule.

At breakfast the following morning, I was far more relaxed than I'd been in Madrid, the work I'd done with Enda paying clear dividends. There was a group of Irish athletes there and just after I arrived, James Nolan said, 'I think we're gonna get another medal today!'

But this time, such expectation floated right over my head. I was calm, confident. I ate slowly, not having to force my food down, enjoying the fact I was preparing for a major final. I went out for a jog then rested up.

Later, Nick came over to talk through the race. 'Top two at the bell,' he told me. 'He's in lane six, he's running blind, so he's going to go out hard. Get as close as you can, be top two at the bell and then go and win it.'

The warm-up area in Birmingham was a large hall underneath the arena. After we checked in, all six finalists were ushered into a lift, crowding together as we made the trip up a level to the second call room. Once there, I could hear the roar from the crowd – the place was packed – and catch that familiar scent of the track. I did some breathing exercises to stay calm and tried to keep my legs warm with some high-knees drills in the tiny space we had to move around. I felt assured about my training, and I'd been racing so well. The fears faded away.

As I walked out for the final, the first thing I felt was the noise: it was *loud*. There were lots of Irish in the arena and they made their presence felt, but I kept my head down, looking at the track, running the race in my head one last time.

The fire is lit. Run through that wall in the first five metres.

Swillims was a formidable rival, one who certainly looked the part: tall, strong, with wavy blond hair and a golden tan. He came out in different versions of the German kit for each round, and for the final he showed up in a full-body speed suit. *Jesus, I dunno if I'd be comfortable in that.*

He looked the quintessential German, while I was Paddy Irishman: singlet, shorts and a farmer's tan.

I got a flying start, gaining half a step on Swillims on the first bend. But down the back straight, he surged ahead, and around the second turn, I saw an unwanted sight appear on my left: the yellow vest of Sweden's Yohan Wissman, who had great 200 metres speed and was putting it to good use, trying to get to the break in second.

Top two at the bell. Do not let him get ahead.

I put in a surge coming down off the bend and moved across Wissman, shutting the door, owning the space. I wanted to be as close as possible to Swillims, without tripping over him, as we headed out on the second lap. But he had a metre on me. Down the back straight I tried to get closer, but his robotic running style looked as flawless as ever, the margin staying fixed, as if there was an invisible, immovable stick between us.

Then, entering the last turn, I gained an inch. That's all it was – no more – but it changed everything.

I have him. I fucking have him.

The difference was tiny, but we could both sense it, with him better able to hear my steps and my breathing, and me spotting the first sign of weakness in his stride. It's like when you're fishing and you feel the line twitching: you're not there yet, but you know you're on to something. It lifted my spirits, just as it had in Madrid, and I sling-shotted wide off the last bend, going for broke.

But Swillims had a lot more in the tank than Canal. He didn't lose his form and kept pumping away, his arms like pistons. With 30 metres left, I still had half a metre to find and the gap was closing slowly, slowly, slowwwwly, but the line was also approaching – fast.

Then things got ugly. My teeth were out, eyeballs bulging, neck straining. *Do you like Linford Christie?* I closed another inch, finally drawing alongside him with 15 metres to go. He tried to respond but there was nothing left, and I edged in front and leaned for the line.

First.

This was everything I'd visualised, so much so that when I finally crossed the line for real, it felt like I'd done it before. It felt so … normal.

I threw my arms in the air, then ran over to the advertising hoarding, shaking it and let out a massive roar. Then I kept roaring, the emotion spilling out of me. I knew why: it wasn't because of the gold medal so much as it was about my decision to leave Ireland, uprooting myself and rolling the dice on what was, ultimately, a big gamble. But now it had paid off. I turned around and saw Swillims hunched over, deflated, taking a seat on the track. He'd run a massive PB of 45.62 for silver and I felt for him. I had pulled out the race of my life, running 45.52.

As I was celebrating, I saw a green missile appear in my peripheral vision and I stuck out a hand, plucking the tricolour out of the air. As Con Murphy said in the RTÉ studio, 'I don't know what was better: his run or the flag catch.' Then I spotted Rooney, who threw me the green and white jester's hat. A deal is a deal: I stuck it on my head for the lap of honour. All my friends, family and relatives were in the stands on the back straight and seeing them jumping up and down remains one of the best moments of my career. There was joy – pure joy – on their faces, and whatever satisfaction I got from my own performance then multiplied several times over.

In the mixed zone, the Irish press pack was waiting. We hugged. Then the pain started to hit. I had to lie down against the wall, the ecstasy turning to agony, the 400 metres finally exacting its inevitable revenge.

I had been called for drug testing and the chaperone was there with me, waiting patiently, but I couldn't stand, instead lying down in a deep state of distress. I eventually did get up and followed the chaperone to the drug testing room, where I drank as much fluid as I could. But racing a 400 metres that hard – going completely to the well – puts you in a dehydrated state. I was stuck there for an age, trying to provide a urine sample. With little to do but drink and reflect, what I had achieved started to sink in.

This felt so different to Madrid. That had all been brand new and there wasn't any expectation. But this time, winning is what I wanted, what I *expected*. In between, I'd had the failures of Gothenburg and Moscow, the frustration of being unable to extract the performance I was capable of. But now I'd done it, nailed it, with a time that elevated me to a new level. The negative voice, at last, went silent.

It was a couple of hours later when I got back to the hotel. The doors opened and a horde of Irish erupted in celebration. One of my best mates, Mark Donlon, was there and he started crying when we reunited, having been on a bit of a journey with me – there through all the bad days – in the years before.

The group headed out to an Irish bar and when they eventually shut the doors on us, we continued the party back at the hotel, singing rebel songs into the night.

I wasn't planning to go back to Ireland after Birmingham, but the team managers said it'd be great if I did: doing some media rounds and utilising the spotlight while I had it.

They were right. The next day, I hopped on a flight and was handed a newspaper with my photo on the front. There was another big welcome at Dublin Airport, with Colm Murray – the sports reporter with RTÉ, who I'd spent a lifetime watching on TV – walking up, handing me another newspaper and telling me: 'Frame that.'

I was a guest on *The Late Late Show* and did a horde of other interviews. Nick – who was my agent as well as my coach – got to work looking for sponsorship deals and trying to get me lanes in higher-quality races. He was delighted with the race – it was exactly what he wanted – but he also wasn't keen for me to spend too long in Dublin: he thought I'd be going on the piss.

'Go home, enjoy,' he said. 'But it's back to work next week.'

We both knew it was a whole different beast outdoors and we didn't want to lose sight of that. I stayed in Ireland a few days longer than Nick wanted, trying to take opportunities to earn a bit of cash and put myself out there for endorsements. Ultimately, having some financial reserve would allow me to commit to athletics and stay the course for several years.

Sponsorship soon came my way in the most unlikely of places: a men's bathroom.

In the wake of the Birmingham gold, I got a message from someone at White's Hotel in Wexford, offering me a free stay and the chance to try out their new cryo-chamber, which sportspeople sometimes use for recovery. While there, I got into the lift with a couple and the man recognised me, congratulating me on the gold. We made some small talk before parting ways.

A few days later, I was at the Red Cow Moran Hotel in Dublin for an engagement and I arrived bursting for a piss. I parked up, made a beeline through the lobby for the bathroom. 'Ah, there he is!' said a voice from behind, a man who followed me in and pulled up at the urinal next to me. It was the same guy from that lift in Wexford: Seán White.

'Are you looking for sponsorship?' he asked.

'Yeah,' I said.

'Well, I'd love to help you out.'

He gave me his business card and said, 'Have your guys get in touch with my guys.' We shook on it – after we'd washed our hands – and lo and behold, he ended up supporting me throughout my career. Incredibly, he never wanted anything in return. No logos on my kit, no shout-outs in the media. Nothing. He had just seen me on TV and liked the way I spoke. 'I love seeing Irish people doing well,' he said. 'I just want to help you out.'

Suddenly, doors started opening all around. The second gold medal, and my fast winning time, had pushed me to a new level. It led to my first professional shoe contract. Before that, I had had some support from Asics but it wasn't an actual contract: they just sent me free shoes, spikes and gear from their Irish distributor. In Gothenburg the previous summer, I went to the Asics hospitality and was offered a contract, but there was no money in it. To get paid, I needed to run 44 seconds for 400 metres and I was still miles off that. I chose not to sign the contract, preferring to remain a free agent rather than tie myself into something that was worth very little.

I was still thankful to have the free shoes and gear – it saved me buying them – but the first thing you crave in the elite athletics world is a paid, professional contract: a status symbol that meant other athletes took you seriously. Birmingham opened a huge door on that front. Joe Rafferty – who had told me in Paris that I just wasn't running fast enough – was working with adidas by then and after the European Indoor final, he came to my room with a bottle of champagne.

He soon helped sort a contract with adidas: a one-year deal that guaranteed me €20,000, with extra bonuses if I hit benchmarks like running under 45 seconds, broke a national record or made a world final.

Once you sign that kind of deal, you can't wear anything from a rival sports brand, so it was OK to walk around in an Abercrombie & Fitch hoodie, for example, but a pair of New Balance shorts or Nike socks were off limits. As part of the deal, I'd get a winter kit drop, a summer kit drop and a competition kit drop, with all the latest pro racing gear. I could also call up and order more anytime I wanted it. The kit drops were substantial. It was like Christmas day when the delivery man showed up to my house with a tower of boxes, with shoes stacked from floor to ceiling.

By then, I was on a grant of €20,000 from the Sports Council, while Seán was giving me €10,000 a year. Anytime I was home, I'd meet him for a coffee and, invariably, he'd pull out a wad and go, 'Here's a few bob for you.' One time he hopped up, went across to the bank, came back and handed me around €1000: 'Here's a bit of spending money.'

Given my sudden earning potential, I had to quickly grow a business brain. Derval O'Rourke put me in touch with an accountant who showed me how to set myself up as a limited company, taking a wage so that when I had a good year, I wouldn't immediately lose half of my income to the taxman. Derval worked a bit with Horizon Sports Management, a marketing company based in Dublin, and she set up a link between us, telling me they were good at getting her commercial gigs. I gave them a call and they got to work, looking for opportunities. Not long after, I was back in Loughborough when I got a text message from Conor Ridge, founder of Horizon: 'Great news. Secured Spar. Yourself and Derval. Eighty grand to you.'

Holy fuck.

It was a one-year deal, with Derval and I part of an advertising campaign that would run through the Osaka World Championships. When the cheque arrived in the post, I could barely believe it was real. I was 23, but decided the best thing I could do with that money was to think long term. Given how happy I was at Loughborough, I decided to buy a house, which cost £180,000. An Irish bank gave me a mortgage for £144,000 – the Celtic Tiger clearly still alive and well, given my income wasn't exactly reliable. Once that purchase went through, I was back to having next to nothing in my account so I rented out the spare rooms and the downstairs sitting room to meet the repayments. I needed to guarantee myself a steady income no matter what happened on the racing front, given how one bad year could see me return to just scraping by.

But as things stood, it looked rosy. I was finally earning a proper living from athletics and had all the backing I needed to reach the top. I was healthy, happy, settled in my environment and training with a great coach and several world-class athletes. There was a little over a year until the Beijing Olympics. I would have no excuse for coming up short.

CHAPTER 8

CLIMBING THE LADDER

Training camps can be incredibly boring, but that's kind of the point. As former US miler Marty Liquori said, 'You've got to be a little bored to be doing really good training', the implication being that when the session is the most interesting part of your day, the quality goes up a notch.

For sprinters, training camps are all about getting some sun on your back and recovering better. Being based in England, vitamin D levels are an issue for much of the year as, in warmer weather, your muscles, tendons – everything – just functions better, allowing you to step up the quality and hit faster times better than you could when it's 12 degrees and raining.

Towards the end of March 2007, I flew to Los Angeles to join Rooney, Nick and Kemel Thompson for a four-week training camp. We rented a place in Irvine, a leafy suburb in south LA, and trained on the blue track at the University of California, Irvine. Kemel was Jamaican, and he brought a laid-back wit and chat to our environment. He was a lovely guy, and vastly experienced, showing me and Rooney the ropes, giving us pointers on how to live like a professional. Training camp meant lots of hard, high-quality sessions, while the rest of the time was spent recovering.

People at home would say, 'Wow, LA! What are you seeing there?'

'Well, nothing, really.'

You can't go on the beer, nor can you spend the breaks between sessions in tourist mode, which drains energy you need for training. Grocery shopping would feel like a big outing, as would a trip to a local coffee shop, where we'd sit and chat for hours.

We did two sessions a day: on the track in the morning and in the gym in the evening, doing core work, weights or circuits. We often squeezed in a physio or chiropractic session in between.

I arrived a few days later than the lads and, as a result, wound up sharing a room with Nick. Little did I know, he snored like a horse. One night it broke me. I woke him up. 'Nick, shut the fuck up!' The lads found it hilarious. Rooming with Nick was a kind of initiation to the group. The following year, I paid more just to have a room by myself.

On rest days, we'd drive down to Newport Beach or go shopping, spending money on things we didn't need at Abercrombie & Fitch. But our sessions were ramping up steadily, and we didn't have much energy for anything beyond training, resting, eating and sleeping.

In the media, some journalists were looking at my 45.5 indoors and suggesting I would run 44.5 outdoors. *No pressure.* But the sessions were going well and sub-45 seemed realistic. I opened my season in early June, with a rust-busting 46.33 in the driving rain of Glasgow. The following week, I went to Geneva, where I was 100 per cent sure I'd break 45 seconds, given the times I was hitting in training. I didn't, though it was still a big breakthrough: an Irish record of 45.23, with Rooney third in 46.02. I didn't get any faster in my next few races, one of which was at the Cork City Sports, where I was disqualified for a false start. I just wasn't quite connecting the dots in races, lining up all the parts that needed to be executed well to nail the big one.

In July, I got my first taste of the top-tier professional circuit: the Golden Gala in Rome. That meeting was part of the Golden League, which was even more exclusive than its current incarnation, the Diamond League. The latter has 15 meetings, but the Golden League had just six and Rome was one of the best, staged in the massive Stadio Olimpico, a 70,000-seater stadium that hosted the Olympics in 1960 and the World Cup final in 1990.

These days, the circuit is delineated with levels that give athletes a clear barometer of their place on the professional ladder, with the Diamond League at the top and then the Continental Tour below, the quality of athlete and prize money dropping as you descend from gold, silver to bronze level.

Back in 2007, a lane at a Golden League was a sign you'd

reached the sport's elite tier, and the treatment was different to what I was used to. At lower-tier events, you often paid for your own flights and hotel. Sometimes you'd get picked up by organisers, other times you'd be at the mercy of public transport, trying to navigate your way to a random hotel without the help of a smartphone.

At a Golden League event, however, *everything* was taken care of. In Rome, I arrived at the airport and was welcomed by volunteers dressed head to toe in the meeting's official merchandise, who walked me to a shuttle transfer to the meeting hotel where I was greeted with a gift bag. The hotel was top end and the quality of food at the buffet was also a cut above. In the lobby was a desk with all the details of transfers to the stadium, and there was a physio room where you could book in for treatment – all free of charge.

On the circuit, it's typically two athletes to a room, except for the special few superstars who get their own double. If there was another Irishman competing, the organisers would usually put me in with him but, if not, it was down to the luck of the draw. I quickly learned not to be too precious, but I would still do my best to stack the deck in my favour, going to the check-in desk upon arrival, scanning the names and asking to get put in with someone I knew. Otherwise, you could be in for an awkward few days.

One time in Salamanca, I was rooming with an Australian long jumper, Fabrice Lapierre. He was a grand fella – shy and quiet – but it got to a point as we passed the hours, resting on our beds, where I thought: *Fuck, will you speak?* The day of the meeting, he couldn't find his camera and was looking for it non-stop. He was in Europe for the summer so had a horde of baggage with him. I was relaxing on the bed as he was rummaging around, then he turned to me.

'Have you seen my camera?'

'Sorry, I haven't seen it.'

'Well, I had it,' he said, looking annoyed.

'Well, I haven't seen it.'

He continued rooting around, then turned to me again.

'Have you seen my camera?'

'Mate, I haven't seen your camera!'

I got the impression he thought I'd nicked it, and while I wanted to tell him I didn't touch his poxy camera, I also didn't want to make an enemy so I left it at that. Eventually, of course, he came across it in one of his bags.

I'd always be nervous when arriving at an event, wondering who I'd be rooming with. Some athletes are happy to sit there in silence, others would need to chat. Being Irish, there weren't many of my compatriots on the circuit and the only Brits I really knew were those based in Loughborough. But when you see an athlete you know, they become your best friend, someone to go to dinner with and avoid the awkwardness of eating alone – or worse, with a table full of athletes who don't speak to you.

In Rome, a year later, I was rooming with Chris Thompson – a British distance runner who was often around Loughborough. We had great craic. We watched an Indy 500 race from start to finish the night before the meeting, laughing about how this was the *only* scenario in which we'd ever sit through that. At the time, beetroot juice was all the rage, with some research emerging that it improved performance. The recommendation was to take one shot. Chris decided to double or triple that. Big mistake. The bathroom in our room was like a murder scene all day. He was running in and out constantly, going, 'What have I done?' We had one hell of a laugh over it.

Another great roommate was Marcin Lewandowski, a Polish middle-distance runner who was as sound as it gets. I shared with him in Monaco, the Rolls Royce of professional meetings, and our room overlooked the hairpin turn on the Formula One circuit. Looking out, we knew just how lucky we were to do this for a living. Marcin was like me – a student of the sport – and despite being in a different event, he knew all about my career. We traded stories about training, races, championships, and the hours passed with ease.

It's not always so comfortable. One time, I was put in with a guy from Austria who made a habit of walking around the room bollock naked. My abiding memory was him sitting on the side of his bed, wearing tiny, Y-front underwear, legs open, chatting away. Meanwhile, I'm talking back, awkward as hell, trying to look anywhere else.

Another time, I was rooming with a sprinter from the Bahamas who, despite being in Europe, was still living on Caribbean time. He brought a PlayStation with him, hooked it up to the TV and was tapping away into the early hours of the morning. Meanwhile, I'm trying – and failing – to sleep just two metres away. I quickly learned to bring earplugs on the circuit, doing what I could to control the controllables.

It was the same with food. Most events provided breakfast, lunch and dinner at the athletes' hotel, but the quality varied widely. On the day of a race, I always liked to sleep in late so if breakfast closed at 10, I'd usually miss it. I'd bring my own breakfast, weighing out 80 grams of oats in a bowl, adding hot water from the kettle in the room and mixing it with whey protein. Once I arrived, my first port of call was always to find a local shop, stocking up on water and bananas. And I'd always bring lots of snacks, such as tinned fish in tomato sauce, which drew some strange looks when I'd crack one open on the plane.

The faster you run, the better the meets, the fancier the hotels, the nicer the food. It all spawns from a simple metric: how fast you are. But if you're coming back from injury or on the decline, all those little comforts very quickly disappear.

The day before the race in Rome, I visited the warm-up track, Stadio dei Marmi. It's one of the most beautiful tracks in the world, the seating area made from white Carrara marble, with sixty marble statues around its perimeter. It felt like being in the Colosseum.

Suddenly, the A-list stars of athletics were all around me, sharing the bus or a ten-person round table in the dining room. There was Asafa Powell, the 100 metres world record holder; Eliud Kipchoge, who at that point was still focused on the track, long before he became the greatest marathoner of all time; there was Sanya Richards, who went on to win Olympic and world titles over 400 metres. Then there was me. I felt so inferior. Some athletes would walk into the track with their entourage: a masseuse, a coach, an agent. I was flying solo.

Do I deserve to be here? Am I gonna be found out?

Jogging around, I was cautious of getting in anyone's way, while on the bus back to the hotel, it was like those movies where a kid is nervously walking down the aisle, eyeing who to sit beside. *Sorry, there's someone there.* It felt like the first day of school.

The favourite for the men's 400 metres in Rome was LaShawn Merritt, who was 21 at the time and had run a scorching 44.14 the previous year. I was drawn in lane one – the last lane I'd want, but beggars can't be choosers.

I had just signed my deal with adidas and the only competition kit they sent me before Rome was a speed suit, which wasn't my usual style, but I didn't have much choice.

The day of the meeting, the bus to the stadium was given a police escort, with cars and motorbikes leading the way with blue lights flashing, sirens blaring, carving a path for us through Rome's rush-hour traffic.

After I warmed up, we were led through a long tunnel into the stadium and, as I walked out into that vast openness, I looked around in absolute awe. This is where I always dreamt of being. Before I set up my blocks, I glanced at the pitch: to the exact point where, in the 1990 World Cup quarter-final, Italy's Totò Schillaci broke Irish hearts with the goal that ended our tournament. I was a few days shy of my seventh birthday at the time, and that goal ruined my week.

Not many Irish athletes got to race at Golden Leagues and so I felt a representative of my nation on that start line, flying the flag. There were nine athletes in the race and given the lane draw, and my inexperience at that level, I was pleased with my performance: eighth place in 45.81, with Merritt winning in 44.44.

After the race, as I was walking back to the warm-up track, I recognised an athlete whose photo I'd had pinned on my wall for the previous ten years: Michael Johnson, the two-time Olympic 400 metres champion and then world record holder, who was an agent at the time. I walked up to him, nervous and in awe.

'Mr Johnson, any chance I could get a quick autograph?'

'No,' he said, turning and walking off, having made me feel like a right tool.

That night, there was a barbecue at the hotel, alongside the pool. I sat at a table alongside the Australian sprint hurdles star, Sally Pearson. I didn't know anyone there so I tried to make conversation, asking how her race went. 'Shit,' she said, before looking down and playing with her food. Then she got up and walked off.

Maurie Plant, an older Australian who was a fixture on the circuit, was alongside us. 'She's just pissed off, mate,' he said. 'She ran shite.'

I knew how she felt. I had been there many times. The night after a race, an athlete's performance is usually written across their face, the bright smile or the dark sulk clear for all to see. You learn to be empathetic and understanding with others, especially when it comes to your roommate. With the combination of caffeine and adrenaline, it's always hard to sleep the night after a race, and you often end up chatting with them into the early hours. One time, I had a great run and was full of beans, but my roommate, Tim Benjamin, had a poor run. I was banging on about my race for an age and, nice guy that he was, he didn't call me out on it, but he was probably fed up. Later on, I realised just how annoying that is, when you just want to press the ejector button and get the hell out of there.

Despite finishing eighth in Rome, it was one of my better paydays, earning me a couple of grand in prize money. I wanted a faster time, and to be closer to the world's best, but I thought, *at least I got a few quid.*

At most levels of athletics, eighth place earned you nothing.

I returned home for nationals, winning in 46.34, then had two solid if unspectacular races in Belgium and Switzerland, not threatening the 45-second barrier in either, chiefly because I wasn't getting it right in the first half, which always made the second half a grind.

The big event of the year, the Osaka World Championships, was up next. The Irish held a training camp beforehand in Matsue, a small coastal city a few hundred kilometres from Osaka. It had a strong Irish connection, being the one-time residence of a famed writer on Japanese culture, Lafcadio Hearn, who was of Irish descent.

Holding camps were a feature for most major championships, a chance to get acclimatised to conditions and get rid of any jetlag before you went to the line.

Japan was a proper culture shock, but in a fun, fascinating way. There was a young Irish guy, an intern at the local city hall, who served as a mediator between us and the locals. The only issue: his Japanese was terrible. One night there was a banquet at the hotel and he had to get up and give a speech in Japanese, but the poor chap could barely string a word together. We were all trying to hold in the laughter and most of us succeeded, though Patsy McGonagle, our team manager, failed in a big way.

Our hosts had A4 pictures of us and one lady came up to our table, asking, 'Which one are you? You all look the same.'

Matsue was a quiet, sleepy city, but the tranquillity was perfect to get me in the right headspace to compete. Enda had made the trip with me and the morning of my 400 metres heat in Osaka, he slipped a note under my door. 'You've done the work. Go out there and chop down the tree.'

Working with him, I learned how to avoid going down the wrong path with my mindset. If I was getting uptight in the hotel, I'd go for a walk. When the nerves hit, as they inevitably did, I allowed myself to embrace them, repeating positive affirmations and reminding myself that nerves were a sign I was up for this. I wrote down all the doubts and, without a garden in which to burn them, I ripped up the page and tossed it into the bin.

My heat was in the morning and when I walked out of the hotel at 7.30 a.m., the temperature was well into the thirties. It felt like being back in Kingston, the heat and humidity almost suffocating. This was my first World Championships as an individual, the biggest event in athletics outside of the Olympics, and I felt the difference in size and scale to the Europeans or World indoors. But I wasn't daunted by it. I felt calm and confident.

I was drawn alongside Olympic champion Jeremy Wariner, with Rooney also in my heat. Wariner coasted to victory while I beat Rooney to the third and final qualifying spot for the semi-finals, running a strong 45.35. Making the final was always a huge longshot, but the following day I backed up my run by finishing sixth in my semi-final in 45.37. I could walk away with my head held high.

The championships marked a step forward, showing that I had what it took to make the Olympic final in 2008. I finished off the season with two 400 metres races in Italy, unable to break 46 seconds in either. But I didn't care. Athletes are often like that with post-championship races on the circuit: it's just about earning a few quid, getting through it. You feel it in both body and mind.

I'm done. I need a break.

I didn't go on holidays, but returned to Dublin and went on the lash with my friends for a couple of weeks, blowing off some steam. That's important, too. After eating crap and drinking steadily for long enough, I'd start feeling terrible. But it gets to a point where you get sick of that way of life and crave the return to a healthier, cleaner existence. At the end of those two weeks, I was fully ready for the pendulum to swing back.

There was a huge year ahead, an Olympic year, and I was refreshed and recharged, ready to commit like never before.

Back in Loughborough, one of my priorities over the summer had been to find people to rent the rooms in my house, helping to cover my mortgage repayments of £1200 a month.

In athletics, you just never have full financial security. You're always one injury away from unemployment. I'd been sharing an apartment with Graham Hedman so he was the first to move in and I turned one of the downstairs living rooms into a fourth bedroom, meaning I had two spare rooms to rent. Loughborough is a small place so when I put it out there that I was looking for people, it wasn't long before we heard back.

I heard from a girl in Nick's student group. We did circuits and *fartlek* together so I knew her already, and she had a friend who was a middle-distance runner who could also move in: Charlotte.

They seemed like ideal housemates, and they moved in a few days before I returned from Dublin, entering a house with no furniture. The first time I met Charlotte, she and Graham had just come back after a trip to Tesco to buy bins and when she walked in, she asked me, 'Why do you have a foreign reg?'

'I'm Irish,' I said.

'Oh, OK.'

I had my eyebrow pierced at the time, and she told me later that, after committing to moving in, she had looked through my Facebook page with her sisters to get a sense of who she'd be living with. They concluded that I was gay.

Straight away, I liked Charlotte. She was from Sunderland and was good looking: tall, blond, slim, athletic, with a radiant energy, always smiling and laughing. That first weekend, it was just me and her in the house for a while and we got to know each other while assembling flatpack IKEA furniture. Conversation came easy. I liked her.

There was some chemistry, she was a bit of a flirt, but I thought she was like that with everyone. She was my housemate so I wasn't going to try it on, get rejected, then have to live with that awkwardness. Another big factor: I was heading into an Olympic year and I didn't want to be shitting on my doorstep. In the group, I'd seen several relationships blossom and then fail and it always got awkward. I just wanted to train and didn't want anything in the way.

So even though I liked Charlotte, I did absolutely nothing about it.

I got back training, hammering all my sessions in those first few weeks. But soon my body started to struggle. I went for blood tests and sent the results to Brian Moore, a specialist in sports haematology. He called me when he saw my results. 'David, these are some of the wildest numbers I've seen. You need to pull back on training.'

But I was stubborn. 'Ah, it's just because I'm back into training, my body is a bit tired, sore. It's adjusting to the routine.'

'Yeah,' he said. 'But you need to listen to your body.'

I didn't and within a couple of weeks my Achilles flared up. That led me to Limerick, where I spent a week with the renowned physical therapist, Gerard Hartmann. He spent hours treating me each day, then I'd go to his assistant, Ger Keane, and do a load of core work. It was exhausting but productive. Each night, as I walked back to the house I was staying in, I would think: *that was a fucking good day.* When you get an injury in a big year, it's very easy to slip into crisis mode and feel like you're falling behind, but Hartmann had an ability to reframe everything as a positive. He gets into your body but also your mind. I returned to Loughborough a healthier athlete, hungrier than ever to get back to work.

In the weeks prior, Charlotte had been on a few dates and while that made me a bit jealous, I knew I couldn't object as I'd given her no indication that I was interested. When I was going to Limerick, she had dropped me to the airport and at the time, there was another athlete – Adrian Hemery, son of British great David Hemery – who was interested in her. Graham was always a great man to stir the pot, telling me, 'Hemery asked her out on a date!' I put on a front, acting like I didn't care, but on the way to the airport I decided to stand up for myself.

'Just to be clear,' I said to Charlotte. 'I don't fancy you.'

I was lying through my teeth, of course, and said it so flippantly before getting out of the car. After that, she went on a date with Adrian, thinking I had no interest. The reality? I was jealous of him having the courage to ask her out and instead of just telling the truth – that I liked her – I did the opposite, giving her a cold shoulder and seeing if it provoked a reaction. I was a typical, stupid, Irish bloke: afraid to say what I felt. But at the back of my mind, I was also afraid what would happen if I went for it and it didn't work out.

As the weeks wore on, and we spent more time around each other, I grew to like her more and more. We were still just friends, but I was happy in her company. I was relaxed and never felt like I was walking on eggshells. It was placid, comfortable, balanced. I was my true self. I wasn't acting and I also wasn't in awe of her. Sometimes that can happen in relationships: you're looking up at the person in some way, either personally or professionally, or they're looking up at you. But we were on the same level. Like me, Charlotte could be stubborn and she would hold me to account if I was out of line. She ticked every box, but I was afraid to make a move.

In December, I was invited to the RTÉ Sports Awards in Dublin, where I was nominated for sportsperson of the year. I initially turned it down but RTÉ were very keen for me to attend, offering to pay for my flights. Without thinking it through, I turned to Charlotte.

'Do you fancy coming to Dublin?'

'What?'

'Well, I'm up for these awards. I have a plus-one. Do you want to come?'

'*You're* gonna bring *me* to Dublin?'

'Yeah, but we'd be staying in my house with my folks.'

Amazingly, she said yes, and I told Mum on the way over, 'I'm bringing a friend.' We had a fun night at the awards, and slept in separate rooms at my parents' house – no messing. But while sitting in the living room late that night, I kissed her for the first time, waiting until I was 99.9 per cent sure that she'd kiss back. (Again, very Irish.) The next morning, we took an early flight back to Loughborough. I did the *fartlek* and then drove back to Dublin, via the ferry, for Christmas.

After I returned in the New Year, no one knew anything was going on between me and Charlotte and we only went on our first official date midway through January. I invited her to dinner and left the house a few minutes ahead of her, driving around the block a couple of times before pulling up outside to collect her. Casanova stuff.

There was a house party not long after where we got caught kissing on the stairs, and everyone knew about us after that. Soon enough, it became an official relationship.

With Charlotte, it felt different. Nothing seemed to get her down. She never came into the house with doom and gloom but had a positive, uplifting energy. She'd been a very good underage athlete, winning English Schools' titles at 800 metres and 1500 metres and beating the likes of Lisa Dobriskey and Fionnuala McCormack at Schools' Internationals. She had finished university by the time we met but stayed in Loughborough to continue training. She understood performance, and that constant quest to reach a higher level. She also understood that athletics was my priority. I wasn't the easiest to live with and, as the Olympics approached, she didn't hold it against me that my focus was somewhere else.

It was a different type of relationship to what I'd been used to. Normally at 23 or 24, you go out and have a few drinks, which eases everything in those early stages. But for us, it was an older lifestyle. In hindsight, it was a better way of getting to know each other, with both of us showing our true selves. Loughborough was a town, but there were lots of lovely rural areas around, places to go for a stroll and have coffee or lunch.

What would resonate more if you had a girlfriend: going to the pub or going for a walk?

My physio, Paula, was one of many to caution me about a new relationship. 'You've gotta be careful, this is a big year for you.' Lots of others said similar in the group: 'Housemates? There's no getting away from them ... '. I knew the danger: my priority was running fast and I didn't want to mess that up chasing women, but I *liked* being in a relationship. It gave me structure, routine.

When you're single, there are more distractions: you want to go out and there's a performance impact to that. Charlotte and I were both moving away from the student lifestyle and because our friends were athletes, socialising wasn't about going for pints. It was: 'Come on over, we'll make dinner.'

In Dublin, I struggled with saying no to nights out. If I went out and didn't drink, then I was the odd one out, the boring one. The lifestyle in Loughborough was a complete shift, which was no disrespect to anyone at home, but in Dublin being dedicated to athletics often left me feeling like a weirdo.

'Are you drinking tonight?'

'No.'

'You're boring.'

Then they'd go off and talk to someone else.

CHAPTER 9

THE TOOTHPASTE INCIDENT

On New Year's Eve 2007, with an Olympic year about to dawn, I took out my training diary and wrote the following:

I'm the driver of where I want to go. If I do not put in the petrol, I will not go anywhere. I want to develop and become the best athlete I can be. To run to my potential at an Olympic Games. To be at my very best when it's needed.

The road to doing that started with a training camp in Lanzarote. Things had gone reasonably well since the Achilles injury but, mentally, I felt like I was playing catch-up. Rooney was in good nick, which exaggerated my unease. He was beginning to gap me in sessions; I'd tie up on the last rep and didn't feel as strong as I had the previous year. It was starting to get into my head. I'd been taking creatine at the time, a legal supplement that had potential benefits for performance and recovery, and I loaded up on it during our training camp. But it caused me to retain water and my weight went up by 2kg. Rooney blitzed me in one of our sessions: 450m, 350m, 250m, 350m, 250m, 150m. That night, I pulled out the diary again.

> I've decided to knock the creatine on the head, it's not giving me any positives, only negatives. I'm dehydrated: legs feel heavy, there's always cramps. I tried it out. Didn't work. Move on.

I started to become incredibly strict with rest, recovery and food. *It's Olympic year, I need to do everything right.* In every area, I chased perfection. I had zero balance and, truth be told, I wasn't enjoying day-to-day life. All I could think about was August.

I bought an iPod Nano early that year and because it included free engraving, I got 'To Be Perfect' inscribed on the back: my motto for 2008. But things were not perfect. Far from it. I felt slow and heavy in Lanzarote, miles off where I needed to be. I was highly strung. I didn't want to go out for a coffee or lunch or do, well, *anything* outside of training. If my next hard session was on a Tuesday, then Sunday would be spent resting up. I over-analysed every detail of training, and life, searching for ways to find an edge.

Because it was Olympic year, I decided to skip the entire

THE TOOTHPASTE INCIDENT

indoor season, ignoring the World Indoors in Valencia, where my time from Birmingham the previous year would have been enough for gold. But that didn't bother me: *all that mattered was Beijing.*

In early March, things started to turn a corner. I did a session of 3x350m in Loughborough, and the British 4x400m squad were on the track at the time, watching every rep. I absolutely spanked the session, running my last 350 metres in a rapid 38.8 seconds. The British guys came over. 'Jesus, I never did that,' said one. Nick did the calculations on what the session would translate to for a 400 metres: 44.4 seconds, a time that could win an Olympic medal, if I could just nail it on the day in Beijing.

A few weeks later, we went to LA for our last training camp before the track season. We were opening our racing schedule at the Mt SAC Relays in Walnut, California in late April, with Rooney and I entered in the same 400 metres. I did some solid sessions in LA, but during the camp the evidence was clear: I wasn't quite returning his serve the way I had the previous year. I convinced myself I'd get closer to him in the race. But I didn't. Rooney won in 45.88. I was fourth in 46.39.

Bollocks, I'm not where I want to be.

Still, there had been progress. I was healthy and getting fitter each week. There was still almost four months until the Olympics: lots of time for things to click. When I arrived back in Loughborough, I opened my training diary and started writing:

> I need to start believing again or else I'm going to really let myself down. Think of why I'm here, why I'm doing this, why I decided to leave home, leave friends, break up a three-year relationship. Why I did what so many other people wouldn't do: in business, sport and life. Stand up to the plate. Be counted. I am Gillick: I work my tits off for everything I have. I'm the one who put me in this position, the one who runs the fuck out of myself. I'm the one who doesn't go out on the piss, who gives up a Saturday night. Why do I do it? To be perfect. To look in the mirror and say: 'Fair play to you.' I'm the one who matters. Nobody else. Time to free flow. Stop thinking, start doing. Go with it.

My next race was a 300 metres in Loughborough, in which I blasted off far too fast and blew up in the last 100 metres. Then I went to Geneva for a 400 metres, finishing second to Rooney in 45.65. The following week, I raced in Crete, winning in 45.78, and then onwards to Ostrava, where I again ran 45.65, and again finished second to Rooney. I knew I was in much better shape than that, but it just wasn't coming out. On 12 June, I wrote in my diary:

> Success – what is success? What is being perfect? Medals and records are a byproduct of running well. When things just flow, there's no thinking involved. You just do what feels natural, instinctive, like it's what you were put on the planet for. For me, that's running.

With the Olympics coming up, people talk medals and yes, a medal would be great. But it goes beyond that. It's about self-fulfilment. Being able to walk off the track knowing you did everything you could possibly do: you gave it your all. Then you can look yourself in the mirror and say you did well. I'm ambitious, I know my strengths. I want success. I want that feeling of being perfect more than anything else. I do believe in destiny, as stupid as it sounds. I do. I'm on the path that is leading to one particular day. Maybe my whole life was planned for this single day. I can't see into the future, so I'm going to grab this day and seize the opportunity.

Two weeks later in Lille, I seized the opportunity, winning against a decent field in 45.12, smashing my Irish record. *At last.* I took the Eurostar train back to England after the race and plenty of people at home had noticed the result, with text messages landing from Irish rugby international Bernard Jackman and former world 5000 metres champion Eamonn Coghlan. 'Great run, we're getting close to the 44,' wrote Coghlan. 'Well done.'

I pulled out my diary on the train and started writing:

I'm delighted: it takes a weight off my shoulders. It always feels good to see improvement, but things to keep check of: running well will mean pressure. I need to be aware of this, it's very important. I was nervous before the race and my self-talk wasn't that positive.

THE RACE

It was one extreme to another: retirement to winning. Confidence is high right now, but little things need to be nipped in the bud. Mount Olympics. I've climbed mountains before. Reach the top.

No pressure, then, David. Jesus Christ. But that paragraph sums up my approach: I was never relaxed, always looking for more. I'd put pressure on myself to run well and if that happened, all I could think was: *Fuck, this is more pressure.*

I was intense about everything – all the time. One bright summer's evening, Charlotte was racing in Manchester and I decided to drive her over and cheer her on. Her dad, Keith, also went along. After the race, as we sat on a bench, chatting about Charlotte's performance, her dad was munching away on a punnet of chips. I couldn't take my eyes off them. The restrictive perfectionist mindset told me to restrain myself, but my longing was so obvious, Keith turned to Charlotte and blurted, 'Christ, get this poor lad some chips.' I told her, 'No, do not!'

My next race was in Madrid, but I felt a niggle in my knee while warming up and withdrew, trying my best to dodge the meeting promoter for the rest of the night, given he'd wasted his money on flights and accommodation only for me to leave a lane sitting empty. Thankfully, the niggle was nothing serious and I got back on track a few days later at the Golden League in Rome, finishing sixth in a field that was worthy of an Olympic final, running 45.52. My last race before Beijing was a couple of weeks later in

Crystal Palace, London, where I felt the 44-second time was coming. But once again, I came up short, running 45.35, with Rooney winning in a PB of 44.83.

On the drive back to Loughborough, Nick tried to brighten my mood. 'Look, you're disappointed and you ran 45.3,' he said. 'You'll get there. Just give yourself a bit of time.'

But I didn't have that luxury. The Beijing Games were just a few weeks away.

It's different, Olympic year, in ways you only truly understand once you've gone through it. On the surface, the job is the same: get yourself in shape, sharpen your form, hit your peak at the right time, then hold your nerve and nail your performance against the world's best. But so much is different. It doesn't matter that the athletes are the same ones you race at the World Championships. There's extra hype, extra interest, with various requirements and distractions and nonsense you'd rather avoid. But it's all part of the job.

In 2008, there was a sudden influx of media requests, with journalists coming to Loughborough for sit-down interviews and various photo shoots.

The Olympic Council of Ireland (OCI) had been annoying me with persistent emails in the spring, telling me to come back to Dublin at a specific date and time to get measured for the suit that Irish athletes would wear for the Opening Ceremony. I was hesitant to do that, given it would mean an interruption to training, and I wasn't even going to the Opening Ceremony, given I'd be in the holding camp in Matsue, Japan at the time. I told them I didn't want to lose a day of training but severe pressure was put on me to come back. I finally relented. In the end, they gave me the wrong size suit, one that was far too big. Dad picked it up for me and when he realised, he rang them back, asking if he could get it resized. They said they couldn't do it, that I would have to bring it to a tailor. I left it at home, gathering dust. It was a piece of shit anyway, all white and without any inner lining. It didn't even have the Olympic rings on it.

A few months before the Games, the OCI also asked me to go to London for a photoshoot for one of their sponsors.

'Do I get paid for it?' I asked.

'No.'

I told them I wasn't going to drive three hours to London, and three hours back, missing a day's training to get nothing in return. They eventually came back and gave me a nominal fee, but it was indicative of how the OCI operated at the time, taking it for granted that I'd do it for free.

Four years later, on the build-up to the London Olympics, the OCI held a preparatory weekend for athletes in Tollymore, Co. Down. They asked everyone who might make the team to attend but I looked it up on Google Maps: it was in a forest park with no track around. I didn't fancy missing two key sessions to listen to various talking heads for the weekend so I turned it down. Sonia O'Sullivan was the Chef de Mission at the London Games and she texted me when I declined the invite.

THE TOOTHPASTE INCIDENT

'I really think you should come.'

So I texted her back, 'There's no way you would have gone.'

For the 2008 Olympics, the OCI wouldn't fly us directly to the holding camp in Japan, and so I had to go first to Beijing and spend one night in the Olympic village before going onwards to Matsue. That was a pain, but we didn't have a say in it. I arrived at the holding camp on 4 August, two weeks out from the race, and I spent most of that fortnight thinking about it.

At that point of the season, if you periodised your training correctly, it all starts to feel easy, like a 3D jigsaw clicking into place. Your workload is reduced, your legs are fresher, and there's an explosive pop in each stride. I was waiting for that feeling to arrive in Matsue, but it was nowhere to be seen. I felt heavy, lethargic.

Our hotel overlooked the sea and there was a greenway running along the coast. I went for a walk there one evening and told myself to get my head into it. *Stop thinking about your race. Look around: enjoy where you are.* But all I could think of was that 400 metres heat: the lap of the track that I'd worked towards for years. Forty-five seconds that would define my career.

On a camp like that, the biggest challenge is killing time. It's something many athletes struggle with, but it's a critical skill for elites: the ability to do nothing. Tom Chamney and I broke up the monotony by going for haircuts. I opted for the usual – blade two, back and sides – while Tom sat down beside me and told the barber: 'All off.' The guy didn't speak English and hadn't a clue what he meant, so Chamney took the razor and did it himself, shearing a blade zero down the top of his head. Then he handed it back to the barber: 'All off!' he told him again.

I think the boredom finally got to him.

We had our own single rooms in Matsue, which were tiny – budgets must have been cut since the previous year – and I watched the Olympic Opening Ceremony alone while lying on my bed. We weren't racing until the second week of the Games so there was no reason to be there for the start; I preferred the peace of Matsue, where we could focus on our training before entering the chaotic, distracting circus that is the Olympic village.

I did a 200-metre session on a gorgeous day and it went well. I felt good as I hopped into the inflatable paddle pool that we set up on the track that was filled with ice water. Fellow 400 metres runner Joanne Cuddihy was training at the same time and told me I looked 'really strong and fast.' I kept reminding myself of that in the days after.

I'm turning a corner. It's coming together.

But my next session brought me back down to earth. The times were OK, but I was absolutely wrecked at the end, delirious as I hauled myself into the ice bath.

Fuck, I should not be feeling like this.

In truth, I hadn't been feeling myself all week but couldn't point to anything specific, and didn't say it to anyone, telling myself it must be the travel, the weather or the jetlag. I was giving myself excuses, like that dog in that old meme where he's sitting, and smiling, as the house is burning down around him.

This is fine.

It was, after all, the Olympic Games. This was no time to wave a white flag.

On the plane to Beijing, I realised I was breaking out in mouth ulcers. That was a sure sign something was amiss: they only popped up when I was run down. Over the summer, I'd also been getting rashes on my feet but I ignored them, thinking it was athlete's foot.

I arrived at the Olympic village clinging to hope, but devoid of real confidence.

The village was just as everyone said: overwhelming. It's a gated community that houses 11,000 athletes and 5,000 team staff, with all shapes and sizes wandering around in their tracksuits. Every body type you could imagine, only accentuated like comic-book characters: towering basketballers whose limbs look like they'd been stretched; hulking weightlifters who carried their arms around like a burden; tiny gymnasts, whose astonishing athleticism was packed into such short, petite frames. It was a melting pot of athletic outliers from 28 sports and over 200 nations: the best of the best from every corner of the planet.

Every nation is designated a specific block in the Olympic village, and the Irish one had tricolours draped around it. Four athletes shared each apartment, which were devoid of any character or personality with bland, whitewashed walls. I walked into my bedroom and there was a load of freebies waiting on the bed: a top-of-the-line phone and various other bits of Olympic memorabilia. Someone told me to get a fob for the Coca-Cola machines, allowing me to get as much as I wanted, whenever I wanted.

Normally, before major events, I liked to spend most of my time in the hotel room, but in the Olympic village, the rooms were so small, boring and sterile that I felt the need to escape. But it was so hot and humid outside, and I was cautious about managing my energy, wanting to save every bit of it for what mattered.

The food hall is the great social hub of the Olympic village. Picture an area the size of the pitch in Croke Park, with several hundred tables, thousands of chairs and a marquee thrown over all of it, with any food you could possibly think of available at each station: from Asian to Mediterranean to the most popular spot of all, a full McDonald's restaurant. All of it was open 24/7 and you didn't pay a cent. The food hall was where we'd sit for hours, killing time, sharing stories and people watching.

Usain Bolt rocked in one day and it was like a president had entered the room. The murmurs started rippling through the crowd and lots of athletes ran over, asking for a photo or autograph. Some of the NBA stars from the US team came in another time and I walked past Jason Kidd, who had always looked so small on TV when playing for the Dallas Mavericks, but in real life I was staring up at him.

The currency of the Olympic village is pins. Upon arrival, every athlete gets a bag of their nation's souvenir pins and those tiny metal objects are at the heart of a barter system, with volunteers and athletes constantly approaching, asking if you had any Irish pins. The more obscure the country, the bigger the collector's item.

The Irish Chef de Mission was Dermot Henihan, and he wasn't popular with the athletes. He'd constantly tell us to be quiet, acting like a headmaster, making us feel like kids on a school tour rather than professional athletes at the Olympics.

There was a communal space in front of the Irish apartments and one day I sat out there, tense and thinking about my race, when the boxers walked out. They did some shadow boxing and, as I watched them train, what struck me was how they all had smiles on their faces.

They're enjoying this.

They were working with psychologist Gerry Hussey and they all walked around with an aura: a giddiness, an enthusiasm, an energy. *That's what I want.* Anytime I met them, they had a bounce in their step and were fun to be around. In the food hall, my stress would melt away in their company and the same was true if they came into the common room to play the PlayStation. You'd forget where you actually were – the magnitude of the event.

I was still in touch with Enda and he was very positive, drilling home all we'd practised over the previous two years. 'Look at all the work you've done,' he told me. 'These are all facts, things that have happened.' He was trying to get me to think positively, but anytime I'd be alone with my thoughts, the negative thoughts would barge in like a lout.

I went to the warm-up track for training and that's when

it finally hit me. I looked up and saw the colossal Bird's Nest Stadium alongside, with the flame burning bright on its roof. *Oh my God, I'm actually at the Olympic Games.*

I had trained on countless 400-metre tracks but due to the massive stadium alongside, this one somehow felt smaller, shorter. I met Rooney and Nick and went through a light session. Seeing them brought some familiarity, a sense of ease in an unfamiliar environment. But it all felt daunting. Instead of excitement, I kept thinking how, amid some bright spots here and there, the season had slowly gone to shit. I needed to find something.

Two days before the race, I met up with my family and friends. They weren't allowed to access the village so I got a taxi to a nearby hotel, walking into the lobby to a cheer from the group. Three of my mates – Mark Donlon, Paul Ryan and Conor Rowan – had cycled to Beijing from Dublin, a journey that took almost 10 months. They left Ireland in September 2007, and I met them in Munich a few weeks later for Oktoberfest. After three days together on the beer, they hopped back on the bikes, destined for Beijing, while I returned to Loughborough, getting back to work to begin my own journey there.

It was great to see the three lads, who had certainly enjoyed themselves on the trip. They must have been the only guys to cycle across the world and gain weight. One of their favourite countries was Iran, where they were absolutely loved by the locals, who were blown away by their story. They were invited to stay in the police station and local churches and given free meals at every turn by the locals. While riding through Turkmenistan, they reached a river where the bridge had washed away and it could only be crossed by train. After a long wait, the three were loaded with their bikes into the cargo container, and when the door opened, they saw about fifty locals sitting in there on the ground. In they walked to a sea of staring eyes and stony silence, which was eventually broken when one of the locals said the two words of English he seemed to know, 'Hello Moto', the slogan from a Motorola ad. The whole crowd cracked up, and on they went on their journey.

Listening to their stories from the road was a nice distraction from my situation, and it was also great to see my family and, of course, Charlotte. She could tell something was up, however, and after the Games she told me, 'Fuck, you did not look well.' I didn't feel well, either. But I didn't tell anyone that or about the ulcers, as if keeping them a secret would mean they weren't real.

I struggled to put on a facade and socialise while, inside, I felt like a lamb being led to the slaughter. They were all asking how things were going in training, what life was like in the village, and I just wanted to talk about anything but the Olympics. I was nervous and Charlotte could sense it. 'Do you want to head back?' she asked after a short while. She understood me completely, knew I needed to get away. The nerves had begun several days before, my mind racing every time the race popped into my head.

Shut up and get on with it. You're racing the Olympics. This is what you dreamt of as a kid, what you wanted all your life.

But now that I was here, why was I not happy? Why was I not up for it?

The night before my 400 metres heat, I sat on my own in the apartment and watched the men's 100 metres final on a tiny TV, jumping up off the couch and, like many others around the world, saying 'holy fuck' when Usain Bolt crossed the line, thumping his chest, in a world record of 9.69 seconds. He had come a long way from the gangly 15-year-old I'd seen at the World Juniors six years earlier. Back then, I had seen Bolt also run a leg of the 4x400m for Jamaica and, as I watched him in Beijing, part of me thought: *Thank fuck he never ran 400s.*

Even though he wouldn't have a notion who I was, I felt a certain connection to Bolt: firstly because of Kingston being our first major championship, but also because he'd had lots of issues as he transitioned to senior level, and I could empathise with that struggle. But he'd overcome all of it and then did *that*.

It was the iconic moment of the Games, and all anyone was talking about in the days after. Later in the week, I had a catch-up with Joe Rafferty, who was sharing an apartment in Beijing with Bolt's manager, Ricky Simms, a Donegal native. Simms had Bolt's golden spikes from the 100 metres final sitting in the apartment and so I took my chance, snapping a pic with them, knowing they were now probably worth far more than me.

The morning of my race, I woke up at 6.30 a.m. When my alarm went off, I briefly forgot where I was but then it hit

Aged 4, in my first year at school at Our Lady's Boys' National School, Ballinteer.

Aged 16, winning the Irish Schools' intermediate boys' 400 metres hurdles title, representing my school, St Benildus College. My first All-Ireland gold medal.

A dream come true. Winning my first European Gold in Madrid in 2005. (© INPHO / Getty Images)

With Jim Kidd, enjoying awards season after my 2005 European Indoor win.

Tasty Tuesdays – getting stuck into a tough track workout with the lads in Loughborough, UK.

Retaining my European title in Birmingham in 2007 – one of the good days! Pure elation and an element of relief. I knew I was in form to run fast, but you have to do it when it matters most.
(© INPHO / Morgan Treacy)

A bet is a bet! Popping on the jester's hat Rooney threw to me from the stands after winning in Birmingham in 2007. (© INPHO / Morgan Treacy)

Making my way through the mixed zone to the warm-up area after falling in the semi-finals of Euro Indoors in 2009. I had been going for three in a row. I lost the head in the warm-up area afterwards! (© INPHO / Morgan Treacy)

Closing in on a personal best and Irish record in Madrid, July 2009, with a time of 44.77 – my first run under 45 seconds.
(© Dani Pozo / AFP via Getty Images)

The B of the bang. Setting off in the 400 metres final at the 2009 World Championships in Berlin. (© Brendan Moran / SPORTSFILE)

Some days it just clicks. My first race of 2010 at the Birmingham Indoor Grand Prix, the easiest of 45-second runs, where to my surprise I equalled my national record. (©INPHO/Getty Images)

Letting it flow in the first round of the 400 metres at the European Championships, Barcelona 2010. (© Brendan Moran / SPORTSFILE)

Tying the knot. Our wedding day, August 2014, Barnard Castle, UK. (© Sarah-Jane Ethan Photography)

One last dance – representing Ireland one last time at the European Championships, Amsterdam 2016. Oscar came to watch. (© SPORTSFILE via Getty Images)

Enjoying some downtime in between sessions at the 2021 Tokyo Olympic Games.

Mo chlann ... our first holiday as a family of five. Me, Charlotte, Olivia, Louis and Oscar, June 2022.

Celebrating my 40th with a 10km run around London with Charlotte, July 2023.

Grabbing a post-interview pic with Ireland's 4x400m relay team after their qualification to the Olympic final, Paris 2024.

THE TOOTHPASTE INCIDENT

me. *Fuck, Jesus, I'm racing today.* The heart rate jumped, adrenaline flooding my system, the butterflies going to work in my belly, ready to put in another long shift.

I walked across to the food hall and had breakfast alone before Patsy, the athletics team manager, joined me. It was quiet at that time of day: too late for the partying athletes to be up and too early for anyone who wasn't competing. I had struggled to sleep the night before, the village getting that bit louder as each day passed, with more and more athletes going into celebration mode.

I had brought my own oats to Beijing and made porridge in the food hall, then took sodium bicarbonate three hours before the race, mixing it with water and knocking it down the hatch, followed by a few jellies and chewing gum to get rid of the taste.

'Bicarb' is used by most 400 metres athletes as it's a lactate buffer, balancing your PH levels and helping to neutralise the acidosis in your muscles in the latter half of the race. But you had to be careful with it, given how it interacted with other foods. On the drive to the Mt SAC Relays, I learned the hard way that bagels tend to sit in the stomach and there was a nasty reaction when I added bicarb. I had to tell Graham Hedman to pull over *immediately* due to sudden, vicious diarrhea. The night before races, I learned to stick to the tried and trusted: white meats, fish, plain pasta. Red meat was also a no-go with bicarb, as I'd learned once in explosive fashion before a race in Turin.

After breakfast, I returned to my room, got my kit ready, then met the team managers to hop on the bus to the stadium. They could see I was nervous, so didn't try to make conversation. I put in my headphones, closed my eyes and started to focus on what was ahead. I met Nick at the track and, as I began my warm-up alongside that imposing, intimidating stadium, one thought reverberated in my mind: *This will define you as an athlete.*

Just before I headed into the call room, Nick gave me a hug. 'Right, Gilly, best of luck. Get out there and show them what you can do.'

I was in the last of seven heats, and the qualification procedure was simple: first three across the line in each race went to the semi-finals, everyone else went home. I was ranked second in my heat based off my season's best of 45.12, and I knew something near that would be good enough to advance. In the second call room, alongside the track, I watched as those in the preceding heats were led out, one by one. I was getting closer and closer to the moment of truth.

The race was in the morning and when I walked out in the Bird's Nest, the sun was high in the sky, the track the most vibrant red I'd ever seen. It looked different, felt different, to every other stadium I'd been in. I stood behind my blocks, awaiting the starter's command and, again, the voice of insecurity started to clear its throat.

This is it. This is what I'm going to be defined on.

I was fighting to get back to that natural, relaxed flow state – my mind devoid of thought – but it wasn't coming. When the gun fired, I told myself the usual cue: *run through that wall.* But from the first few strides, something was off. I wasn't springy, fast, energetic. It was laboured, lethargic.

THE TOOTHPASTE INCIDENT

The perfect 400 metres? You're explosive in the first 20 metres and from 50 to 100, you're still driving, building speed. When you hit the back straight, you get tall, relaxed, getting the shoulders down and the hips up. It's a float, but a fast, relaxed float. At halfway, you go up a level, shifting from fourth to fifth gear as you enter the bend. The water jump for the steeplechase is at 150 metres to go, on the inside of the track, and when you pass that it's a cue to give another push, to get the hips nice and high because you want to be rolling off the bend, into the home straight, with a long stride. If your hips are low on the last bend, tilted, then your stride will shorten. That's an early death for a 400 metres runner. With 120 metres to go, you push again and then it's nice and tall, drop the hammer, into sixth gear, as you enter the home straight. At that point, all that's left to do is rev your legs like propellers, hold your form and get to the line as fast as humanly possible.

In Beijing, there was no flow, or float, down the back straight. Jeremy Wariner, the reigning Olympic champion, was the heavy favourite in my heat and I wasn't worried about him – he was a class apart – but I became far too aware of the others, those I'd be battling for second and third.

Fuck, he's opened up a few metres.

On the last bend I wasn't fluid, I was fighting, and I could see people moving away from me. It was depressing, demoralising, but there was nothing I could do. I was in fourth and had three metres to find on Belgium's Cédric Van Branteghem to grab a top-three spot, but my legs were gone, missing in action, absent without leave. I crossed the line fourth, clocking 45.83, seven-tenths of a second slower than my PB.

I was shell-shocked. I walked through the mixed zone and could see the RTÉ interviewer waiting and probably thinking: *How the fuck do I open this conversation?* I couldn't articulate what went wrong. I poured my heart and soul into the build-up and didn't have a bad season. I had punched some good numbers and any of the times from my previous three races would have been enough to qualify. But I couldn't even manage *that*. I toed the party line in the interview with RTÉ. 'It didn't really happen for me today … .' Blah, blah, blah.

Inside, I knew I wasn't myself, but I wasn't going to make excuses or tell them about the mouth ulcers. Not at the Olympics. 'I didn't perform,' I said. 'And I don't know why.' Then it was onwards to the print journalists, who follow athletics more closely and I could sense the disappointment from them. There was empathy. *Fuck, now I'm gonna be one of those sympathy cases: an athlete who went to the Olympics and did nothing.*

As I walked to the athletes' area, I started thinking about everyone I'd let down: the mates who cycled from Dublin to watch me run like a donkey. The aunts and uncles and cousins in the stands, wearing green and white T-shirts with 'Go Gillo' printed on them. They'd spent thousands to be here, only to see me fail. In those moments, you're so vulnerable, so isolated. It's like a knife was plunged into my chest and twisted. As I gathered my kit, Wariner came up and gave me a handshake. Then Rooney emerged from around the corner, buzzing and energetic as he'd qualified for the semi-final. He presumed I had, too.

'It's done,' I told him.

THE TOOTHPASTE INCIDENT

'What? What the fuck?'

I sat there, unable to speak. It was like someone had ripped my heart out. I wanted the ground to swallow me up. I dreaded meeting everyone else. But I had to get out of there. I slowly made my way to the warm-up track, which is the worst place to be when things don't go well. Your bad result is written on everyone's face as they greet you. They don't know what to say, and nothing they could say will make it any better.

Nick was so disappointed. He gave me a hug. 'Hard luck,' he said and left it at that. You can't shine a shite and there's no point trying. This had been the biggest moment of my life and it all went wrong. That's when a realisation hit with the impact of a heavy, blunt object.

That's it. That was your 45 seconds. It's over. Go home.

Charlotte was staying in a hostel in Beijing and in the afternoon I went to meet her. Soon after I walked into her room, I had a complete and utter meltdown. She calls it 'The Toothpaste Incident'.

'I'm fucking useless!' I shouted. 'I've let everyone down. Here I am at the Olympics, and I'm an also-ran – one of those Olympic tourists. That's not me.'

I picked up her toothpaste and launched it off the wall, trying to release the anger. She was standing there, in silence. What could she possibly say that would soothe the pain? Eventually, she tried.

'It's not that bad. It doesn't matter.'

But I was only getting started on my rampage of self-hate. 'I ran shit! I've let everyone down. Everyone came over to see me and I ran the worst race of the season. Why now? Maybe I just don't have it in my head. Maybe that's the end of the road.'

This self-hatred had all been pent up from the moment I crossed the line. I was like a caged animal. I didn't want to be the one coming back to the village ranting and raving, and it was only around the people closest to me that I could really open up. Charlotte, unfortunately, bore the brunt of that, watching her toothpaste fly around the room like a missile and then exploding. She didn't know what to say or do, backing herself into a corner of the room and waiting for the storm to pass. But she was exactly what I needed at that moment: someone who cared, someone who allowed me to vent. Someone who understood.

In sport, and especially as a sprinter, there's a pressure not to show any weakness – to be that cool, calm, alpha male who's strong and able to cope with everything that comes your way. But on the build-up to big events, so much is happening beneath the surface, with tension and stress and anxiety building like the inside of an active volcano. When it doesn't go the way you planned, all that pressure is released. It would have been hard to fully vent around my coach or teammates, who were still in competition mode, with their own jobs to do. Charlotte, for me, was the safe space, someone around whom I could just let it all out and express how I was truly feeling. At the time, I didn't think of how hard it was for her to be in that position – I was that selfish athlete, wallowing in my own self-pity – and it was only long after that incident that I understood how awful it must have been to be around.

THE TOOTHPASTE INCIDENT

That night, the lads got me to go out, even though it felt like the last thing in the world I wanted to do. Maybe it was an Irish thing in times of misery. *Let's just go on the piss.* Charlotte and my family went too and we all headed to an Irish bar, the worst place to be because there were lots of familiar faces, the kind I wanted to avoid. We did a load of shots – some horrific type loaded with tabasco – but it did little to lighten my mood. I was playing pretend, forcing the odd smile and trying to just get through the night.

I had another week in Beijing, but I just wanted to get out of there. I tried to make use of the time, doing some sightseeing and visiting the Great Wall, but everything was tainted by my performance. When I look back at the pictures, I can see it on my face: it's a mask. I went to watch the boxing and some athletics, sitting in the stands for the 400 metres semi-finals alongside Charlotte, having debated all day whether to go. I was hollow as I watched it – absolutely hollow.

On the build-up to Beijing, I had gone through all the previous World Championships and Olympic results and, on average, the time you needed to make the 400 metres final was 44.8 seconds. That was within reach, but I didn't break 45 or even get close to it. Rooney *had* made the final, running 44.60 to qualify, and he went on to finish sixth in 45.12: the same time I'd run in Lille.

Sitting in the stands, watching the races under the lights, I was ashamed of myself. It's always better inside the ropes but there I was, frozen out, like a kid who didn't get invited to the party but then had to watch from afar. I looked around at that vast, stunning stadium, feeling the electric atmosphere. This was the stuff I dreamed of as a kid. But now I was just a bystander, a spectator.

A failure.

A few days later, one of the lads said to another of my mates, 'I'd have thought Gillick would be over it by now.' That friend then said it back to me. They didn't mean any harm, but it showed the lack of understanding. If it was a footballer at the World Cup, everyone would get why I was still crushed four or five days after being knocked out. And this was my World Cup. I was cut so, so deep. People didn't know what to say but their knowledge was also limited. How were they supposed to understand the vast chasm between 45.1 and 45.8 seconds, how one was a massive success and the other an abject failure.

I couldn't understand why I'd regressed. *How could I have dropped 0.7 in a few weeks?* Something just didn't make sense. I'd been reluctant to tell anyone how I felt in case I was seen to be making excuses, but in the village one day I told Nick about the ulcers. He said, 'Let's get some bloods.' I went for tests in the medical tent at the village and the doctor told me there's something there, but they didn't know exactly what. He advised me to get a stool test when I went home.

I ran a few more races after returning to Europe but they were all even worse than Beijing: I felt flat and slow. I didn't really care at that point. I had no desire, no fight, and was just going through the motions. I wanted to get as far away from running as I possibly could.

When I was back in Dublin, I went for a stool test in

THE TOOTHPASTE INCIDENT

the Mater Hospital and then Charlotte and I drove to the west coast, going on holidays on the island of Inishbofin. I was there when I got the results over the phone, the doctor telling me I had a viral infection and that the rashes on my feet and the ulcers were likely symptoms of foot and mouth disease. That gave me some comfort.

That performance wasn't me. I'm better than that.

I knew something physical had been amiss and it wasn't just that I didn't cope with the pressure. Before Beijing, I felt for weeks that my body wasn't 100 per cent, but me being me, I was also making things worse, worrying and over-analysing. Was it bad luck? Or had it been my fault? Maybe both. But deep down, I knew the reason my immune system probably crashed was because I'd spent every waking hour on edge, stressing myself out.

Charlotte and I went for a walk along a clifftop in Inishbofin and had an honest chat about the year. By then, the flames of self-hate that enveloped me in Beijing had started to fade. I knew I'd made mistakes, and now I was able to step back from the wreckage and see them. Everything had been so regimented all year. I couldn't switch off – ever.

Charlotte told me I had been a nightmare to live with. One time, I was walking up the stairs in the house, she was walking down, and I was so fixated on training that I brushed right past her like she didn't exist. She told me she had turned around and given me the finger. I've never once seen Charlotte give anyone the finger, which highlights just how much of an asshole I must have been. But I didn't realise that at the time.

Another day, I came in from a session and she asked if I wanted some lunch. 'Do you want the usual? A Spanish omelette with sweet potato.'

'That'd be great,' I said, as I went off for a shower. I returned to the kitchen and was presented with the omelette, but as I was eating it I realised there was a lot of sweet potato in it.

'How much did you put in?' I asked.

'The usual.'

'What's the usual?'

'A hundred and fifty grams.'

I lost the plot. 'The usual is a hundred grams.'

We had a blazing row, over fifty grams of sweet potato, and she didn't talk to me for two days.

The big issue was that, ultimately, I had stopped enjoying what I was doing. It was all about times, performance, outcomes, rather than relishing the process and the feeling of doing something I loved around like-minded people.

I was 25 at the time, but if I wanted to have a long career in the sport, to race at the top level until the age of 30, I had to start enjoying it and appreciate how lucky I was to do it for a living. Looking out at the Atlantic Ocean, as the waves crashed off the rocks below, I could see it all with such clarity. There and then, I made a promise to myself, and to Charlotte.

I'm going to start enjoying this. Next year will be different.

CHAPTER 10

'JUST FUCKING RUN'

To make any real impact in the 400 metres at global level – to reach finals or win medals or earn decent money – you need to run 44 seconds. It's not a nice-to-have, it's an *absolute must*. So, as I started planning out the 2009 season with Nick, we gave ourselves an ultimatum: if I didn't break 45 seconds, I was switching to the 400 metres hurdles in 2010.

I had no interest in just qualifying for major events and then being a championship tourist. I would challenge Nick, banging on his door and walking into his office, asking: 'What are we doing here? Are we content to run low-45s or are we going to get into the 44s?' He liked that ambition, he shared it, and was never afraid to hit me with home truths when necessary.

We had both learned a lot from the Olympic year. When you taste some big highs and then crash land at rock bottom, getting destroyed at the biggest event in sport, in ways it can be a good thing. From there, the only way is up, and you'll do just about anything to avoid going through it again.

At the end of the 2008 season, I took a long break, clearing my mind and refreshing my body. I returned with a new approach: I stopped writing long, detailed notes in my diary about every session, just noting the reps and times – nothing more. I stopped weighing my food and started seeing it as fuel, not obsessing over every morsel as I had the previous year. If I fancied a beer, I had one – maybe two or three, if I wanted. If I fancied going out with friends, then I went out, guilt free.

A few years before, I had run into Eamonn Coghlan, a legendary figure in Irish athletics, at the Texaco Sports Awards in Dublin. Enda had often told me that if I ever got to meet athletes of that stature – Eamonn was a former world 5000 metres champion, and had set multiple world indoor records – I should be like a kid in their company, asking as many questions as possible, always following up with: 'Why?' One of the many things I asked Eamonn was whether he paid close attention to nutrition. 'Ah, I had a coach, Jumbo Elliott – did you ever hear of him?' he said. 'Jumbo would say to us: "Lads, just fucking run."'

I nodded along, even though I thought: *That makes no sense.* But it was only years later, after Beijing, that I finally understood what he meant: how we can be far too detailed, too anal, to the point of sabotage – paralysis by analysis.

It had been part of my downfall at the Olympics, and 2009 called for a new approach.

Just fucking run, I told myself. *Do your job, work hard, look after yourself, but Jesus Christ, enjoy it.*

My attitude over the previous year had been reflected in my diet: it looked great on paper but was loaded with so much stress and obsessiveness that it was actually *unhelpful* to my performance and well-being. During my years in Loughborough, I went further and further down the nutrition rabbit hole, seeing it as one more area where I could excavate a tiny percentage gain.

My nutritionist, Martin McDonald, was brilliant at what he did. When we started working together, he took me shopping, following me around Tesco as I did the usual, throwing white rice, white pasta into the trolley. Then he taught me better options, more nutrient-dense carbohydrate sources like sweet potato, quinoa or bulgur wheat, taking me down the aisles I'd never visit. Such foods are common these days, but at the time my training partners would give me strange looks: 'What the fuck is that?'

I used to stick to basic vegetables – carrots and broccoli – but Martin got me into green, leafy veg: kale or rocket, which were more nutritionally dense. He taught me the importance of timing. The day before a big session, I'd add in more carbs. He taught me when and how to use whey protein. I'd make spelt pasta at home, put it in Tupperware and bring it with me on the plane to a race, knowing it was better than what I'd get on the road. The whole idea was for me to be able to stand behind the blocks, knowing I'd left no stone unturned, controlling all the controllables.

I was lucky when it came to diet: I didn't put on weight easily. I was typically 85kg for most of the year and, as summer approached, I'd naturally drop to 82kg, but I wouldn't have to restrict myself. My training load would reduce so I wasn't eating as much and, with the nerves of competition, you just don't feel as hungry. I trained with one lad who, if he so much as looked at a weight, would blow up like a blimp. He'd have to restrict his diet to keep things in check, but thankfully I never had to, apart from when I was injured. *That's* when my approach became unhealthy.

I'd stress myself about eating an apple, searching online for how many calories it contained. I'd be starving for most of the day and then eventually crack, sticking a spoon into the peanut butter. Before I knew it, I'd have eaten the whole jar.

But even when I was healthy, some obsessive habits crept in. When I wasn't training in the evening I'd think: *Well, then I don't need carbs this evening.* That became an issue if we went out to eat: I couldn't control what was on the plate so I just stopped going out. I'd stay home and make Charlotte a typical dinner, then make myself just an omelette, looking across at her spuds with envy. I had the same lunch almost every day: chicken and a salad with spinach, rocket, feta cheese and quinoa, making my own healthy dressing.

At the elite end of athletics, there's a wide variety in how seriously people take nutrition. Some Olympic medallists eat junk food daily; others won't touch a square of chocolate. On one trip, I sat across the table from an endurance athlete who barely ate at all, at least from what I saw. All they had at breakfast were four tiny sachets of jam. I didn't pass comment, but was looking across the table, wondering: *How the fuck are you able to run?*

Dietary habits varied by event. High jumpers want to be as light as possible to be better able to spring into the air, and I'd often see them smoking outside hotels on the circuit, trying to suppress their appetite. I saw some elite 100 metres sprinters doing the same.

Me? I often struggled to eat before races due to nerves, but always loved the buffet afterwards, pulling a chair up and milling through the desserts: everything in moderation, including moderation itself.

When it came to supplements, I took fish oil and a multivitamin, while I'd also have a whey protein shake with my porridge every morning. Being based at Loughborough, a sports-oriented university, I'd get the latest research and advice and so I tried things like beta-alanine and creatine. Under Martin's supervision, I did tests on bicarb and caffeine, working out what amount worked best in the hours before a race.

We took caffeine for reaction times: heightening the senses and helping me move on the B of the bang. The amount was calculated off body weight and I'd take Pro Plus tablets in phased amounts, knocking back eight of them in the hours before a race. Coupled with the bicarb, it meant one hell of a cocktail in my stomach and the first thing I'd check when arriving at the track was the location of the toilets, which would be visited early and often.

Caffeine could also make you dehydrated so I was always cautious of getting enough water. If it was a semi-final, I wouldn't take the full dose of caffeine because otherwise I'd be lying in bed that night, staring at the ceiling, and the lack of sleep would have a knock-on effect in the final. I'd drink chamomile tea, listen to some music and do a body scan, trying to relax and drift off. Sometimes it worked. Sometimes it didn't.

That year, our training group would get together on Wednesdays to watch the Champions League. We'd gather at someone's gaff and pig out on Pringles and chocolate. 'They're not calories if they're in someone else's house,' we'd say. I came to understand you need that balance, the ability to switch off completely, which enabled you to switch back on when it really mattered. Jumbo Elliott had clearly understood that, as had Eamonn Coghlan. And now I did, too.

Stop analysing things and just run, I'd tell myself. *And don't be a miserable dick.*

I'd finish training and that was it: done. Park it. Move on. Whereas before, I'd analyse everything that happened. I started to enjoy the hard work again through the depths of winter: the masochistic misery of those Saturday-morning *fartleks* in wind and rain and hail and sleet. The worse it was, the more I'd think of the Americans and Jamaicans, training away in their warm, glorious sunshine.

I'd relish every squelchy step through the mud, knowing it was taking me forward.

The winter was a consistent one – no setbacks or injuries – and 2009 started off with another training camp in Lanzarote. There was one key session there that showed me my labour was bearing fruit: 2x300 metres with 15 minutes recovery. I absolutely smashed it, running 32.6 seconds for the first 300 metres and 32.3 for the second.

Rooney had a niggle, so he didn't do the session, but he was always great for encouragement. As much as we were competitors, we were also training partners and friends. After I finished, he walked up with a little smile, giving me a wink. 'You have it now, you've cracked it,' he said.

Something had clicked – the connection I'd been searching for between getting out of the blocks, setting it up and running strong. We had brought a physio to Lanzarote, Ciarán Fitzpatrick, who'd known me since I was a teenager, and he also noticed the change: 'I never saw you move like that before.'

I wanted a huge summer, so I wasn't worried about indoors. But I was clearly in good shape. Nick and I decided we'd again do one race in Düsseldorf and re-assess. I won that, in 46.18, which wasn't bad but wasn't amazing either. The European Indoors were a few weeks later in Turin and I wasn't too pushed about going – my eyes fixed on the summer – but it *was* a chance to win a third straight title, something which, in the end, I couldn't resist.

In late February, I watched the Italian Championships

on a computer in Nick's office, and saw Claudio Licciardello win the 400 metres in 46.03. *Fuck, now I have to run faster.* But I knew I was capable of that. I went to Turin without tapering off my training and I tried not to engage with the media narrative about a third straight title. I did some interviews but gave the usual one-liners: 'I just want to run to my potential.'

I won my heat, feeling good, and I just had to be top-three in the semi-final to secure a spot in the showdown. I was drawn against Johan Wissman, who I knew would blast the opening lap. I wanted to be top two at halfway but I didn't get the first lap right, hitting the bell in third, with Wissman out front and Romania's Ioan Vieru in second.

On the final bend, I moved wide to attack them and was running on the outside of Vieru, who in turn was outside Wissman. Vieru veered out and there was a tangle of legs. I hit the deck.

He did nudge me, but I was on the outside and when you're wide on a bend like that, you're deemed to be the one putting pressure on your rival because you're at the higher height, leaning in. Ultimately, it was my fault for putting myself in that position. I should have committed more over the first lap, putting myself closer to the front, but when that didn't happen, I should have waited until the home straight to launch an attack – doing it on a bend was a recipe for disaster.

I was furious. I went to walk off the track but Big Red, who was trackside, shouted at me to finish the race – a necessary step if you want to appeal, which I didn't know.

I eventually sauntered across the line before walking into the mixed zone, where I passed Vieru.

'You fucking tripped me,' I told him, but he shrugged it off. To be fair, there had been no malice in what he did. That just happens in the indoor 400 metres. I walked into the warm-up area, ranting and raving, and took off my spikes and launched them down the track. Everyone was looking at me, in silence, then I had the embarrassing moment of having to walk up the track and retrieve them. The Irish team put in an appeal on my behalf, which was denied. My three-in-a-row chance was dead and buried.

It was a different kind of disappointment to Beijing: annoying as hell but not as hurtful, given it wasn't a terrible performance, just one where I'd made a big tactical error. Nick came to my hotel and kickstarted the moving-on process. 'You know what shape you're in for this year, you know how training has gone,' he said. 'Forget about it.'

One of my best mates, Mark, was also there. 'Are you not fucking bulling?' he asked.

'I am,' I said. 'But I'm also in good shape, I'm running really well, so I'm not going to dwell on it.'

The summer was ultimately what mattered, the be-all and end-all, and things were very much on track to get that right.

There's a cost that comes with failing at a major championship, and it runs just as deep as the emotional scars. At the end of 2008, my one-year, €20,000 contract with adidas was up, replaced by another one-year contract for just

€5,000. I couldn't complain, of course, knowing I hadn't produced on the big stage. But the only way to change things was to make an impact at the big event of 2009: the World Championships in Berlin.

The track season began in familiar fashion, with a training camp in LA followed by my first outdoor race in Mt SAC, where I won the 400 metres in 45.81, my quickest ever season opener.

If I can run that now, what can I do later?

That year, I had started working with psychologist Gerry Hussey, having admired what I'd seen in the boxers in Beijing. I wanted to develop that same, buoyant attitude they had on the big stage. But between Gerry and Enda, I soon felt like I'd learned all I needed to know about the right mental approach. It was just about putting it into practice. In the end, neither could run the race for me.

In June, it felt like things were really clicking: I took wins in Switzerland, Greece and Italy. In the latter race in Milan, I lined up against Oscar Pistorius, the 'Blade Runner', a double amputee from South Africa who used carbon-fibre prostheses in races.

At that point, Pistorius was still allowed to line up against able-bodied rivals, with studies ongoing into how much of an advantage, if any, his blades provided. I won in Milan in 45.51, with Tim Benjamin second in 45.54 and Pistorius sixth in 47.24. There was a media scrum around Pistorius after the race. 'Fucking hell man, you won the race and all they're after is him,' laughed Tim. 'No one wants a piece of us.'

I sat beside Pistorius on the bus to the stadium and,

despite his global fame, he seemed normal, friendly, but his story took a dark turn a few years later. He was convicted of culpable homicide after killing his girlfriend, Reeva Steenkamp, in his home, shooting her through a door, claiming he mistook her for an intruder. I got a fright when I heard the news as Rooney was over in South Africa training with Pistorius. He left 24 hours before the gun shots rang out.

During his career, the talk around Pistorius was around more trivial matters. The consensus in athletics was that his blades were unfair, that he was running on springs that were far more efficient than other athletes' lower limbs. His final 100 metres was his fastest of the race, whereas for the rest of us it was our slowest.

Pistorius ran in lane eight due to the gentler curve and athletes would grumble about him getting preferential treatment. Still, his times weren't overly fast, so most people weren't up in arms about his presence. But the consensus was that one of these days he *would* challenge us because of his tools. In January 2008, the IAAF (now World Athletics) had outlawed the use of such prostheses in top-level competitions, but Pistorius overturned that at the Court of Arbitration for Sport. He went on to compete against able-bodied athletes at the London Olympics in 2012, but in the years since the rules have tightened, with athletes like him needing to prove there is no advantage if they wish to use prostheses, while also providing scientific backing for their claims.

In June, the quickest of my three victories came in

Thessaloniki, where I was just outside my PB with 45.16. *Are we content to run low-45s or are we going to get into the 44s?* Next up was Madrid, where I'd failed to even make the start line the previous year. I was shocked they invited me back. But I knew it was a fast track, with perfect weather: a big chance.

In the gym, I was stronger than ever and I also started doing Pilates and added core work. As a result, I was able to hold the right body positions in the key part of the race where fatigue puts you in a vice grip. That all meant a faster path to the finish.

Before the race in Madrid, I was nervous, but it was the *right* amount of nerves. I felt the adrenaline but was still calm, confident. I focused on the first 50 metres, trying to set it all up, and from there I clicked into a beautiful rhythm. It felt easy, *effortless.*

I turned into the home straight out front, in splendid isolation, and with 50 metres to go I thought: *I could be on for something big here, go for it.* I crossed the line and saw the time: 44.77. A massive wave of relief washed over me, closely followed by an intoxicating rush of euphoria.

Thank fuck I finally broke 45.

A week later, I was back in Rome and, two years on from my Golden League debut, the impostor syndrome was long gone. I felt I belonged. I ran another great race, getting pipped for the win by Chris Brown by just one hundredth of a second, clocking 44.82. I was buzzing, knowing Madrid wasn't a flash in the pan. Nick had been at the British Championships that day and when the result came through from Rome, he literally fell off his chair, then punched another chair in delight.

Finally, we seemed to have cracked the 400-metre code.

One of my favourite things in athletics is that when you're running well, the vast majority of people – even your rivals – are delighted for you. John Steffensen, an Australian who'd finished fourth in Rome, came over after the race. 'It's fucking great when you're on it,' he said, high-fiving me. 'You've got it now. You'll go far. Best of luck.'

Earlier that summer, Jana Pittman, a two-time world 400 metres hurdles champion from Australia who was based in Loughborough, came over after watching me do a session of 120-metre repetitions. 'Fuck, you're in the form of your life. You're gonna run 44,' she said. It meant the world when people at the pinnacle said stuff like that. I'd grab it, hold it, treasure it. Most of all, I'd believe it.

I flew back to London after Rome, but on the way there I started to feel unwell. I'd been due to race next in Lucerne, Switzerland, but started vomiting after arriving in Loughborough. 'I need to bring you to the doctor,' said Charlotte, who drove me to a medical centre. As I explained my symptoms, the doctor grew uneasy. 'I think you've got swine flu,' he said, handing me a mask, writing a prescription and then leading me out the back door of the clinic, not wanting to cause a panic if people saw me in the waiting room. He told me he'd have to sterilise everything after I'd left.

I spent a horrid night in bed, tossing and turning, but the following day my symptoms vanished. I got my test results back: it was a false alarm on the swine flu and just another 24-hour bug that caught me. Annoyingly, I was forced to miss a meet in Switzerland, organised by five-time Irish Olympian, Terry McHugh, who very kindly offered to fly my parents out to watch me run along with an appearance fee of €2,000 plus prize money.

Before the World Championships, my last 400 metres race was in Monaco, where I got to experience the vast difference in treatment athletes get when they're running well. The night before such meetings, there's always a technical meeting at the athletes' hotel where organisers sit with managers and sort out which athletes will run in which lanes and what the pace will be in middle-distance races.

Because Nick was also my manager, and he didn't travel to most races, I usually wasn't represented in the technical meetings. But the night before the meeting in Monaco, I was approached in the hotel lobby by an Italian manager who I'd never met. 'Lane three,' he told me. 'They tried to put you in seven, but I fought for you to be in three.' Paul Doyle, an American manager I knew who was always helpful to Irish athletes, had done similar for me at other meetings, fighting on my behalf, but to have a manager with no connection doing so was something new. 'You're fast,' the Italian told me. 'You deserve to be there.'

The race was a good one. I finished third in 45.34, a decent time given the strong winds, with LaShawn Merritt winning in 44.73. As Nick said: 'If you're going to Monaco and getting top three, you're in good form.'

I walked back to the hotel that night with some British

athletes, stopping in McDonald's along the way. Monaco is a surreal place: we walked past glistening yachts, shiny supercars and a succession of women who looked like supermodels. It was like a make-believe place. I took a moment to appreciate where I was, and how lucky I was to do this for a living.

A few days later, it was back to my roots, running a 21.43-second 200 metres into a huge headwind at the nationals in Dublin. That night, I went for a few pints with friends – something I'd previously never have done before a major championships. But I was a very different athlete this time, knowing when to flick the switch on and understanding when it needed to be off. I was stronger physically and more assured of myself mentally.

I felt like I belonged among the world's best. Now I just had to prove it.

From the moment I touched down in Berlin, I felt a good vibe, a positive energy. The Irish team was staying in a big hotel, well outside the city centre – an ideal spot to chill out ahead of the World Championships.

I ran well in my heat, finishing second in 45.54 to secure one of three automatic spots in the semi-finals, where the level went up a notch. That magic number to reach the final was stuck in my head – 44.8 – but the difference in Berlin compared to Beijing was that, this time around, I had already done that. Twice. But doing it on the circuit and doing it at a championship are two very different things.

The following evening, I was back on track, drawn in

the most loaded of three semi-finals: alongside heavyweights like Jeremy Wariner, Michael Bingham, Leslie Djhone and Ramon Miller. Only the top two made the final automatically, with two extra spots available for the fastest third- or fourth-place finishers across the heats. I knew Wariner would be out front, alone, but it'd be a dogfight between the rest of us for second.

The day started with a light jog, then I had breakfast, got a massage and did some stretching. The race wasn't until 6.15 p.m., so I spent the afternoon in my room. The Olympiastadion is a vast, ominous place, which had a capacity of around 100,000 when it was originally built for the 1936 Games. While it's had a few facelifts over the years, the place is much the same today: austere, imposing.

Alongside it is a public pool, which hosted the swimming events at the 1936 Olympics. As I walked past it ahead of my semi-final, and heard kids shrieking, laughing, playing, it was a juxtaposition with the stressed-out sentiment in my head.

Why didn't I choose another career?

It had been 12 years since the last Irish sprinter, Susan Smith, reached a final at a global outdoor championship, but I knew that was within reach if I could nail every part of my race as I'd done in Madrid and Rome. *I'm not asking you for anything different. Just set it up.*

It was a beautiful, warm evening in Berlin, the setting sun shrouding the stadium in golden light. I was drawn in lane six, with Bingham outside and the rest of the big contenders in the lanes to my left.

'JUST FUCKING RUN'

When the gun fired, I had the quickest reaction of all – 0.14 seconds – and I exploded through the first 50 metres, trying to hit top speed as soon as possible. But you can't sprint for 400 metres straight – well, you can, but you'll be waddling home, punch-drunk, if you try – and so I started to relax, coasting down the back straight in a fluid rhythm.

As I hit the final bend, the cavalry came charging on my left, and I turned into the straight wedged in a line of athletes who were all hunting for second place behind Wariner. There were inches between us as the line drew closer, but I was down in fifth place, which meant certain elimination. Then, suddenly, Miller seemed to go backwards, as if he'd run face-first into a brick wall. I flashed across the line with a haze of bodies around, not knowing where I'd finished.

My first thought: *What the fuck happened to Miller?*

I finished fourth in 44.88, but only found out when I walked through the mixed zone, given that I couldn't read the big screen that was on the opposite side of the stadium. I held the second of two time-qualifier spots, but more than likely only temporarily. There were two more semi-finals and if the third-placed finisher in either ran faster than me, I was gone. *Game over, go home.* I knew it was out of my hands. I had done my part, hit that magic number, 44.8. All I could do was hope.

In the second semi-final, the guy who finished third ran 44.93. I was hanging on for dear life. One race to go. By this point, I had arrived in the lower part of the mixed zone, underneath the stadium, and one of the guys from

Flotrack, a US athletics website, asked if he could film me as I watched the third semi-final. I agreed. I was a nervous wreck during it but when the winner hit the line in 44.95, I erupted in celebration, leaping around and giving Flotrack some great content.

I'm a world finalist.

To me, this was as good as any gold medal at European level. Most importantly, I'd backed up my performances across the year. It's all well and good to run well on the circuit but, in reality, all that matters is that your best performances happen when they need to: at championships.

And now I had done it. I was ecstatic.

After the initial outburst, I soon came back down to earth and tried to keep a lid on my emotions. I went back to the hotel, got my game face on. I didn't want people patting me on the back just because I made the final. After all, I went in ranked fifth in the world. *I should be making the final.* I was sharing with Paul Hession and when I got back to the room, he pulled up two images on his laptop. One was from that semi-final, with me running down the home straight looking tall, strong, shoulder to shoulder with the world's best. The other was from the Osaka World Championships in 2007, where I was a wimpy athlete, head hanging to the side in the home straight, dying a slow death. Hession put the two pictures side by side on his screen. 'That's some two years there.'

I was wired that night and struggled to sleep, but thankfully I had a rest day before the final: a chance to recharge.

'JUST FUCKING RUN'

I had a chat with Nick and he wasn't exactly jumping up and down.

'You've done what you needed,' he said. 'But there's a lot of work still to do.'

While on the bus to the stadium before the final, a text message pinged on my phone. It was from Finbarr Kirwan, who had sat and listened to me three years earlier as I made my case for extra funding. By that point, he had moved on from the Irish Sports Council and was working in the US, but still paid close attention to my career. 'We're all really proud of you,' he wrote. 'You said what you were going to do.'

Later that night, after a thunderstorm delay, a dead-silent call room and a curiously timed handshake from a beaming LaShawn Merritt, I stood behind the blocks for the most important race of my life: the world 400 metres final. I was drawn in lane two so when the gun fired and a thousand cameras flashed in the night sky, I had a birds-eye view of the world's fastest men right in front of me.

I knew Wariner and Merritt would probably have a lock on gold and silver, but bronze looked up for grabs. *Why not me?* I got out fast, blasting past Rennie Quow of Trinidad and Tobago in the lane outside on the opening bend. But that didn't mean much: Quow always went out conservatively and finished like a bullet train. I kept the hips high on the back straight and glanced ahead to see Merritt and Wariner pulling away. *That's OK. That was expected.* I attacked again on the final turn, but then Quow surged up beside me from the lane outside.

THE RACE

Wariner and Merritt turned into the straight just about dead level at the front, with Chris Brown a metre or so behind them but starting to tie up fast. I was in a line of five athletes another few metres back, with a bronze medal *right there* for the taking. I gave it everything, but just couldn't keep pace with Quow as he whirred his legs like propellor blades in the lane alongside and left me behind, taking bronze in 45.02 behind Merritt (44.06) and Wariner (44.60).

I hit the line in sixth, running 45.53. When I saw the time that won bronze, my mind instantly went to the what-ifs. *Maybe if I'd been drawn in a different semi-final? Maybe if I got a better lane?* My mind was a cocktail of hypotheticals as I walked into the mixed zone and, these days, when I'm interviewing people, I sometimes think back to Berlin and wonder: *What jumbled shit is going through this athlete's mind as I'm trying to ask a question?*

I met Nick at the end of the mixed zone and he was disappointed, deflated. 'I thought this was your time,' he said. He had coached people to world finals before but never clinched a medal. I didn't expect him to be so down – I hadn't run a bad race, after all – but his reaction was a sign of the faith he had in my ability.

A big part of me couldn't help thinking about a medal, how it wasn't very far away at all. But another part of me – a bigger part – was proud of what I'd achieved. When I looked at it clearly, calmly, there was nothing more I could have done.

*

Berlin was a great championships for the Irish, with Olive Loughnane winning silver in the 20km race walk, which was later upgraded to gold due to the Russian who crossed the line first getting disqualified for doping. The Irish sprinters had a breakthrough championships, with Paul Hession just missing the final of the 200 metres, finishing tenth overall and Derval O'Rourke finishing fourth in the 100 metres hurdles final. In a lift at the hotel, a German coach asked me: 'What has happened with the sprinters in Ireland? What are you guys doing? What is the system?'

'I'm not sure there is a system,' I told him. Derval was based in Ireland but doing her own thing, with coaches who worked outside 'the system'. Hession was based in Scotland, training under Stuart Hogg, while I was based in England. But regardless, it was clear Irish sprinting had come a long, long way from five years before, when my Jamaican friend at the World Indoors looked at us like we'd landed on the medal podium from outer space. 'Ireland? Where's that?'

After leaving Berlin, I had a few more races to close out the season: I finished fourth at two of the best Golden League meetings, Zurich and Brussels, before racing the World Athletics Final in Thessaloniki, Greece.

In between, I went back to Dublin for a corporate gig and Nick wasn't happy with that decision, but the money was good, €5,000, and given the main event of the season was behind me, I decided it was worth my while. I didn't run well in Thessaloniki, finishing a memorable season with a race to forget.

THE RACE

I was physically and emotionally spent, starting to run on fumes, and it showed. I came home sixth in 46.09. Soon after the race, I got a text from Nick: 'What the fuck was that?'

CHAPTER 11

UNSPORTSMANLIKE BEHAVIOUR

There's a ripple effect that occurs when you start running well, and the rewards are visible long after the initial impact. Towards the end of 2009, the head of adidas in Ireland called me out of the blue.

'David, you've had a great year,' he said. 'Do you want to go shopping?'

'Yeah, sure.'

'Right, get yourself down to London and I'll put £2500 behind the till.'

Adidas had two flagship stores in London: a performance, sportswear shop and an originals, leisure-wear shop. Charlotte and I got the train down and were greeted by a personal shopper, who guided us around as we spent £1500 in one store and £1000 in another. I felt like the big cheese, at least until Nicolas Anelka, a French footballer who played for Chelsea, walked in with his own personal shopper. That evening, Charlotte and I hopped on the train back to Loughborough with bags upon bags hanging off us – an unexpected perk of making a world final.

Another time, when I had just signed with adidas, I was invited up to their warehouse in Manchester where they stored tens of thousands of pairs of shoes and apparel. I was sample size so, for me, it was as good as a shopping spree, with no limits on how much I could take. 'Right, you have an hour,' I was told. 'Off you go.'

In the end, treatment like that goes back to the numbers: the times that define your worth in the eyes of major brands. Run fast and you'll be rewarded. If you don't, it can very quickly be *sayonara*. My performance in Berlin had shown adidas I was now a contender for world and Olympic medals and, having been on a one-year, €5,000 contract in 2009, Nick negotiated for my first multi-year contract, which guaranteed me €20,000 per year through 2010, 2011 and 2012.

The summer of 2009 had been a good one, but it was missing something, and when I sat down to plan the following season, I told Nick, 'Next year, we're getting medals.'

As much as I'd run well, I was left with nothing to show for it. But 2010 offered two golden opportunities: the World Indoors in Doha in March and the European Championships in Barcelona in July. I wanted to be on the podium at both.

The winter went well, but there was one, small issue that was starting to bug me: a bit of noise from certain people in Irish athletics. Rooney and I were on a collision course at the Europeans, with both of us capable of gold, and the likes of Stephen Maguire, Patsy McGonagle and Joe Rafferty, who all had plenty of experience working in elite athletics, flagged up their concerns which could be summarised as follows: *Rooney is British, Nick is British. Is it not more in Nick's interest to get Rooney to win?*

Outside the group, that's what people were thinking, but inside it I never once felt I was being treated any differently. But still, the thought began to seep in. There was some added tension between Rooney and me because we knew we were both going to be at the pointy end of the European final, maybe standing right in each other's way of gold.

We went to South Africa for our training camp in January, putting off the decision about an indoor season until I knew what shape I was in. If I was ready to go to Doha and win a world indoor medal, then I'd go. If not, it would be full steam ahead for outdoors.

There was one day when the choice became obvious: I did three sets of 350 metres, 250 metres with three-to-four minutes' recovery between reps and 10 minutes between sets. All the 350s were run in 43 seconds, which is … *fast*. Afterwards, I collapsed on the side of the track and the British hurdler Andy Turner came over and asked Nick about my session. Nick showed him the rundown on his stopwatch. 'Fuck!' said Turner.

After that, we decided to race in Birmingham, where I broke my Irish indoor 400 metres record, winning in a world-leading 45.52 seconds.

'Felt really strong the last 100,' I wrote in my diary. 'I eased down the last 20. There's a lot more there.'

I weighed 85kg at the time, heavier than my usual racing weight, but it showed me I could run fast off hard training. I didn't need a massive taper or to hit a specific weight.

What's more, the race felt so *easy*. I still hadn't done any real speed work or blocks training – the icing on the cake that brings an athlete to their peak. The decision was an easy one: I was going to Doha.

I then started looking around to find out how my rivals were running, sitting with my laptop, refreshing the results from the US nationals. Bershawn Jackson, a world champion and Olympic medallist in the 400 metres hurdles, had won the 400 metres in 45.41. It was slightly quicker than I'd run in Birmingham, but their nationals were staged in Albuquerque, where the altitude helps sprinters run faster due to lower air resistance. I knew that, in Doha, there would be very little between us.

From the start, Doha felt like the opposite of Berlin. It seemed a pop-up city in the desert, devoid of much culture, and instead of the peaceful tranquillity of that hotel in the Berlin suburbs, we were staying in apartments in a noisy, concrete jungle.

But I wasn't there for a holiday. My mission was straightforward: win the world indoor title.

I got off to a great start, winning my heat in a controlled 46.72. That evening, I was back on track for the semi-final, drawn alongside Jackson. Winning the semi-final was crucial as it'd give me lane five or six in the final. But I didn't do that. Jackson got to the front at halfway and while I tracked him through the second lap and attacked up the home straight, I came up inches short of winning, clocking 46.15 to his 46.13. That meant that instead of drawing for lanes five and six, I'd now be in a draw with the second-place finisher in the other semi-final for lane three or four. A while later, I was lying on the physio bed when the news came through: I got lane three.

Bollocks.

It wasn't impossible to win from three, but to do so I'd either have to go out in kamikaze fashion on the first lap, trying to get to the front, or accept my fate and slot in either third or fourth at halfway, hoping the right gaps would open as I tried to navigate traffic.

I didn't sleep a wink that night, with the sleeping tablets I took failing miserably, and when I finally arose I was groggy, sluggish. It was no surprise that when the gun fired in the final, my reaction time was slow: 0.24 seconds.

I made a big mistake in the blocks. There was a lot of noise in the arena at the time due to the men's pole vault taking place and I was distracted as I crouched, waiting for the 'set' command. I should have put my hand up, forcing the starter to reset us, but I didn't. As a result, I was behind the others from the very first step.

As we broke from lanes towards the end of the first lap, I was languishing in fifth place. I surged up to fourth as we approached the second turn, but had to hit the brakes as the second American, Jamaal Torrence, cut in across me.

THE RACE

In the back straight, with a little over 100 metres to run, I moved wide and steamed past Torrence, leaving just Jackson and the Bahamian, Chris Brown, in front of me. I moved in across Torrence entering the final bend, trying to save a metre by not running wide, and then surged up on the inside of Jackson, who'd left a big gap as he tried to move wide to attack Brown for gold.

But as soon as Jackson saw me coming, he drifted left to cut me off. I ran into the back of him, stumbled badly, and the collision cost us both several metres.

As a result, the three athletes behind us came steaming past and by the time I got going again, it was too little, too late. I crossed the line fifth, in 46.62, with Jackson sixth and last. Brown took gold in 45.96, and I was sick when I saw that time – almost half a second slower than what I'd run in Birmingham.

Jackson walked into the mixed zone ranting and raving. 'You fucking bumped me, man.' To me, it was the opposite. 'Ah, fuck off,' I told him.

The US team put in an appeal to try to get me disqualified and elevate Jackson to fifth. 'Twice in the final 150 metres, athlete 194 from Ireland obstructed and jostled athletes from the United States, seriously affecting and impeding their progress,' the appeal read. 'Both US athletes finished with bona fide efforts. Action requested: disqualification of athlete 194 and any other appropriate action.'

It worked. I got disqualified. I was later handed the decision, which was handwritten: 'The Jury accepts the appeal and rules that David Gillick, the athlete from Ireland, be disqualified and the final places be adjusted accordingly. The jury members noted that the athlete has been the subject of concerns about ~~unsportsmanlike behaviour~~ physically aggressive tactics in previous races.'

I read it, especially the crossed-out part, and thought: *Fuck you.* But part of me also loved it. To do well in the indoor 400 metres, you *have* to be physically aggressive. As angry as I was, I saw it as a badge of honour and I stuck that decision on my fridge as a source of motivation, a reminder of the whingeing Americans.

I'm gonna fucking show those pricks.

I was devastated after the race. The collision cost me a lot financially but my anger was due to losing something far more valuable: a global medal. I got the bus back to the apartment and was by myself, crying.

My dad and sister had surprised me by coming to Doha and Mark, as always, was there, but I didn't want to be around anyone. I was too pissed off. That was my moment to get a world medal and I knew I had the beating of that field, but the championships just didn't flow together.

My reaction time was off in the final and I didn't set the race up, and there was that moment of panic at the last bend. *Should I have waited?* I could have held my fire and gone wide, but that would have meant hitting the brakes and I would have had no chance then of reeling in Brown. I wanted gold, so I went all-in on a daring inside route. High risk, but potentially high reward. It backfired spectacularly. Still, I didn't regret going for that gap. Still don't. You won't win world titles by playing it safe.

Despite our exchange in the mixed zone, with the red mist descending, I didn't have any lasting bad blood with Jackson, and nor did he. Later that year, we crossed paths in Crystal Palace and had a chat and a laugh about the incident. We both knew it was part of what we signed up for in the indoor 400 metres – very much a contact sport.

After Doha, Charlotte and I decided to get out of Loughborough so I could clear my head before preparations began for the outdoor season. We joined her parents on a trip to Keswick in the Lake District.

Charlotte's dad was a businessman and he was always open about finances. On the drive up, he asked me how much I'd lost due to that incident on the final bend in Doha. I started adding it up between the prize money and the medal bonuses in my contract. 'Sixty to seventy grand,' I said, and that was before we got to endorsements or sponsorship doors a global medal would open.

He almost stopped the car. 'What!?'

A few weeks later, I got a call from Rooney telling me that LaShawn Merritt, the reigning world outdoor champion, had been busted for drugs.

I was stunned, as were Rooney and Nick, but after taking a few moments to process the news, I thought: *This is what everyone has talked about with the sport. Why would my event be any different?*

Merritt recorded three positive tests between October 2009 and January 2010 for a steroid hormone, DHEA, and pregnenolone. His explanation was up there in the pantheon of doping excuses: he blamed it on an over-the-counter penis enhancement product called ExtenZe that contained the banned substances. He was given a 21-month ban, having relied on testimony from the clerk in the 7/11 store where he allegedly bought the product. The arbitration panel said the clerk's testimony was 'devastatingly convincing,' adding it was 'confident that enhancing his sports performance was the last thing on Mr. Merritt's mind when he purchased ExtenZe.'

We laughed about his story: *Dick pills! It's so elaborate, maybe it's actually true.* But to me, it all just seemed too convenient, a level of carelessness that was hard to believe from a man who was earning a massive salary and who was the reigning Olympic and world champion.

The banned ingredients were listed on the label of the supplement and despite athletes at elite level being warned time and again about the risk of supplements, apparently he'd just been knocking them back, various times, across several months? There are, undoubtedly, many doping cases that are caused by accidental ingestion – some cold remedies will trigger a positive test – but I've no doubt also that some athletes, after they test positive for a certain substance, will go searching to find what everyday supplements or products it's contained in.

Then they can create a story around that, give someone money to stand up at a hearing and verify their version of events, and if you convince an arbitration panel it was just a careless accident, you get a reduced ban.

Reading the details of Merritt's case brought me back to

the call room in Berlin. I imagined myself sitting in that room, looking around, wondering: *Who in here is clean?*

Rooney and I used to chat about that a lot in training, fully aware that some of our rivals could be having the same debate about us. *Gillick made the final in Berlin, he could be on the gear as well.* If you're not inside the sport and you just see the headline – 'World champion busted for drugs' – it's very easy to paint with a broad brushstroke. *Sure they're all on it.*

But that always pissed me off because I *knew* I did it clean. Yes, there was an element of doping in the sport, but I didn't think it was that dirty because I hadn't seen anything – either in the UK or on the circuit. But Merritt getting busted opened my eyes, changed my view.

I had finished sixth in the world final but started to think: *Where did I really finish? Maybe I'm the fastest clean guy on the planet. Just how dirty is this sport?*

The drugs thing always fascinated people, and I'd often get asked about anti-doping procedures, which vary a *lot* by nation.

Some countries, like Ireland, test their top athletes regularly. Many others do not, their lack of anti-doping procedures usually blamed on a lack of budget, which is a useful excuse when you've no interest in finding out the truth about your stars. That's where athletics' governing body, the IAAF, had a big role to play, stepping into the void to test athletes from such nations out of competition.

Once you reach a certain level, you get added to their

testing pool. For me, that happened in 2009, while Sport Ireland had been testing me since 2003. At times, I'd look across at certain rivals and wonder, knowing they were from countries where there was little or no drug testing. But I'd acknowledge that and remind myself: *Focus on yourself.*

On average, I was tested 10 to 12 times a year, but the frequency varied a lot. The Irish system is one of the strictest in the world and, ahead of a championship, I was sometimes tested three times in a week. I'd start to wonder why they're showing up so much. *Are they suspicious?* But in a sense, I took it as a compliment when they cranked up those visits: it meant I was running well.

The whereabouts system is a key part of anti-doping. We had to designate one hour each day when we'd be available for drug tests and provide detailed information every quarter of the year: listing your home, your work, your training venues, the normal duration you'd be at each place, along with your overnight address, which had to always be up to date.

The drug testers could still show up outside of your one-hour window, and they often did, but that was the one part of the day when you *had* to be where you said you would. I picked my slot early in the morning, knowing I'd always be at home.

For my first drug test, in 2003, I was so nervous. You go into the bathroom with the doping control officer, drop your underwear to your ankles, pull your T-shirt up, then pee in a cup. In the early years of my career, you didn't have to be so explicit, the officer would just take a casual glance, but then it got more intrusive. Part of that was because some dopers figured out a creative method to provide a clean sample: putting a balloon of clean urine up their ass before a test and then using a fake, prosthetic penis to pass it into a cup.

During the test, women would have to squat down and the drug tester would squat with them, checking for any such gizmos, while for me it was about making sure the tester had a full, unobscured view of everything – *everything* – as I provided the sample.

If something came up at the last minute and my plans changed, I'd update my whereabouts by text message. The testers would give us little whereabouts stickers so I put one on my front door, a reminder as I left the house to make sure things were up to date. If you weren't where you said you'd be and the testers showed up, that was one missed test. Three of those in a 12-month period and you'd get a two-year ban. One time, I was in the airport, flying to a race, and Charlotte called to say the testers had shown up at home. *They couldn't be, I've updated it.* But for whatever reason, the text message had been sitting in the outbox of my messages and hadn't gone through. Thankfully, I was able to show them that and avoided racking up a missed test.

If you get three strikes like that, it taints your whole career – whether you're clean or dirty. But while a lot of innocent athletes might rack up one missed test, sometimes two, you'd have to be exceptionally careless to get three in a year. When I see that happen, I always assume the athlete is cheating.

The system can be annoying at times, but it's not that hard to stay up to date with and I get pissed off when athletes moan about drug testers calling or having to update whereabouts. It's part of the job, a small price for clean sport.

The testers usually took both blood and urine. The blood test was simple – a two-minute job – but if you couldn't pee when they arrived you might be sitting around, drinking water and chatting, for an hour or two. Once, I drank so much water that I gave samples that were too diluted, so had to wait another hour or two for my urine to return to normal.

I was always paranoid about making a mistake, whether with my whereabouts or my supplements. We had a website where we'd check the legality of any supplement or medication, and for things like my protein, I'd always put in the batch number of the product and read the report. It was the same if I got sick: there was paranoia about what I could and couldn't take, with some cold and flu medications containing banned substances. During each drug test, I'd write down every supplement I'd taken, from vitamins to paracetamol. It was always in the back of my head: can I be 100 per cent sure this is legitimate? That it's not produced in a factory where there's cross contamination?

One study found 35 per cent of supplements contained banned substances, many of which were not listed among the ingredients, so it does happen. You've got to make damn sure any supplement you're taking is legitimate. The market has grown so much and it's still poorly regulated but when an athlete tests positive and blames a supplement, I still put the blame on them for not taking adequate care. You're supposed to be a professional. What you put in your body is part of the job.

One time, I was drug tested while at a gathering of Charlotte's relatives at her countryside cottage. The testers came in and Charlotte's mum was like, 'Do you want a cup of tea?'

I replied, 'No, Audrey, they want a cup of piss.'

The relatives were full of questions after they had left and couldn't get over the fact some random man had followed me into the jacks and stared at my penis while I peed in a cup. What a glamorous life we led.

One of my first big eye-openers about doping was through reading Dwain Chambers' book. He was the leading British 100 metres runner in the early 2000s but was often coming up just short of global medals, and so he moved to California to train under Ukrainian coach Remi Korchemmy.

In August 2003, Chambers tested positive for THG, a designer steroid that was at the heart of the BALCO scandal. BALCO (Bay Area Laboratory Co-operative) was a company based outside San Francisco that, on the surface, offered blood analysis and food supplements, but its hidden business was supplying elite athletes across a range of sports – from baseball to American football to athletics – with performance-enhancing drugs. Anti-doping authorities only became aware of the designer steroid in the summer of 2003 when Trevor Graham, a rival coach who was fed up of his athletes getting beaten, anonymously sent a syringe containing the substance to the US Anti-Doping Agency.

A test was soon developed to detect it and Chambers was one of those who tested positive. He was handed a two-year ban, but he didn't do the usual for an athlete in that scenario – claiming innocence – and instead dished the dirt on exactly how he'd been drawn to the dark side: what he took, when he took it and who helped him source it. When his book came out in 2009, I read about the web of lies he'd got himself into and how well things were orchestrated. *That's not a one-off*, I thought. *How many people are in that world?*

Plenty of people had got caught for drugs, but there were very few cases in the 400 metres and so, until 2010, I had a certain naivety or perhaps a bit of delusion.

People would say it to me, 'They *must* be on something', but those sweeping assumptions pissed me off because I knew I wasn't. But anywhere there's fame and fortune, there are cheats. The news about Merritt started to change my perspective.

Don't be so stupid, David. Why would your event be any different?

The road to the outdoor season in 2010 began in the now-customary fashion: with a training camp in LA. I raced a couple of 200 metres races in California, clocking a PB of 21.20, though given the improvements I'd made in the speed department, I had been hoping for sub-21.

My first 400 metres was in Geneva – against Rooney. We were the two big names in the race and the night before, we were given central lanes: I was in four, Rooney in five.

When I got to the track on race day, I was still in four but Rooney had been switched to three. Previously, I'd had the advantage as I could judge my pace off him, but now he had it and would know exactly how to expend his energy, given he could use me as a gauge. I was pissed off at the late change and I approached Nick. 'What's the story here?' He didn't know.

As it turned out, when the lane draw was released, I was told that Rooney had approached the meeting director to switch to the lane inside me. Even though we were rooming together, he hadn't told me. *What the fuck?* I started to think back on the whispers from the Irish camp and whether it really was the best thing to train alongside one of my biggest rivals, wondering whether Nick had helped negotiate a favourable lane for him at my expense. We'd always been friends and were obviously competitive, but this was the first time I thought: *OK, so this is how it's going to be.* I asked Rooney and he shrugged his shoulders, neither confirming nor denying that he'd done that. Years later, it came up in conversation and he told me he had requested to be in the B race so he'd have a better lane. The meeting director wouldn't allow that, but did change his lane for the A race.

Rooney was a different character to me. We got on very well, and we're still good mates, but he was different – more confident. In 2010, he was under pressure. He'd torn his hamstring the previous year and had his contract cut, then had to listen to lots of people whispering that he wasn't handling the transition to senior level. He needed to hit certain numbers to preserve his Nike deal and so I understood why he did what he did in Geneva, even if that didn't lessen my annoyance.

I'd have liked to be tracking him too but if I was drawn in the lane outside, I wouldn't have manipulated the race to suit my needs. And if that's what he wanted to do, then at least he could have admitted it when I asked him. It planted an extra seed of competitiveness, adding some bite to the race. He won it in 44.99, while I finished second in 45.32. That day, more than most, I was pissed off to lose to him.

My next race was at the European Team Championships in Budapest, where I finished second in 45.29 to another big European rival, Jonathan Borlée of Belgium. I needed to get back under 45 seconds and I did that at my next two races in La Chaux de Fonds, Switzerland, and in Barcelona, winning in 44.98 and 44.95.

La Chaux de Fonds was at altitude and it's renowned for fast times, and while I didn't get any prize money, I did win a nice watch: a Ulysse Nardin. It was many years later before I learned just how nice it was. I was renting a house in Dublin which got broken into and the watch was sitting on the mantelpiece, but the burglars obviously didn't know much about watches either as they left it behind them. After that, I decided to get it insured and was told it was worth seven or eight grand.

The race in Barcelona was just over a fortnight before the

Europeans, which were being held in the same stadium, and I had the perfect preparation: winning on my twenty-seventh birthday, with the organisers handing me a huge trophy and playing 'happy birthday' over the tannoy. Things were clicking.

I might have been training with one of my big rivals, but Nick was great at managing the dynamic between me and Rooney, always giving us specific target times, trying to keep us from punching ourselves out in sessions. If Rooney wanted to drop a bomb on the last rep, I didn't let it bother me, trusting Nick's plan to have me right where I wanted on the big day. A diary entry from that time summed up how I felt about the rising tension with Rooney:

> Park these things until the end of summer. The agent side of things needs to be addressed. Move to Ricky (Simms) or Paul (Doyle). Nick can focus on being my coach. Group size is too big at the moment: young athletes with not the same focus to be world class. Surround yourself with world-class athletes. Needs to be a focused number of athletes: no more than 10, max. Focused, elite, hardworking. One shot at life. Get what I want. Rooney? Leave him at it. Not going to annoy me. It's up to me if I want to let it get to me.

I travelled to Barcelona feeling more assured than ever about my form. I'd spent years trying to solve this 400 metres puzzle, but I finally knew how to put all the pieces together. I just had to slot them into place on the day it mattered most.

CHAPTER 12

THE BURGER INCIDENT

Athletics, on a fundamental level, is an individual sport. Which is not to suggest team events don't matter: in secondary school, after all, the only thing that kept me running was the prospect of a cross country medal with St Benildus. And one of my fondest memories remains the 4x100m relay win in Santry alongside my classmates from Our Lady's National School.

But ask any athlete what they'd prefer, an individual Olympic medal or a relay medal, and you'll soon find out where their priorities lie.

Still, everyone loves relays. They're a fun way to finish off championships, and as enjoyable for athletes as they are for fans. But there is one exception: when committing to them will impact your individual performance. These days, such debates are had around Rhasidat Adeleke or Sharlene Mawdsley, and there's generally an understanding – at least there *should* be – that while it's nice for Ireland to do well in the mixed relay, it *can't* come at the expense of an individual medal chance.

On the build-up to Barcelona, the relay started to cause me some headaches. Because I'd reached a higher level, and there was decent depth in Irish 400 metres running, the London Olympics were a possibility for the men's 4x400m team. But to qualify, we needed two fast times that put us in the world's top-16. The best place to achieve them was at major events like the World Championships where, with everyone at their high point of the season, we stood a significantly better chance of running fast.

The only issue? There was no proper plan in place to make this happen. At the start of each year, I'd always sit with Nick to plot out the course to our peak race. In 2010, that was the European 400 metres final in Barcelona. We worked back from that, slotting in various checkpoints along the way. Gareth Devlin was the High Performance Director for Athletics Ireland at the time, but communication was patchy through the early part of the year. That was a trend with Athletics Ireland: they'd make no mention of relays during the crucial planning phase, then we'd get to April or May and suddenly there'd be a phone call: 'Oh, we're trying to get some teams together.'

I didn't like that ad-hoc, oh-shit-let's-pull-something-together approach, and I flagged with Gareth the pressure it would put on me. The lack of planning was unprofessional, haphazard and disrespectful to the athletes and coaches who were trying to hit their peak.

THE BURGER INCIDENT

Still, I *wanted* an Irish relay team to get to the Olympics, and so I lined out for a 4x400m with my Irish teammates in Loughborough in late May, then again at the European Team Champs in Budapest in late June. We ran 3:07 on both occasions: solid but not what was needed. When the countdown was on to Barcelona, I told Gareth my priority was on the individual 400 metres. *I'm trying to win the fucking thing.* The heats of the men's 4x400m were scheduled for the morning after the individual 400 metres final. My logic was that, by then, I'd have run three rounds of the 400 metres in four days, that I didn't know what shape I'd be in the morning after the individual final, so it'd be worth preparing for the relay heats without me. Then I'd be available as needed if they made the final.

'We need to sort this,' I told Nick as Barcelona approached.

'That's all good,' he told me. 'Gareth is on board with that plan. Just concentrate.'

From the conversations Nick and I had with those in the Irish camp, we assumed everyone understood the lie of the land: the Irish would run the first round without me, and I'd slot back in if they made the final.

But assumption, of course, is the mother of all fuck-ups.

Soon after I arrived in Barcelona, I walked into the dining hall at the team hotel and one of the 4x400m team, Gordon Kennedy, handed me a pair of sunglasses. 'What are they for?' I asked. 'We're all gonna wear the same ones for the relay,' he said. It was a nice gesture, don't get me wrong, but I had a lot of running to do of my own before I started thinking of sunglasses and 4x400m relays.

Soon after, Stephen Maguire, one of the Irish team coaches, came up to me laughing: 'The 46 runner telling the 44 runner what to wear in the race.' I knew Gordon didn't mean any harm and his excitement was understandable. It was, after all, a big opportunity to kickstart the qualifying process for the London Olympics. But, for me, this was a European 400 metres title I could *win*. It was *my* be-all and end-all. Once the championships got under way, the relay didn't enter my mind.

I had arrived two days before the first round of the 400 metres. At the track the next day, Sara Slott Petersen, a Danish 400 metres hurdler who was based at Loughborough, came over for a chat. 'Your race is gonna be the race of the championships,' she said. 'So many guys packed together!'

It was true. The men's 400 metres had six or seven athletes who could win and there were only a few tenths of a second between our best times that season. The margin for error would be tiny.

I coasted through my heat, winning in 45.84, and feeling effortless, having eased off the gas with 60 metres to run. The following night, I was back on track for the semi-final, and I measured that perfectly, running relaxed and fluid, tall and strong. I outran Michael Bingham in the home straight to take the win and was stunned when I saw the time, 44.79, just outside my Irish record of 44.77.

After the race, Bingham said, 'You didn't need to push for the line.'

I was like, 'I *didn't* push for the line, I just dipped.'

That ensured I got the win and a better lane for the final. What I didn't tell Bingham was just how controlled I had felt, how easy it had been.

Replicate that, I told myself, *and you're gonna win.*

I had a day off before the final, which I spent mostly relaxing and sleeping, as well as going to the beach for a bit with sprinter Jason Smyth to help get my mind off the following day. The day of the final, I went out for a jog, did a couple of strides and saw two of my big rivals, the Borlée twins, Jonathan and Kevin, doing the same. We exchanged a simple smile and nod, and part of me thought: *It's just my luck that there's two of them.*

At the warm-up track that evening, the Irish tent was busy, chaotic, with lots of people milling around. This bugged me, as various coaches were loitering who didn't have athletes competing. I was highly strung, agitated, knowing how much was on the line.

Before I headed into the call room, a British coach, Lloyd Cowan, came over and gave me a handshake. 'Go do what you do well,' he said. Next, they led us into the stadium via a land bridge, which we reached via a flight of stairs. *Power up these fucking steps,* I told myself, not wanting any negative ideas about heavy legs leaking in during those final minutes.

There were a lot of Irish fans around and I heard a few shouts as I walked across the bridge – into another fabled stadium, which had hosted the 1992 Olympics. The track was an ocean blue and it shimmered under the lights, the stands crackling with electricity from tens of thousands of fans. This was the race I'd spent ten months training for.

'On your marks,' said the starter, and I stamped on the blocks one last time.

'Set.'

The dynamite is lit. Run through that wall.

Bang!

I was drawn in lane four, with Leslie Djhone just outside me in five. He always ripped through the first 100 metres and he did the same here once we were unshackled from the purgatory of the blocks.

I also got out hard, gaining a half-step on Jonathan Borlée on the lane inside, who many saw as the favourite after he won his semi-final in 44.71. But I couldn't see the ground I'd gained on him, only the ground I had lost to Djhone. Into the back straight, when I should have been relaxing, freewheeling, I had a split second where I thought: *Shit, he's getting away from me.* It was nothing new; Djhone always went out fast and later came back, but it was just enough to upset my rhythm, to lose focus on what *I* was doing.

Around the last bend, I was firmly in the hunt for gold, knowing Bingham and Djhone – who'd both blasted the first 250 metres – were now coming back. Rooney was in lane one, the worst draw imaginable, but with 120 metres left he suddenly appeared to the left in my peripheral vision.

Fuck, Rooney's up.

We hit the home straight with two metres covering the first seven men, with Russia's Vladimir Krasnov bringing up the rear in eighth. I tried to move and attack, but the extra effort only caused me to tense up.

At that point of the 400 metres, the key is holding your form, keeping your stride long and making sure everything is linear – any side to side motion is wasted energy. But that's easier said than done. My shoulders were tightening, my head was going forward, as if being tugged by an imaginary string, while my core was crumbling. Jonathan Borlée surged past and I tried to match him. Djhone was starting to go backwards but still just ahead of me, hanging on for dear life.

Then, suddenly, Kevin Borlée came steaming past us all out in lane six, with Bingham and Krasnov also flying home from the outer lanes. I was surrounded by athletes, with inches between us, as the line got closer and closer. Instead of doing what I should have – relaxing – I tensed up more, my hips going forward. I was leaning, striving, *lunging* for the line, all of which cost me speed. The first seven flashed across the line almost in unison. I collapsed to the track, not knowing where I'd finished. All I knew was I didn't win.

Then I lay there, wheezing for air, awaiting my fate on the big screen. The lights illuminated as each name flashed up, starting with the winner.

First place, bang! It's not me.

They lit up again. Bang! Still not me.

One medal to go. Bang! Again, it's fucking not me.

Kevin Borlée took gold in 45.08, with Bingham winning silver and Rooney the bronze, both of the Brits clocking

45.23. Then it was Krasnov, who'd come from way back to snatch fourth in 45.24, and then me, in 45.28.

Fifth.

Fuck, there goes my moment.

I laid back on the blue track, hands clasping the back of my head, and surveyed the scene from what felt – almost two years on from Beijing – like a return to rock bottom.

The others were high-fiving, the medallists grabbing their nation's flags. I got up, shook Rooney's hand, and then stood and watched as he headed off on his lap of honour. I had never got to do that at an outdoor championships in a big stadium. Maybe now I never would.

Another mixed zone of doom, gloom and regret was awaiting: a place of dark thoughts that I'd try my best to suppress as I stood in front of the cameras. I told the journalists I just didn't connect the race up as I'd have liked, that I was in a tricky position with 50 to go: giving them the usual party line.

Only when I escaped the stadium, and met Patsy McGonagle, did the dam burst on my emotions. I started bawling crying. 'What the fuck has just happened?' I said. 'What the FUCK has just happened?'

Patsy grabbed me and led me to a quiet corner, outside the stadium walls, where we could be alone. Then he hugged me as I continued to cry. 'Get it out,' he said.

I was still in tears on the bus journey back to the hotel, the same way I'd been in Doha – my head buried in that comforting cloak of my hands. My mind was overrun with regrets and what-ifs. *I wish I was more relaxed down the back straight. I wish I just ran my own race.*

Did the pressure get to me? Maybe. But all it takes is a split second of doubt and suddenly you're questioning yourself. When other runners are up on you and you're not expecting it, it unsettles you, rattling your best-laid plans.

In the 400 metres, your race approach is pre-programmed across hundreds of sessions that you've done at the requisite pace. But if you throw that away in the moment, trying to react and respond to others, tightness creeps in. You've *got* to maintain your form, which dictates your stride length and efficiency, but I didn't. With 120 metres left, I had changed the dial, trying to reprogramme the computer, and the computer didn't just say no but *hell no*.

Then it started to shut down.

The mediocre winning time, 45.08, only rubbed salt in my wounds. I was just 0.2 seconds away from gold, and only 0.05 off the bronze. Which only made me feel worse. *Could you not just have beaten me easily?* It took many years to watch that race back. Over a decade and a half on, it remains the one race that still replays in my mind, the one race I still run, searching, hoping, for a different outcome.

Four or five years after the final, Rooney got everyone bar the Russian and the Pole together on a video call, each of us talking through what was in our heads as we came up that home straight in a line.

It was one of the best European finals ever, with seven of us in the hunt for gold with 40 metres left. Kevin Borlée said he felt his form was good coming up the home straight and he got a sense everyone else was tying up. Rooney felt he'd nothing to lose so decided to just leg it to 300 metres and see what happened. Bingham said he didn't push his semi-final against me, knowing a second-place finish would get him an outside lane and he was comfortable with that as it'd allow him to run his own race in the final. That might have been an inspired move because, as it turned out, it was the athletes in those prized middle lanes who struggled the most, having gone to war with each other, trying to react and respond to moves.

I was livid with myself for letting that happen, and the night of the race, I wallowed in self-hate at the hotel. Patsy came over to me in the lobby, telling me that David McCarthy, who'd been due to run the relay the next morning, had gone home. 'We don't have a sub,' he told me. 'Are you going to run?'

'I was *never* going to run,' I told him. 'You know that and the high-performance manager knows that.'

'Well, we're going to have to pull the team,' he said.

'Don't put that on me now. I'm not running. That was always the agreement. I've been through this so many times. I'm not running.'

With that, I headed out to Burger King to meet Charlotte and my family. The atmosphere was like a funeral, all of us sitting around in quiet, solemn mourning of my medal chance. My sister, Eileen, was on her phone, responding to texts from back home.

'Right, what is it?' I snapped. 'What are they saying?'

THE BURGER INCIDENT

'They're just really upset for you,' she said.

'Just put the phone down, will you?'

My parents had watched the final alongside Jim Kidd and, as we sat in Burger King, my mother chose a very bad time to pass on his critique. 'Jim says if you had more speed, you'd be able to finish the races better.' I erupted and had a blazing row with my parents.

'You don't have a fucking clue what you're talking about! You're taking someone's opinion about what I need to do. What does he know?'

I was annoyed with Jim. It wasn't his place to tell my parents what I should be doing. It's one thing to tell me, but not my parents because they put him on a pedestal: he was the one who brought me through. At that moment, in the stadium, during the most crushing near-miss of my career, there was no need for it. It was all too raw.

Mum and Dad, in fairness, didn't understand how hurt I was and the consequences of not getting a medal. But this was a time when I needed them to just listen, not to tell me what to do. I was as low as I'd ever been, and that's when my mother brought up the relay.

'Will you not just run it?' she asked, which led me to lose the rag again.

'You just want me to please people! *I'm* the one who's cut at the moment.'

Charlotte was in the middle, trying to play peacemaker among the Gillicks. 'OK guys, we need to relax now.' But I wasn't letting it go. This was not the place and certainly not the time to tell me what I should have done or what I should do next. I slammed my burger down on the table and told my mother to 'just fucking shut up!' Then I stood up and walked out, still fuming as I walked back to the hotel alone.

I was disappointed that in such a crushing moment, my mother was questioning my reasoning, that she couldn't see it from my perspective and didn't seem to have my back, pressuring me to do something that wasn't in the plan to make other people happy. I shut myself off from my parents after that, cutting off all contact, and it was several weeks later when my sister got us all together for a coffee, acting as mediator, that we finally cleared the air. We still disagreed about what happened in Barcelona, but agreed to let it be and move on.

I didn't regret my little blowup and I didn't feel guilty, but I was disappointed by it. It was one of those unfortunate moments when your job spills over into your personal life, impacting relationships with those you love.

Charlotte had seen it before, and she would see it again. She still refers to that as The Burger Incident.

The next morning, I awoke and watched the heats of the 4x400m on TV in my hotel room. The Irish had drafted in a 200 metres runner, Steven Colvert, to run the final leg, joining Gordon Kennedy, Brian Murphy and Brian Gregan. They finished sixth in 3:07.21, two seconds away from making the final, with Colvert tying up badly on the home straight of his leg. I felt sad watching it and had the inevitable thought: *Maybe I should have run*? But then

THE BURGER INCIDENT

another thought took its place: *This was all planned; it was known. Where was the understanding?*

But all of a sudden, I was public enemy number one in Irish athletics. It felt like everyone forgot about the world final, the European indoor wins, about me running 44 seconds. All they wanted to know: *Why didn't you do the relay?* I was sitting in the hotel dining room early that afternoon when Joanne Cuddihy came in and joined me.

'Why didn't you run?' she asked.

'I'm not getting into this.'

'The Borlees were down there.'

'Joanne,' I said, in absolutely no mood for a lecture, 'fuck off.'

Her face dropped, and the following day she apologised, saying she shouldn't have given me a hard time about it. But that was only my first sliver of seeing how much my absence had upset people.

During the day, I got a sense around the hotel that people weren't warm; they were blanking me a bit. I walked down the stairs and bumped into Brian Gregan and he told me I'd stopped them from realising their Olympic dream. Gregan was young, only 20 at the time, and so I didn't hold what he said against him. But I also wasn't accepting it.

'I'm here to do my job,' I told him. 'That's really unfair. You can't pin that on me.'

This was the final day of the championships, and that night most of the Irish went to the same bar. After arriving, I walked down to the table where two of the relay team, Brian Murphy and Gordon Kennedy, were sitting. I said hello and, as soon as I did, they stood up and walked out, not so much as acknowledging my existence as they left. After that, I went to Patsy McGonagle. 'What the fuck is going on here?' I asked. 'I'm getting blanked now. People are blaming me for the relay. You guys need to put out a statement.'

Patsy did just that, writing up a statement for Athletics Ireland in his hotel room to basically say that they supported my decision to not run the heats of the relay and this had been agreed in advance of the championships. He also called a team meeting for the following day to clear the air and remind everyone what had been agreed prior to the championships. None of the others showed up. On the bus to the airport the next morning, people were looking the other way when I walked down the aisle. It left a sour taste in my mouth. I felt isolated and, thankfully, I wasn't flying back to Dublin with the team, but to the East Midlands. I needed to get the hell away.

The whole championship, on the track and off it, was one of my worst experiences in athletics.

At the end of the day, it's an individual sport and all the choices I had made across many years were to get an Irish vest to European or world finals, all so I could fight for a medal on behalf of my country. But suddenly, I had to hear that I was the one who'd ruined other people's Olympic dreams. The decision not to run that relay is one I've never been allowed to forget, and if I had any inkling of how big a deal it would become, then I would have abandoned what was agreed and just run the damn thing.

THE BURGER INCIDENT

Just last year, I posted something on social media about one of the current Irish 4x400m relay teams and someone popped up in the replies: 'Unlike you – not stepping up for your team in Barcelona.'

Back in 2010, people at home were saying they should pull my grant, cut my funding, even though 100 per cent of my grant money was based on my individual performances and none of it on relays. Soon after the championships, there was a two-page spread in the *Sunday Independent*, a story that painted me as a complete arsehole who'd let my country down, essentially saying I'd spat out my dummy and didn't want to run and that I was the reason the team wasn't going to the London Olympics.

One of the athletes had gone to a journalist and slated me, anonymously. My parents kept the cutout of that story and when I was back in Dublin, I sat in the bedroom of their house and read it. That cut me – deep – as the things said in the piece weren't accurate or in any way fair. But I knew many people would believe them. I was livid.

A couple of years later, I did an interview with Cliona Foley and she said, 'I was told you were cut adrift and no one wanted to talk to you, that you spent the whole time by yourself.' I was like, 'What?' But it wasn't a million miles from the truth during my final day in Barcelona. I never spoke about what happened and never lashed back at the teammate who slated me (without having the courage to put his name to his words). I decided to just take it on the chin and thought: *Right, at least I know now where I stand with other people.*

One of the lads called me a few months later to clarify that it wasn't him who was behind the story while, to this day, I still haven't been told by anyone in Athletics Ireland exactly why David McCarthy went home, hearing two different tales at the time. Of course, there was no review or reflection on the communication issues during the build-up, which was typical of Athletics Ireland at the time. It was out of sight, out of mind, with no lessons needing to be learned. *Next.*

But, for me, there was lasting damage. I'd been made out as someone who didn't care about representing my country, that I wasn't a team player. But I had flown everywhere I was requested to for the relay through the years before, and earlier that season – sometimes to the detriment of my own career.

I had thought, at one of my lowest moments, there would be some level of understanding, that people would be there with support. But Barcelona taught me the truth in that old saying: success has many fathers, but failure is an orphan.

In the wake of my fifth-place finish, that nagging issue reared its head again. It was said to me several times in Barcelona that I was training with a British coach, alongside a British athlete, and that it was more in Nick's favour for Rooney to do well than me.

'None of you have ever come to my training to see how we work,' I said.

Still, the goal of 2010 had been to get on a podium and I'd come up short – twice. Rooney *did* get a medal, and so

THE BURGER INCIDENT

amid the many scrambled thoughts I had after that final, one was to the fore: *Maybe I do need to change things.* Before leaving Barcelona, I went for a coffee with Chris Jones, a high-performance consultant with Athletics Ireland. Again, the issue of my training group was raised, with Chris suggesting it could be a good idea to go elsewhere.

I was tied into a contract with adidas until 2012, so my choices were limited, with so many of the top coaches in the sport aligned with specific brands and therefore unable to coach athletes signed to other brands. I didn't know any of that before, as I wasn't looking around to join other coaches. But after Barcelona I started doing some research. I wanted to go where there were fast people over 100 metres and 200 metres so as to improve my speed and sprint mechanics, knowing that would translate to a better 400 metres. If I wanted to get on the podium at the London Olympics, I needed to give myself two years in a new programme, making sure I was settled heading into Olympic year.

There was an obvious choice when it came to improving my speed: Lance Brauman, an adidas coach who guided a slew of the world's fastest sprinters in Florida. The guys at adidas were very happy to see my interest in moving there. In more recent times, Lance has coached Olympic champions like Noah Lyles and Shaunae Miller-Uibo, but his stable was just as world-beating back then: he coached Jamaica's Veronica Campbell-Brown to Olympic gold over 200 metres and US star Tyson Gay to world titles over 100 metres and 200 metres. The group was based in Amsterdam during the summer, a good jumping-off point for races around Europe, and so that's where I travelled to meet Lance for the first time in August 2010.

I arrived at the Olympic stadium not knowing what to expect, then watched some of his athletes train before going back to the apartment Lance was renting. He flipped open his laptop and talked me through his programme. I had some imposter syndrome as he was talking. *Does he even know who I am?* But on paper, it all looked good. There was no red flag to suggest his training would be remarkably different to what I was used to. He was warm, friendly and he seemed interested. For every question I asked, he had answers. He referenced a few other 400 metres runners he'd worked with, explaining how he'd taken them from here to there, from this time to that time. Everything looked, and sounded, great. At the airport before returning home, I called Charlotte and told her about the meeting.

The decision was made before I hung up the phone: I was leaving Loughborough and moving to Florida.

CHAPTER 13

LOST IN TRANSLATION

It was time for another of those awkward conversations: to break up with my coach. I dreaded telling Nick I was leaving, given how much he'd done for me in the previous years. But it had to be done.

He took the news in his stride, wishing me well at the end of our chat. If anything, I'd have liked him to plead with me a bit more, convincing me to stay and explaining how we could improve. But deep down, I knew this had to happen. I needed a break, a change, a fresh start. I spent a month training with his group before I left, which was a bit awkward at times, but the athletes I respected most, like Rooney, understood why I was going. Sometimes, you just need to change.

Charlotte and I were committed to each other so we decided to do a long-distance relationship, and she threw a surprise party before I left, inviting everyone I trained with. As departure day came closer, I started getting sad and stressed. I didn't have a place to live in the US. I had no bank account so I couldn't get a lease on an apartment, and that great unknown made me anxious. I got emotional while packing and had a huge, nagging doubt.

Is this the right thing to do?

Charlotte dropped me to Manchester Airport and the mood on the way there was sombre. I said goodbye, kissed her, hugged her, then turned and walked away. I was distraught. I went into a cubicle in the toilet and started bawling. This time, I was truly going it alone, moving a long way from home. On the plane, I kept reminding myself: *This is what you have to do. This is part of chasing the dream.* I wrote in my diary: 'Blue skies will come.' I couldn't turn back now.

I landed in Orlando and was picked up by one of the athletes in the group, Shalonda Solomon, who I'd never met before. I spent my first night in a Holiday Inn, then spent the next few weeks staying at Lance's house until I sorted somewhere to live.

Lance was strong, stocky – a former sprinter – with silver hair and a southern accent. He was typically American, but not in that sweet-as-apple-pie sense, more like a brusque, no-bullshit, straight-talking high school football coach. He was businesslike, and not the kind of fella you'd sit down and chew the fat with. Not that I cared. I wasn't looking for a friend. I just wanted to run fast, and he had a record of helping dozens of athletes get to the very top. Lance knew the kind of personality I was – driven, committed – and as he drove me around town, showing me the training venues, he warned me how that could have a downside. 'You're intelligent,' he said. 'But don't overthink it.'

Clermont is a strange place, a city of around 40,000 people that's just over 20 miles west of Orlando. Not the kind of place a tourist would ever visit, with the Florida Mall being the closest thing in town to an attraction.

The first few days, I was looking around thinking: *What the fuck have I done?* There were lots of houses and apartments, but no one was around on the streets. There was no community. I'd run down the road and people would look at me like an alien had just hopped past on a pogo stick. *Who the fuck is this guy?* Culturally, there was no heart in Clermont, no soul. This was new America, where the roads were long and wide, interspersed with two of the country's great obsessions: retail outlets and fast food joints.

After jumping through several hoops and coughing up a huge deposit, I got sorted with a one-bed apartment, with Lance acting as the guarantor. Setting that place up and finding furniture proved a good distraction in the early weeks, but after that the boredom started to set in – in a big way. The group trained Monday to Friday, then at weekends I would be at a loose end. I spent a lot of time by myself. I'd get up on a Saturday morning, go for a run, then turn on the TV and watch three Premier League games back to back.

There was no social aspect to the group like in Loughborough. People came to practice, trained, then they went home. It wasn't that I wanted a red carpet laid out, but it all seemed so businesslike, so transactional.

I was the only white guy in the group and while that never bothered me, I did wonder if the others would be embarrassed to hang out with me in social settings, being seen with this six-foot-two white guy from Ireland. Most of the athletes in the group were from the Caribbean, and sometimes they'd be chatting in Creole at training and I'd be there like a piece of furniture alongside them, without a clue what was being said.

One of them I got to know quite well was Andretti Bain, a Bahamian 400 metres runner. I'd pop over to his apartment now and again, which was always a hive of activity. Andretti's younger brother was over from the Bahamas and going to school locally, while he also had a mate who was living on his balcony: his bed set up on that tiny outdoor space. The one big social event when the group got together was Thanksgiving, when we were hosted by David Oliver, one of the world's best hurdlers and a great guy.

Debbie Ferguson-McKenzie was like the mother of the group: a lovely, lovely lady. She was Bahamian and had gold, silver and bronze medals from three different Olympics. She was so warm, always asking, 'How are you doing?' when I saw her, seeming like she genuinely wanted to know. When you saw her coming, you'd always be relieved.

One day, there was a huge fight at the track between two of the group members: Keston Bledman and Curtis Mitchell. Curtis was a 21-year-old American who'd just graduated from the NCAA to the pro ranks, having broken 20 seconds for 200 metres the previous summer. He was fun to be around, a proper character, and trained like no one I'd ever seen. He would do his own training on top of what Lance gave him, and sometimes I'd drive past and see him slogging up the hill by the track, alone and in the dark – full-on *Rocky*-style stuff.

He'd always be buzzing at the track, full of energy, but it annoyed some people in the group. He had a car that he could start remotely, and he'd be revving it in the car park as we stood on the track, thinking it was hilarious. Keston was the opposite to him: quiet and subdued. There was no badness in him, but he'd come from a rough spot in Trinidad and Tobago and definitely knew how to handle himself. Curtis was talking trash one day, telling everyone what he was going to run, the races he'd win, and Keston grew tired of it, telling him to shut the fuck up. Then it all kicked off, a full-blown brawl, with both of them saying 'I'm gonna kill you' as Lance ran in to separate them.

There was one tight-knit circle of friends in the group: Tyson Gay, Steve Mulllings and Kelly-Ann Baptiste. Gay and Mullings used to do their gym work separate to the rest of us, with some guy we didn't know. They'd do weight training before coming to the track for a session, which made zero sense to me, but who was I to question some of the fastest sprinters in history?

Gay was the group's star, its shining light. He had won the 100m-200m double at the 2007 World Championships in Osaka and finished runner-up to Usain Bolt in the 2009 world 100 metres final in Berlin, the 9.69 he ran in Shanghai a few weeks later the second fastest time in history behind Bolt's world record. Gay kept himself to himself. I joined the group in November and it was only in February or March when he first spoke to me directly.

'What's your name again?' he asked at training.

'David,' I said, thinking, *I've been here for three months.*

You might think world champions like him are fastidious about everything they do, working harder than the rest. But that didn't seem the case. In those early months, we would do long reps of 600 metres to 800 metres on the grass and if you watched Gay and didn't know his achievements, you'd think it was some lad trying to burn off the Christmas pints on New Year's Day. He and the other 100 metres guys would jog their reps, wearing full tracksuits and hoodies, not caring that the women were well ahead. Anytime Lance's back was turned, they'd start walking. There were certain days Lance wasn't around and, if that happened, lots of the lads would barely even train.

I was the opposite. You tell me to do 10x100m and I'll run every single metre, otherwise I'd feel like I was cheating myself. But when I saw how many others operated, I started to wonder: *Maybe I'm training too hard?*

There was a sloping road down to the track that we'd use for hill reps, which I'd always hammer, but some of the others would literally walk up, one of those being Keston, a 9.86 100 metres runner. In the gym, Lance would walk around, telling people what to do, then leave for a while and some of the athletes would get under the bar and just lie there until he returned. I remember Keston sitting on a Swiss ball, doing nothing, then when Lance walked in he got back to work, having sat out the vast majority of the session.

One week, there was lots of chat in the group about the ESPN *30 for 30* documentary on Marion Jones, one of the most famous drug cheats in the history of athletics. The day after it aired, it was all that was talked about; lots of the athletes were raging, cursing, condemning Jones, with Gay chief among them.

Shit, he's really passionate about this.

But two and a half years later, when he was being coached by Jon Drummond, Gay tested positive for an anabolic steroid. 'I don't have a sabotage story,' he said. 'I basically put my trust in someone and was let down.'

Due to his cooperation with anti-doping authorities, he was handed a reduced ban of just one year. When I heard the news, I immediately thought back to how he was that morning as he talked about Marion Jones. 'Man, she fuckin robbed people's money and medals,' he said. I thought about what headspace he must have been in at that time. Did he only start doping later? Or was this all one huge act, one so convincing that it deserved an Academy award? I wasn't sure, but either way I could only laugh at the hypocrisy.

It was a weird set-up at the track in Clermont. You had Dennis Mitchell's group on the home straight, with Lance's group on the back straight. Dennis was a Nike coach. He'd been banned for doping during his own career in the '90s and coached Justin Gatlin after the 2004 Olympic champion returned from the second of his two doping bans, guiding him to the world 100 metres title in 2017. Lance was with adidas, and he didn't get on with Mitchell. We'd be doing a session and look over and see Dennis flapping his arms, shouting: 'He's stealing my sessions!'

As an athlete, I was the type who thrived on constant feedback. I wanted my coach to tell me what was good, what was bad, to put an arm on my shoulder or give me a kick up the arse. But with Lance, I wasn't getting that. I was paying him $1000 a month for his coaching, but it was very much a hands-off approach compared to Nick. As a result, I started analysing everything, trying to guess what shape I was in during those first few months. Devoid of a social outlet to get my mind off athletics, I started to get into my own head more than ever.

The training was very, very different to what I'd known. In the first month or two, I thought, *this isn't very hard at all*, but after that the intensity ramped up. On Mondays, we'd do a session on grass like two by two minutes with four minutes' rest, followed by three ninety-second reps with three minutes' rest, followed by three by one minute with two minutes' rest. The next day, we'd do hills – 4x200m, 4x100m, 2x300m, with walk back recoveries, followed by weights. I'd smash the 300s and some of the lads would say, 'You don't need to run 'em that fast.' They used to call me The White Ox because I'd hammer everything. Wednesdays were like Mondays – more grass runs – while Thursday saw us do grass runs plus weights. Friday was more of the same, then Saturday was a relative rest day: a ten-minute warm-up followed by some hurdle mobility work.

The thing I hadn't considered before moving: I had no social circle. There were only so many times I could go to the Florida Mall or wash the car. I had too much time on my hands and one thing I had grossly underestimated was the impact of the quality of life in Clermont, what I was going to do outside of training. I never put a value on that in Loughborough – but I realised how much I needed it when it was gone.

I stayed in Clermont until 23 December before returning to Dublin for Christmas, partly because I wanted to get as much good training in as possible and partly because I thought there might be some formal gathering for the group, a bit of a social event before we parted ways.

There wasn't, of course, so I had my own little Christmas party. I went out for dinner by myself, ate two large pizzas, then went to the cinema by myself, filling a giant bag of pick 'n' mix sweets. I came out, went to Cold Stone Creamery and got the biggest ice cream I could find, then woke up the next day sick as a dog. I was in a depressive state, gorging, and it was due to a crippling level of loneliness. There was an element of feeling sorry for myself too.

When I saw the Aer Lingus plane at Orlando Airport the following day, it felt like my saviour. I couldn't wait to get away.

In the New Year, the intensity ramped up in training – a lot. That's when I started to really suffer. The rest and recovery between running days wasn't enough for me. I'd smash five days of hard training, back-to-back – all short and fast – then I'd be in a wreck at the weekend. The non-stop intensity soon caused my weak points to flare up, my Achilles and calves in a constant state of tightness.

If that happened at Loughborough, my physio would do dry needling, which is basically acupuncture but with longer needles that get deep into the muscles, hitting specific trigger points. They worked a treat. But in Florida, a physical therapist or physio wasn't allowed to use needles, only acupuncturists, and the short kind they used weren't getting into my soleus in the same way. One day, it cried surrender.

I was running 300-metre reps with Andretti and felt a sudden jolt in my lower leg, as if I'd been stabbed with a hot rod. My first port of call was the group's massage therapist. She was a lovely lady from Haiti with an upbeat, positive energy, which contrasted with the sadistic way she'd make you suffer on the treatment table: I'd have to wear a gumshield as I'd be biting so hard.

She put a heat pack on my soleus and started rubbing it out which, looking back, was probably not the thing to do in the acute phase of a muscle tear. It felt worse in the days after so I booked in with a physical therapist at the rehab hospital, where I was told it wasn't my soleus but my plantaris tendon (which is nearby). She told me to give it two weeks without training and it'd be fine. I did that, tried running, but it was the same pain. I went back to the physical therapist who told me to give it another two weeks. But it was the same thing: pain once I restarted. So I went back again.

'I don't think this is my plantaris: it's getting worse.'

She was pissed off. 'I have 25 years' experience, I know what I'm doing.'

'Well sorry,' I told her. 'But I think you're wrong.'

Medical care in the US is so much more complicated, and expensive, than in the UK and Ireland, and it took me weeks to get an MRI scan so I could figure out exactly what was happening. Eventually I found a chiropractor who was willing to refer me, and the results were grim. 'You've a massive tear in your soleus,' he told me. 'It's substantial. You're looking at three months here.'

Fuck, that's my season.

Charlotte was with me at the time, spending two months in Florida while she was between jobs. But she was due to leave a few days after I got that news and I dreaded her departure. The two of us were in floods of tears as I dropped her to the airport. I didn't know it at the time, but she was worried about me and told her parents what was going on after arriving in England. 'Just book him a flight, get him the fuck out of there,' said her dad.

She could see that I was starting to fall apart and suggested returning to Loughborough. 'No, I've gotta stay here, get back running and get things right,' I said.

But when she left, everything *did* fall apart. I couldn't run but I'd still head along to training, and Lance would ask how it was.

'The same as yesterday,' I'd say.

'Well, go up and do 45 minutes aqua jogging and I'll see you tomorrow.'

All I was thinking about was when my leg was going to get better, and I was panicking about the consequences of the injury.

I'm gonna miss the Olympics. My funding is gonna get cut.

One day I went on Irishjobs.ie, working out what I'd do if this really was the end. When I got the initial MRI report, I called Joe Conway, the Irish team doctor, and he reviewed the images.

'David, this is quite bad,' he said. 'You've gotta be really careful with your soleus. This could potentially be a career-ender. There's a lot of nerves in there and it tricks you. You think it's better, you'll go out and run, and then do it again.'

That was exactly what had been happening. I had actually torn it three times by the time I had that conversation.

Then, in April, I woke up one day and my foot was the size of a football. I'd been bitten by fire ants and was put on antibiotics for two weeks. No training meant restricted eating as I had a huge fear of putting on weight and falling even further behind. It's normal for most athletes to monitor their weight to some extent through the year, but I started to take it to a whole new level. I bought weighing scales and would hop on them multiple times each day, counting every single calorie I consumed. I developed an eating disorder, gorging myself one day and then completely restricting myself for the several days that followed, building an obsessive paranoia about what I was consuming, which would eventually lead me to crack and binge yet again. I kept it all a secret.

Then the calls would come from home.

'How are you?'

'Grand, yeah!'

But inside, I was a mess. When I wasn't training, I could go days without chatting to anyone. One of the big reasons I chose the group was because there was an Irish connection. Jason Smyth and his coach, Stephen Maguire, had spent a lot of time training with Lance and were due to be there again that year, but due to visa issues they arrived a few months later than planned.

I moved in with Jason and Stephen when they arrived and was glad to have some company as I tried to get back on track. Stephen was so helpful with advice and took an interest in steering me along. Whereas with Lance, the moment I got injured he didn't seem to care. And it wasn't just me. One day, we were about to do sled pulls and Jamaican sprinter Nickel Ashmeade told Lance his hip was sore.

'So are you not gonna train?' asked Lance.

'Well my hip is sore, and with the sled...'

It seemed a reasonable thing to tell your coach if you felt pain, but Lance was furious. 'Why don't you just fuck off home and come back tomorrow?'

With training, I felt like it was Lance's way or the highway. He'd hand you the week's schedule on a Monday and it wasn't up for debate. For a lot of athletes in the group, Stephen filled the good-cop role. One time, Gay came around to the house with his laptop and he and Stephen sat at the kitchen table, analysing his races. I thought it was strange, given Stephen wasn't Gay's coach and here was the second fastest guy in history, coming to this guy from Strabane for advice. I asked Stephen what it was about and he'd say, 'Lance is a tough man; he won't give them any kind of love, so I do.'

The athletes wouldn't show any insecurity on the track and they definitely wouldn't show it to Lance, but Stephen was a guy they could go to and open up. They loved having him around.

When I got injured, it felt like I'd been kicked out of the group. I'd wake up, go to the track and Lance would just tell me to go aqua-jogging. There was no other communication, no checking in to see how I was doing. He'd been warm and welcoming in my first few weeks, letting me stay in his family home, but when things went wrong I was quickly aware how far I was down his list of priorities – if I was even a part of them at all.

Stephen was a huge help, and I'd have honest, open conversations with him. He turned around to me one day in the house and said, 'You need to have a chat with Lance.'

Stephen arranged the meeting and I met the two of them in a dark, dingy sports bar with no natural light. Lance was sitting at the table when I arrived, his arms resting on it, and there were no pleasantries or hellos. He was just staring straight ahead. Stephen started the conversation, then Lance turned to me.

'I think you've a problem understanding me.'

The gist of the five-minute chat that followed was that I needed to shut up, get on with it and do what I was told. I knew from months before that Lance didn't like the way

I'd ask questions, even when it was clear my body was breaking down from his training. When Charlotte was over, Lance's wife had helped her get a job for a couple weeks at a local school, and she told Charlotte, 'Lance is a very good coach, David just needs to trust him.'

I was struggling, physically and mentally, with the season on the doorstep and my outlook increasingly grim. In times like that, athletes are susceptible to all kinds of quacks and apparent miracle workers.

That's how I found myself paying a visit to Dr B.

The name sounded so dodgy. He was a doctor who was big into triathlons; everyone knew him around Clermont, and he would sometimes come to training to watch. He was called Dr B because people went to him for shots of B vitamins. If someone was struggling in training they might be told, 'You need to go to Dr B and get your B vitamins.'

I always thought, *I don't need any of that shite*, but when I was injured, at a low ebb, I was like: *Fuck it, I'm going to Dr B*. I chatted to Debbie about him. 'Dr B will help you out,' she assured me. 'He's cool.'

Then I asked Charlotte what she thought. 'Well, if he's there and seems legit, maybe he can help.'

Dr B was in his forties and had all his medical qualifications plastered on the wall of his clinic. The day I walked in, I had a good look at them. *Are these all legit?*

'So, you're injured,' he said. 'How are you feeling?'

'I'm stressed,' I told him.

'Well, these will make you feel better.'

I visited his clinic twice. During the first appointment, he injected me multiple times with cortisone, an anti-inflammatory, and the second time he injected me with various vitamins.

Both times, I checked everything he was using before I let him near me. 'Are these all legal?' I asked, reminding him that I was regularly drug tested.

He assured me it was all above board. I'd never done anything like that before and I haven't since – I was always nervous just taking an aspirin – but he had such a good reputation in Clermont that I figured it was worth a go.

With the cortisone, he injected me all over my leg: up and down the calf. With the vitamins, he injected me all over my body, about 15 or 20 times in total, with one of them going into my forehead.

A few weeks later, there was a British group training in Clermont and I knew one of the athletes well, Jeanette Kwakye. They had a physio with them, and I was in desperate need of some proper treatment, so I reached out to him. The physio called around to the house for an appointment and, as he was working on me, I told him about Dr B and how trigger-happy he'd been with the cortisone shots. The physio was horrified.

'He was just putting them in? It wasn't X-ray guided? Fucking hell, that's incredibly bad.'

I felt embarrassed that I'd been so reckless with my health, but desperate times led to desperate measures. The next time the drug testers came, I had to write down a list as long as my arm of the stuff Dr B had put into me. There was nothing banned in it, they were all perfectly legal, but submitting myself to a doctor who treated my body like a pin cushion was a sign I was going down the wrong road, getting more and more desperate in my search for a cure.

After three months of being unable to run, I eventually got back on track in May, a few weeks before the Jamaican International, which was due to be my first race of the season.

When the soleus was finally healthy, I went to the track and Lance gave me the programme for the week, which included two all-out time trials over 300 metres and 350 metres. I thought it was madness, throwing me in at the deep end, but I was the athlete, he was the coach, so it was time to just shut up and run. Lance said he'd blow the whistle and he wanted me to go as hard as I could for as long as I could. Inevitably, I blew a gasket on both time trials, running awful times, and my Achilles flared up after the second one.

That day, I collapsed on the track and was lying around, suffering, when Steve Mullings came over to me. In 2004, the Jamaican had tested positive for testosterone and was given a two-year doping ban. He returned from that and rose back to the top of the world, joining Usain Bolt, Asafa Powell and Michael Frater to win 4x100m gold at the Berlin World Championships in 2009.

I didn't know Mullings well, having only chatted a

handful of times while with the group, and that day after my failed time trial was the only time I felt like he gave the slightest shit about me. He had no reason to come over to the area where I was lying down, drawing breath, but when he got there he just stood around, saying nothing. It was weird. It seemed like he wanted to say something but then decided not to. After a while, he left.

I've always wondered what he wanted to say, and that curiosity only grew later that year when Mullings tested positive for Furosemide, a masking agent that dopers can use to quickly excrete traces of more heavy-duty substances, like steroids, from their system. As it was his second offence, he got a lifetime ban.

When Mullings tested positive, one of the group members texted me. 'It's so bad what they're doing to Steve,' he wrote. 'He's the fall guy.' The rumour, according to this athlete, was that Mullings had been a scapegoat for a bigger name in Jamaica.

A couple of years later, I would look back very differently on the clique between Mullings, Gay and Baptiste, a sprinter from Trinidad and Tobago. At the Moscow World Championships in 2013, Baptiste tested positive for a banned substance, which was not identified publicly, and she was handed a two-year ban. That was the same year Gay tested positive, having switched coaches in the meantime to train with Jon Drummond, who was handed an eight-year ban by the US Anti-Doping Agency for the possession, trafficking and administration of banned substances.

In the case hearing, it emerged that Drummond had arranged for Gay to see a chiropractor, Dr Clayton Gibson, who had sent him a number of creams labelled DHEA (the same steroid Merritt tested positive for) and HGH (human growth hormone). Gay said he first used them in July 2012, a few weeks before he finished fourth in the 100 metres final at the London Olympics.

Over the years, I've been asked many times whether I saw anything during my time in Clermont. I didn't. And even at my lowest ebb, I was never tempted to go looking for it. No one ever approached me or offered me anything and not once, through all the injuries, did I ever think: *Fuck it, let's give this a go.*

I'd prefer to fail morally than to succeed immorally.

I never saw anything that made me think my training partners were using banned substances, but when Mullings, Gay and Baptiste all got caught in the years after, I did start to reflect and wonder.

One time, shortly before he was due to race in Manchester, Gay tore his hamstring during a track session in Clermont. It was like someone had pulled a pin on a grenade at the track, given the panic all around. The first person Gay called was his agent, who quickly got him a flight to see someone for treatment. We didn't see Gay for a couple of weeks but then he came back, fully healthy, and did a 120-metre rep on the long straight with a three-point start – halfway between a standing start and the usual 'set' position.

He went through 100 metres in under 10 seconds.

It was run with the wind, and hand-timed, so you could add a couple of tenths of a second to his time, but he was also wearing a pair of running shoes instead of spikes. I thought: *Ho-ly fuck*. Soon after he did it, one of my training partners came over to me as I was stretching against a fence.

'What did you think of that?' he asked.

'Fuck me, man,' I said, astounded that Gay could run that fast so soon after tearing a hamstring.

'Oh, come on,' he said.

'What do you mean?'

'Come on, David. You're not stupid. He got injured, he goes away, comes back and he's doing that? Come on.'

By May 2011, the relationship between Lance and me was hanging by a thread.

After my first failed time trial, he admonished me for the time I had spent warming up. It was an all-out effort so I meticulously went through my usual pre-race routine, spending an hour making sure I was fully ready to fire when the whistle blew. I was nervous and returning from injury so I didn't trust my body. But Lance was furious.

'What the fuck were you doing before that?' he asked. 'This is *training*, why are you wasting all your time warming up?'

Meanwhile, I'm thinking, *I haven't run for three months, and you're asking me to go flat out?* Lance called me a day later, telling me he was pulling me from the race in Jamaica.

I opened my season in early June with a low-key 400 metres race in Clermont. It went about as well as expected:

I finished sixth in 46.80, over two seconds down on my best. A week later, I raced at the adidas Grand Prix in New York and that was just as bad: I finished fourth in the B race in 46.64. I knew I wasn't fit, but Lance would always say, 'Every race, you get further up the track.' I tried to listen, convincing myself it'd come good.

The following weekend, I was racing in Izmir, Turkey, at the European Team Championships. As I was packing up my things in Florida to go back to Europe for the summer, I decided to take everything that was important with me, because by then I was quite certain I wasn't coming back.

On the flight across the Atlantic, I contemplated where it had gone wrong, whether it had been my fault or Lance's fault or bad decisions or just plain old bad luck. But then another thought came in: *Maybe I'm just not that good? Maybe black athletes are just better? Maybe white athletes can't sustain that same level? Maybe I just don't have it?*

I ran even worse in Izmir, finishing sixth in 46.95. On the bus back to the hotel after the race, I texted Nick: 'I've just made the biggest mistake of my life, I should never have gone.'

He told me not to worry about it, saying I should come back to Loughborough and that we'd figure things out. I was due to go to Amsterdam to join Lance's group at their summer base, but instead I flew to London. I didn't have much of a plan at that point, but I knew I needed some familiarity – a place where I felt comfortable. When I saw Charlotte in the arrivals hall at Gatwick Airport, I burst into tears. Deep down, leading up to my departure to the

US, I knew I had been making a mistake. But I followed through on it anyway.

While I was gone, I had sublet my house in Loughborough and there was no longer any room at the inn, so I crashed in Loughborough with my nutritionist, Martin McDonald, who had a spare room. I was embarrassed to return with my tail between my legs, but it was the best place to get back on my feet. My next race was at the Diamond League in Lausanne, where I was drawn in lane eight, right alongside the crowd. There was a lot of noise and distraction as I waited for the gun, and I twitched in the blocks. False start: disqualified. I felt like an idiot.

I had another race a few days later: in the thin air of La Chaux de Fonds, a place renowned for fast times. Of course, given the form I was in, even the altitude couldn't save me. I finished fourth, and last, in my section, clocking a miserable 47.21. It had been seven years since I ran a 400 metres that slow outdoors. A few days later, I was back in Loughborough, writing in my diary:

OK, this is bad. Time to plan out what needs to be done right. Now. Not in one month's time. I arranged to meet Brauman: I'm not returning to the US in November, I'm not going to Amsterdam. No need to explain why. It'll be short and sweet. Think of myself. You can't keep going on like this. You're going to be happier here, in a routine with people focused on you. Number one, you have to walk away from the track. Be selfish.

Nick was great during those weeks, welcoming me back without a trace of bitterness, which he could have been entitled to have.

'You have to try these things,' he said. 'You went to America to better yourself, it didn't work out, but we'll get you back on track.'

I had barely heard from Lance in the preceding weeks. When I did text him after a race, I might get a one-line response. I had to bite the bullet and decided to give him a ring.

'I'm not gonna come to Amsterdam, I'm gonna stay here,' I said. 'I'm gonna leave the group.'

In response I got another one-liner, the kind that typified his bluntness. 'Well, if the head's gone, then the head's gone.'

Then we hung up, the call lasting about 25 seconds. We haven't spoken since.

CHAPTER 14

THE MATTRESS INCIDENT

Before the drought came the deluge.
At the end of the 2011 summer, I knew what was in store over the year ahead: a long, hard build-up to the 2012 Olympics in London, during which I'd live an ascetic, disciplined lifestyle, athletics being the sun around which my whole world orbited.

But before I could commit to that, I needed some blowouts.

My head was utterly fried after the track season, riddled with doubts about the future and the potential consequences if I couldn't get back to my best in 2012. I returned to Dublin and spent a couple of weeks boozing with my mates. I did back-to-back days of drinking, putting in weekend shifts where I'd start on a Friday afternoon and would still be drinking on Sunday evening. I was 28 at the time, but that life had largely been alien to me up to that point.

Why did I go so hard in those few weeks? It was an

THE MATTRESS INCIDENT

attempt to escape reality and that looming question of what I'd do with the rest of my life if athletics came to an abrupt stop. I began to understand why people turned to drinking when they're depressed and how that soothing, short-term relief can easily spiral into full-blown alcoholism.

It'd be so easy to continue doing this – and forget about athletics.

Charlotte was working in London and when I told her what I was doing, she said, 'Really?' It just wasn't something I did. But it was another sign that something was off.

I had started to withdraw from Charlotte. We didn't break up, but I just didn't want to see her and I couldn't really explain why. Perhaps because she held me accountable. I grew more and more distant and when I was back in Loughborough a few weeks later, it all came to a head.

She called me, looking for answers. 'What are we doing here? What's happening?' she asked. 'If you don't pull yourself together, I'm out of here. I'm not wasting my time.'

Then she asked something that really set me off: 'Is there somebody else?'

'There's fucking no one else!' I shouted. 'I just don't want to see anyone. I don't want to see you; stay away from me.'

I was a complete dickhead. The most generous explanation I could think of was that, subconsciously, my withdrawal from her was a cry for help. I was struggling badly, beating myself up for the mistake I made in going to the US.

Why the fuck did I get on that flight? Why did I have that kneejerk reaction to not medalling? Why didn't I trust my gut?

I had so much resentment, anger and frustration. In mid-September, as I prepared to start back training, I wrote in my diary:

> I've had the fun, I've made shite of myself. The craic was great. I'll miss it. But deep down, I'm afraid of what's ahead. That's why I want to just continue on the piss. I'm scared I won't get back to where I need to be for next year and I'll look back with regret to America. I'm trying to be positive, but I'm just afraid I'll fail. My confidence is low, I was made to feel shit and small in the States. I need to refocus, to believe in David Gillick. I need to talk to a sports psychologist. I do feel tired of athletics, but one more year could change my life forever. I will get the hunger back. Embrace it, run at your fears, and run through it. One shot, one life. You owe yourself at least that. Be a cunt. Be ruthless. One shot. Best of luck.

For the first time in a few years, money was becoming an issue. I was getting older, my earning potential was dropping off and another year like the one I had in 2011 would mean it fell off a cliff. That worry only grew when I got back training with Nick's group: the lads had moved on in my absence and I was so, so far behind. The young lads were leaving me for dead on the last rep of sessions.

There was a different vibe around Loughborough that year and you could see it at the track. The London Olympics were just over the horizon and the Brits had ploughed huge funding into various areas to ensure they charged up the medal table. There were more massage therapists and physios and performance staff trackside. You could sense an energy, an upbeat positivity, in Loughborough, which had been designated a centre of excellence.

At training one night, the topic of conversation was about which British athlete would get a free ride to an Olympic gold medal. I didn't understand what the others meant at first.

'Well,' said one of the lads. 'Every time there's an Olympic Games, there's some home athlete who comes out of nowhere, wins gold, and they'll be protected from testing positive.'

Loads of names were mentioned in the ensuing chat, but one name came up far, far more than the rest.

By this point, I had become more cynical about doping in athletics, and I wondered whether there was any relationship between my injuries and having chosen to do it clean. Because drugs don't make you faster, per se, but they do make you recover faster and able to train hard more often: to withstand huge intensity day after day after day. *That's* the part of it that enables athletes to run faster, whereas clean athletes have to respect the natural laws of recovery and can only manage high-intensity work with greater intervals.

Over the years, there were often rumours that some athletes were 'protected', but in 2012 it was still just hearsay and innuendo, with no evidence or proof, so I took all that chat with a grain of salt.

But that changed in 2015 when Lamine Diack, the president of the IAAF since 1999, was arrested and charged with corruption. In 2020, he was found guilty, having covered up Russian doping cases in exchange for bribes. Five other senior figures in the sport, including Diack's son, Papa Massata, were given jail sentences for their roles in a programme of 'full protection', in which 23 Russian athletes had their doping sanctions secretly waived in exchange for payments that ranged from €100,000 to €600,000. Gabriel Dollé, the director of the IAAF's anti-doping department, was given a two-year suspended jail term and fined €140,000.

It was sickening to read how those who were supposed to be gatekeeping the sport were actually making it dirtier. It made me more cynical than ever.

And this was just the stuff we found out about. I was shocked by Seb Coe's behaviour when it all came out. He'd been the Vice President of the IAAF during the latter part of Diack's reign but said he knew nothing about the corruption. No proof emerged in the investigation that he did know, but to me it smelled. It was so corrupt at the very top of the sport, and Coe had essentially been Diack's wingman but knew nothing of his deeds?

Coe was elected president of the world governing body in 2015 and has been in that position since, but I did wonder when he got elected: is this just essentially the same regime but under a different name? Yes, countries have been banned and suspended and the Athletics Integrity Unit has been implemented, but part of me feels this was only in response to the Diack revelations, wanting to be seen to be changing things. But I'd question whether athletics is really in a better place regarding doping these days.

I also feel the entertainment and fan experience of the sport hasn't evolved under Coe's tenure. The Diamond League doesn't really capture the public imagination, the best athletes are not competing regularly enough outside of major championships, and the sport is a tough sell to the public, with drug failures still making headlines.

At the start of 2012, Irish athletics was facing another doping scandal.

Martin Fagan, a distance runner from Mullingar and an Olympic teammate of mine from the Beijing Games, tested positive for EPO. Fagan said a combination of depression, financial worries and injury had led to him taking the banned, blood-boosting drug. He also claimed that he did so on just one occasion: the day before his positive test.

I was shocked when I heard the news, but that was probably a reflection of me falling into that parochial mentality. *Ah no, Irish athletes wouldn't do that.*

It had been the same with Cathal Lombard, Geraldine Hendricken and Steven Colvert. Hendricken tested positive for nandrolone, a banned anabolic steroid, in 2003 and put the blame on a food supplement, while Colvert tested positive for the blood-boosting drug EPO in 2014, and also denied any wrongdoing, pointing to issues with the reliability of the test, which some scientists supported.

Whatever the truth, four senior Irish internationals

getting banned in just over a decade was a reminder that this is a global issue. So often, we can be naïve and think, *it's always them taking drugs, never us.*

Fagan's positive test was disappointing, but also annoying. There was that element of: *nice one, Martin, now everyone's gonna think we're all on drugs again.* Fagan did an interview in which he detailed the context that led to him injecting EPO, explaining how he felt like he had no other option. I could relate to what he said because I'd been at that low point, that desperate place, and while I could never condone doping, and I never considered resorting to it, I understood the slippery slope that had led him there.

This sport, for all its beauty and brilliance, can truly break you: in mind, body and spirit.

Without Charlotte, Loughborough just wasn't quite the same. I missed her, and I missed the contented little bubble we had when she was around.

She was committed to staying in London until after the 2012 Games as she was working there with the British Olympic Association. Without having her around for much of the previous year, I realised how important it was to have someone like that in your corner when you're going through the ups and downs of sport: someone who you don't class as part of your support team but who's always there for you, a person I could confide in or just sit in silence with.

She ran herself so she got it when I was nervous, those times I wouldn't want to talk before a big session or a race.

THE MATTRESS INCIDENT

She also had friends who weren't absorbed in athletics so I'd be going out and meeting them, helping to avoid that obsessive, self-destruct mode where I had nothing else to think about.

I went to see her in London, fixing things up between us, but it was hard for me to get down there very much due to training and so she ended up being the one making the bigger effort, coming up to Loughborough on a Friday then going back down on a Sunday.

She held me to account, asked me what the fuck I was doing. She told me she wasn't going to wait around, that she didn't deserve to be treated like this, and that if it continued she would move on. She was right and completely justified. I told her I was just struggling, a bit all over the place, and it had nothing to do with her, that I just didn't know whether I was coming or going. She still tells me today: 'You were such an arsehole.' And I was, but my excuse is that it wasn't really me. When you're in a dark place, as I was, the reality is you take it out on those closest to you – and that person was Charlotte.

On the track, I was also struggling. Nathan Woodward, a 22-year-old Loughborough student, had taken a massive leap forward during the year I was away and he was leaving me for dead in sessions, with the 'lactic sniper' picking me off in the last rep, leaving me staggering, punch drunk, towards the finish. I was hitting Nick's target times in sessions but wasn't taking confidence out of them as Nate would always be a couple of seconds quicker on each rep, which got inside my head.

We went to South Africa for our training camp in early January 2012, where I put in lots of hard work. But nothing was flowing. Maybe it was the environment I was in, with so many running well, but I got caught up in the fact that I used to be ahead of them in training and suddenly I was behind. I gave the indoor season a miss, knowing I needed a long block of training if I was to book my spot at the London Olympics. But I was running out of time. I had no margin for error.

On St Patrick's Day, I did a session on the track in Loughborough: 2x350m, 2x350m. On the last rep, I felt a sudden twinge in my soleus. My heart sank.

'I'm after doing something here,' I told Nick.

'No panic,' he said. 'Let's see how it goes.'

Mum and Dad were over to see me at the time and we went up to Lincoln for a day out, but I didn't tell them the severity of it, hoping it'd be alright. When they asked how training was going, I said, 'All fine, I just have a niggle, but it'll be grand soon.' A big part of me believed that it would, but the MRI scan said otherwise. I had torn my soleus again.

There were under four months to the qualification deadline for the Olympics. In the weeks after, all I could do was rehab, cycle and aqua jog as if my life depended on it, hoping it might come good. In April, Nick's group was heading to LA for the pre-season camp and I decided to join, thinking a change of scenery and some sun on my back would do me good, even if I couldn't run. I got a taxi to Heathrow from Charlotte's place but the traffic was a

THE MATTRESS INCIDENT

nightmare, to the point where, when I checked in, the lady at the desk told me, 'You've gotta run.'

I couldn't run, so I hobbled through the airport with a painful shuffle, just about managing to catch the flight.

Midway through the camp, Rooney made the traditional trip to the Mt SAC Relays, while Graham Hedman and I stayed behind at the apartment. Rooney got up and had a bowl of Frosties before hitting the road. Meanwhile, I was there having my green tea and porridge and nuts. Rooney smashed it in the race, clocking 44.92 to beat Jeremy Wariner. Graham and I watched it while sitting in the apartment.

Fuck the porridge, give us those Frosties.

I liked Rooney, I had so much respect for him, but I couldn't avoid the envy. I wished that was me, healthy and firing at full capacity just a few months out from the Olympics.

I went back to Ireland after LA and checked in with Emma Gallivan, the physio in the Irish high-performance system who had taken over my rehab. She was fantastic, nursing me back to health physically and getting my mind in a better place. The biggest challenge was something I'd been struggling with for some time: facing reality.

On 22 May, I wrote in my diary:

I have accepted where I am currently at. It is May 2012 and that is where I am. I am not the DG of 2009 or 2010. It's 2012. My progression over the last week has been great. I'm feeling comfortable, feeling positive, being at home. I'm taking control, being myself and doing what's best for me. I'm saying no to things and trying to focus on training. The past is history, the future is all mystery. The present is all I have. Accept it. Use senses to bring myself back to present.

But try as I might to stay in the present, it was hard to avoid the Olympic build-up. London was the closest Ireland would ever get to a home Games, so the marketing machine was kicking into overdrive.

Electric Ireland had a big campaign and I committed to that in late 2011. Everyone involved, who maybe weren't up to date with athletics, was very excited about London, asking me everything about it and whether I was looking forward to it. Meanwhile, I knew it was far from guaranteed that I'd be going. The negative voice inside my head got louder.

While I was rehabbing in Dublin, Charlotte came to visit me and one day we did a little road trip to Avoca in Wicklow. As I drove off the motorway, I saw myself on a huge billboard, coming out of the blocks in the Electric Ireland ad. 'David Gillick, London 2012.' I knew by then the chances of qualifying were slim, but most people didn't know that. I'd meet people in Dublin and they'd ask, 'So when are you off?' I'd try to brush it off and say I wasn't sure but in my head I thought, *I'm not fucking going.*

I felt like a bit of a fraud, but I didn't want to give everyone the long explanation of why I wasn't where I should be.

I had to try, but after the season it had been in 2011 the Diamond League was no longer an option. I learned the truth in that old athletics adage that you're only as good

THE MATTRESS INCIDENT

as your last race. My season opener was in Turin, and I was a nervous wreck beforehand. I ran a pitiful 48.36, good enough for eighth and last place.

After that, I went to Moscow, racing in the cavernous Luzhniki Stadium, which hosted the 1980 Olympics. It was obvious that was as close as I'd be getting to an Olympic stadium that year, as I trailed home seventh – and last – in 48.27. I felt like a child running with the weight of the world on my shoulders. Going down the back straight, the track felt flat, my legs heavy. I met British sprinter Christian Malcolm as I was getting the bus back to the hotel.

'I know you've had a tough time,' he said. 'But try keep your head up.'

A few weeks later, I went to Helsinki for the European Championships, running the 4x400m relay, hoping I could help them into the final. I ran the second leg but nothing about it felt good, and as I was running down the back straight, it felt like my body was going to fall apart. In the end, we got disqualified for a lane infringement, which just about summed up my situation.

The qualifying deadline for the Olympics was just after that, on my twenty-ninth birthday, but I was three seconds outside what I needed. In the 400 metres, that's a different stratosphere. The game was up. I wasn't going to London and, with that, I went back to Loughborough to plan the road ahead.

'Less could be more,' I wrote in my diary. 'Happiness is key.'

Underneath that, I jotted out my financial situation: my

savings and my likely earnings after I was dropped by adidas and the Irish Sports Council funding. I accepted that I had a good ride and I couldn't be pissed off with people bringing the guillotine down. They were paying me to race and I wasn't racing – or when I was, I was just bringing up the rear. I contemplated retiring, but that brought me face to face with another terrifying question.

What am I going to do next?

The one place I didn't want to be during the Olympics was London.

Unless I was out there on the track, I knew it'd gnaw away at me if I went as a spectator. I also didn't want to go back to Ireland, knowing it would be overrun with the Olympic buzz, and I'd have to explain to everyone why I wasn't there.

I thought about going up to Charlotte's parents in Sunderland, but soon I got a call from RTÉ, asking if I'd do some TV work in the studio back in Dublin. I figured if I said no, the chance may never come around again. So I agreed, but I regretted it almost immediately.

Watching all the people I'd raced with, and trained with, run in the Olympics broke my heart. But as each day passed, I started to get over that. By the end, it was nice to have done it rather than spending those weeks sulking, and it was good to have had some part, however small, in the Olympic buzz. It had been a record-breaking Olympics for Ireland, with six medals in total. One of them was in athletics, with Rob Heffernan crossing the line fourth in the 50km race walk, which was later upgraded to bronze after a doping disqualification.

I had no idea my media work might lead to something more, but I had enjoyed it – and that at least was something.

Ever since Beijing, I had resented the Olympics and abandoned my long-held plans to get the rings tattooed in the wake of my performance there, feeling I didn't deserve it. But after Berlin in 2009, I'd thought: *These guys are beatable, I can do this.*

Throughout my career, I always thought London would be the Games where I'd peak, where I'd thrive. But the night of the Closing Ceremony, I was sitting alone in the bedroom at my parents' house in Dublin, watching on TV as The Kinks played Waterloo Sunset in the London Stadium.

I cried.

The dream was finally over.

When the Games faded from view, I was sure about nothing in my life except one thing: I wanted to be with Charlotte, to live under the same roof and to build a life together. I just didn't know where that would be. My diary from October that year gives a good window into my mindset.

> Long-term, trying to think of future. Jobs. Money. What do I want to do post athletics? It's a worry. I find myself worrying, it's negative, it weighs me down. I feel under pressure to use my name and past to get work and make money, trying to exploit myself. Time

is almost running out. People will forget me, who I am, what I've done. I've lots of contacts for the future to exploit: master's link; corporate world; Institute of sport; coaching pathway.

Towards the end of 2012, I got a phone call from Athletics Ireland's High Performance Director Kevin Ankrom to tell me I wouldn't be funded for 2013. I had been on €40,000 in the previous few years and had been given some grace with continued support into Olympic year. But then it was cut to nothing.

It was the same with adidas: 'Unfortunately, we won't be in a position to renew your contract.' I knew those calls were coming and had no complaints when they did. I was no longer a promising investment: I was about to turn 30 and my career looked like a busted flush. The sponsorship from Seán White also fizzled away, which was fine. I didn't want any money from him. I told him, 'You've been fantastic, you helped me achieve amazing things.' I wanted to leave all that stuff behind, to no longer feel like I owed anyone anything; I wanted to make life simple, to just crack on with enjoying whatever time I had left in athletics.

I had dozens of ideas about my post-career trajectory, but none of them were concrete and they didn't fill me with the excitement I got from lacing up my spikes. I wanted to get back running and go out on my terms – running well rather than having my season fizzle out, as it had in 2012.

I decided to give it one more year.

THE MATTRESS INCIDENT

Charlotte and I had long wanted to do a stretch in Australia and my initial plan was to give it three months there, from December to February, but then we decided to go for most of the year and just return to Europe for the outdoor track season. I spoke to various people who spent time there and everyone thought the lifestyle was good. Joanne Cuddihy had been coached by Tudor Bidder, a Welshman who was based in Canberra, and so that's where we chose. We left England in October 2012 and Charlotte got an admin job with the Canberra Raiders, a professional rugby league team.

From the start, it was the change of scenery we needed, with beautiful weather and a different culture. The first morning, I went out to the garden to have breakfast and freaked out because I saw a blue-tongued lizard that was the size of a dog. But I loved it.

Another day, I was doing a session by myself: hill sprints in a wooded area. As I took off on one of the reps, I was slowly lifting my head when, in the corner of my eye, I saw a massive, seven-foot, muscle-bound kangaroo that leapt across my path, missing me by inches. As he bounded on to his next destination, I stopped, stunned, counting myself lucky that he'd missed me – and that I had avoided a new and novel way to get injured.

We didn't have much income, and I was steadily burning through my savings, but we lived cheaply, renting a spare room from another couple.

Canberra was expensive as it's the administrative capital and lots of people there had government jobs. When we went shopping, I'd buy the Vietnamese river cobbler because it was the cheapest fish available and we'd do kangaroo stir fries because beef was such a rip-off. We stopped eating peppers as they were so expensive. We bought an old banger of a car for a couple of grand: an '85 Honda Prelude, with 300,000 miles on the clock and lights that came up out of the bonnet. But I didn't give a shit about having a flashy car. I just wanted to stay fit, healthy and enjoy the time with Charlotte. And I did.

I got on with everyone in Tudor's group. He and Nick spoke about how to approach my training, and so he didn't throw me straight into running, instead building up my strength and fitness with a lot of rehab and cross training. Tudor was someone, I soon discovered, who I could have long conversations with, someone who gave me regular feedback on what I was doing. He was so helpful in so many other ways, too. He understood the importance of having a life beyond sport and would invite us to his house for barbecues. He'd send emails with flight offers, recommending places to visit, factoring short breaks into my training cycle so Charlotte and I could explore the country. We spent Christmas in Melbourne. We took a trip to the Whitsunday Islands, flying over the Great Barrier Reef, snorkelling in crystal-clear waters. It was spectacular.

I got into a great routine, my fitness coming along slowly, and I started to enjoy running again. By March, I was flying, and did a brilliant session that finished with a 200-metre rep. But in the last five metres of that, I felt a slight twinge in my Achilles. It didn't feel too bad at the time, but after

THE MATTRESS INCIDENT

I got out of bed the next day, any attempt to walk was met with piercing pain. I went to a clinic and they gave me the diagnosis: I had a hairline tear in my Achilles.

I don't believe this.

I was put in a giant, protective boot and resumed cross-training in the weeks that followed: slogging away in the pool or on a stationary bike. When it felt better, I started back on an Alter-G (anti-gravity) treadmill, a device which essentially suspended you in the air and you could slowly increase the amount of bodyweight, starting at five per cent and very slowly building up to a hundred.

I was due to start my season in late May, with a race in Japan. Given the level I had slipped to, no one was looking for me in their meets, so I arranged the entry myself, spending $500 on the flights before the injury popped up. But as the race approached, I found out that my Achilles wasn't up to it. I went to the track and was about to do a fast 150-metre run but there was immediate pain. I was in tune with my body. I knew it was bad, particularly as this was the crucial time of year for fine-tuning. It's the worst time to get an injury. There was no chance to turn it around.

The game was up. My career was finished.

When I got back to the apartment, I threw a tantrum. 'Fucking injured – again!' I told Charlotte. 'This is a waste of time.'

Because Charlotte and I were only living there for a year, we didn't buy a bed, only a mattress, which was on the ground. She had just done laundry when I walked in and had all the clothes neatly folded and resting on the mattress.

I picked it up and launched it in the air. Everything went with it, the clothes all crashing down at once, and with them my career. Charlotte watched me do it, saying nothing. She'd later refer to this as The Mattress Incident.

'It's all over,' I told her. 'What am I going to do with the rest of my life?'

The day after I got injured, an email pinged into my inbox. It was from someone at RTÉ, asking if I'd be interested in *Celebrity MasterChef*. I was due to go back to Europe a few weeks later anyway and so figured I'd do it, knowing it would help fill the void, allowing me to kick the can down the road about my next steps. Charlotte was enjoying her work and so she stayed in Australia for another few months.

It was weird coming home. I had quietly made the decision to retire but didn't broadcast it. People in athletics would ask and I'd say, 'I'm just injured.' I didn't want any fuss and was content to just let my career fizzle out.

In a way, I was relieved. There was finally peace in the long-running war with my own body. When I left Dublin, seven years earlier, I'd made myself a promise: that when I got to 30, I wanted to look in the mirror and say, 'I gave it a proper crack.' I always thought when I retired, I'd be content and fulfilled. But being back in Dublin on the day of my thirtieth birthday, shortly after calling time on athletics, I felt the opposite. I was lonely. Lost.

My birthday fell during the week and my friends were all at work. Charlotte was still Down Under, but Derval O'Rourke met me for breakfast in Clonskeagh. Our careers had run on almost parallel paths and she had retired around the same time. Those who don't know Derval would think she's got a hard, tough exterior, but she is soft and kind, when you do know her. Derv knew I wasn't in a good place. Coming home injured, unable to participate in a sport where 30 is considered over the hill, is an awful lot to handle. I wasn't overly open with her, but we chatted about what we were going to do next. The thing that struck me was that she had an exit plan, as we called it, whereas I had none.

Later that year, I was a guest on *The Saturday Night Show*, hosted by Brendan O'Connor on RTÉ. Ahead of my appearance, the producer asked, 'Do you have any news? Any update on the decision?'

'What decision?'

'Retirement,' she said, asking if I'd be willing to announce it on the show.

'No, I'm grand, thanks.'

I didn't want to say it publicly on national TV, and in truth, I just didn't want to talk about athletics anymore. Eventually, I made an announcement, more because I was sick of the question: 'Are you still running?' The media jumped on it, which in a way was nice – seeing that there was some interest. I did some interviews and was surprised to see the news come up on the Sky Sports ticker at the bottom of the screen. Must have been a slow news day.

Plenty of messages came through, which were nice to read, helping me remember the good times, but to be honest, I had retired months before, so the overriding feeling was relief to have made it public. A weight was lifted. Time to move on.

I had no idea what to do with my life back in Dublin, but *MasterChef* proved the perfect distraction. I had no expertise in cooking but when I'd still been in Australia, the producer suggested that I try to get into a kitchen before the show, as it'd give me a steer. There was a restaurant close to where we lived, so I asked if I could come in for a week and see how things worked, and they let me partake in breakfast, lunch and dinner service. At the end of the week, I invited Charlotte and my housemate, Alex, to come in and I cooked for them. They were like, 'You didn't make this.' But I did.

I spent a month filming *MasterChef* in the summer of 2013 and loved it. I realised the traits I'd developed in athletics were applicable far beyond the track: I was methodical about the process and perfectly able to handle high-stress situations. It was a hard, intense few weeks. I'd get into bed at night and would be on the phone: 'How do I pluck a chicken?'

I reached the final three, alongside Aengus Mac Grianna and Maia Dunphy. Given the show was sponsored by Emirates, we were brought to Dubai for the final. We cooked for a load of head chefs and some of the chief buyers for hotels in Dubai, and I felt entirely out of my depth. I cooked quinoa-encrusted lamb cutlets with a jus for starter; halibut with a celeriac rémoulade on a bed of avocados for my main course; and a summer meringue with crème Chantilly for dessert, stacked in a tower as a nod to the local Burj Khalifa.

THE MATTRESS INCIDENT

Lo and behold, I won it. There was no prize – you got paid to take part and then paid something extra for each episode you stayed in – but it gave me a massive lift.

Of course, it wasn't long before my old ways crept back in – worrying about the future and how I would support myself. I wondered if I could leverage the win to build a new career, and I did manage to get some work out of it. Soon after, I got an email about doing a cooking demo for a car brand in Galway. I decided to cook healthy pancakes, which at the time were a novel idea. Charlotte went along with me, and she was sitting in the front row when it came time to flip the pancake. Of course, I wasn't a chef and had never actually done that in my life. I tried to flip it, missed the target, the pancake landing half on the pan with the other half splatting on the demo island. There was an audible 'eww' in the crowd. I looked up and saw Charlotte, mortified. I was supposed to be this *MasterChef* winner and I couldn't even flip a pancake. It felt like being back on the track after a bad race.

Get me the fuck out of here.

The summer turned to autumn. One morning in September, I woke up in the box room I'd grown up in, back where it all began, except now I was thirty years old. September is when I would normally start back training, making whatever changes were needed and laying the foundations for the year ahead. But now there was no season to prepare for. I had no purpose, no direction, nothing to get out of bed for. I did have one goal in mind before I finished the year, however: to ask Charlotte to marry me.

I had thought about doing it when we were on the Whitsunday Islands in Australia but one of my mates in Australia talked me out of it.

'You can't do it out here,' he said. 'You'll ask her and then it's just the two of you on a beach. You want people to celebrate it.'

He was 100 per cent right. Charlotte is very close to her family, so I decided to do it when we were around them, preparing to pop the question on New Year's Eve, putting a bright finish on what had been, personally, a difficult year.

We were spending New Year's in the English countryside, at Barnard Castle, with her family. On the afternoon of New Year's Eve, I asked Charlotte to go for a walk by the river. It was the same place her parents got engaged and so I had decided to do it there, popping the question as we sat on a nice stone bench. At least that was the plan, but Charlotte didn't fancy a walk and decided to take a nap instead.

Well, this is all fucked.

I knew she wouldn't want the embarrassment of having me ask her with lots of others around, so in between dinner and dessert that night, I said again, 'Will we go for a walk?' It was pitch black outside, but I was getting desperate.

'Let's just get some fresh air,' I said. 'I'm stuffed after that.'

She agreed. We walked down to the river, reached the seat, and I got down on one knee. 'Where are you going?' she said. 'I can't see you.'

I popped the question and, thankfully, she said yes. It was time to get on with the rest of our lives.

CHAPTER 15

INTO THE VOID

By 2014, my relationship with running could be best described as toxic.

I hated athletics, *hated* it, and blamed it for everything I was feeling. The love I once felt had first dissipated, then outright disappeared, replaced by a burning, bitter resentment.

And yet I couldn't let it go. Couldn't escape it. If I wasn't David Gillick, *The Athlete*, then who was I? Nobody. Nothing. I was thirty years old, living with my parents, and the lads I'd grown up with had their own homes with established careers. I was ten years behind, feeling like I'd invested all I had into this dream and been left with nothing to show for it.

In Dundrum Shopping Centre, not long after I announced my retirement, I bumped into Paul Opperman, the club-mate who'd taken me under his wing at my first World Championships in Paris ten years earlier.

'What the fuck are you doing?' he asked.

'What do you mean?'

'Why the fuck are you retiring? You're only fucking thirty.'

But my mind was beyond changing. Around that time, I dreaded bumping into people I knew. I'd leave the house and they'd ask, 'Well, what are you gonna do next?' I had no good answer, and I got sick of being asked. So I stopped leaving the house.

I had no idea what to do and was just passing time, stuck in limbo. A call from Kevin Ankrom pulled me out of that purgatory. 'This has just come across my desk,' he said, explaining that Athletics Ireland had signed a deal with New Balance and the brand was looking for a marketing rep in Ireland. 'You need to get a CV,' he said. I hadn't done one of those in ten years, but thankfully Ankrom was the king of CVs. He updated his all the time, firing off applications to jobs, and he lived close to Mum and Dad. I called down to him and he helped me construct my CV, which I fired off to New Balance.

The role's remit was to look after the Athletics Ireland account, checking in with stores around the country, helping to stage events and arrange New Balance branding. I got the job. When they put me through to their human resources department to talk about my terms, to be honest, all I cared about was money. I was no longer an athlete and felt the only way I could be seen as a success was by doing well financially.

My team and my boss were based in England, so I was given free rein to do what I wanted for much of the time.

But the role involved a lot of driving, visiting different stores and clients, which meant lots of time alone, in my car, with only my thoughts for company. They were sliding further and further into a dark hole.

Charlotte had returned from Australia, starting a job with Athletics Ireland, and we moved into a rented house in Dublin. One day, I went out for a run and got about a kilometre from the house before stopping abruptly.

What's the point?

Another time, I went up to the local GAA pitch with Charlotte and I started running laps, hammering the lengths and walking the widths. I was going *all out*, trying to hurt myself.

'What are you doing?' asked Charlotte.

I threw a tantrum. 'I fucking hate this.'

I was so frustrated and just trying to make myself suffer, a bit of self-medicating masochism. I stopped running completely, after which it wasn't long before the voice in my head kicked into overdrive.

Why the fuck did you not get a medal in Barcelona? Why the fuck did you go to America? This is all your own fault.

The job forced me to get out and face the world, to put on a facade, acting as if I was handling the transition well. But inside I was falling to pieces. One day, I paid a visit to The Run Hub, a shop in Ashtown, where I met Gary O'Hanlon, a well-known coach and athlete.

'Gillick?' he said. 'What the fuck are you doing here?'

'I work for New Balance now,' I said, before explaining my role.

'What? You ran 44 seconds! What the fuck are you doing this shit for?'

Another time, I had to drive to Limerick to visit Adrenaline Sports in Newcastle West. They were doing a promotional event and asked if I could come down to do some cooking demos. It was a dark, wet winter's night, and after arriving, I plugged in my electric stove and started flipping pancakes a little more successfully than the first time. Then I packed up and made the two-and-a-half-hour drive home, wondering what exactly I was doing with my life.

I'm a dancing monkey.

There was public me and private me, and they couldn't have been more different. One time, I was sitting in my car, stuck at a crossroads in Donnybrook, when two Dublin buses flew past with my big, happy head plastered across the side as part of an ad campaign for a health supplement, Udo's Choice.

I was having an awful day and how I felt was so far from that image. People would say, 'You're on the side of buses! Everything must be going really well,' and I'd smile and nod. But when I got home, I'd have a meltdown in front of Charlotte. I was desperately unhappy and wanted to just wind back the clock to the way things were in Loughborough. I was idolising my past, panicking about the future, and absolutely hating the present.

Although my job had links to Athletics Ireland, no one from there or Sport Ireland had formally reached out to see how I was doing after I'd stopped competing. At the time, there was no support for athletes once you retired. As far as they were concerned, once your spikes were hung up, you sailed off into the sunset. Next.

At home, I was an asshole to Charlotte, a volcano that would erupt without any notice. She was always walking on eggshells, not knowing what David she would get on any given day. I could come in all bouncy and happy or in volatile, horrendous form. In America, she knew straight away what kind of day it'd be once I stepped out of bed, but now it was utterly unpredictable. I'd lie on the bed, staring into space, lost in a world of self-pity and self-hate. One time, I decided to go on a bike ride but couldn't find my sunglasses, which sent me into a rage. I fired various things around the room to vent my fury.

Meanwhile, when I would visit stores for work, I'd pretend everything was rosy. That was exhausting, and when I'd get back in the car, everything I had bottled up would emerge on the long drive home. Charlotte is a bubbly person, always smiling, but when I'd arrive at the house I'd see her peering out of the kitchen, unsure how to act as she'd have no clue what mindset I was in. It was a horrible atmosphere to bring home.

I was searching for something to fix everything, to fill that gaping void athletics had left behind. But I had no idea what that something was.

In August 2014, Charlotte and I got married in Barnard Castle in England and I grew emotional at various points throughout the day. 'Are you crying?' people would ask, unaware that it wasn't tears of joy, but a window into how hollow I was feeling. It was a beautiful day, with all our loved ones present, but a part of me just wasn't there.

I continued working the day job and agreed to some other events at weekends, searching for something – anything – to fill that emptiness.

Charlotte fell pregnant in the middle of 2015, with our first child due in the spring of 2016, and I felt a growing sense of dread about that. At the time I was hopelessly ill-equipped to take care of myself, never mind anyone else.

I decided to pack in the New Balance job, knowing it wasn't helping how I felt, and around that time I re-connected with Enda McNulty. He had a company called Motiv8 that helped businesses implement high-performance and well-being practices through various corporate programmes. He'd been on to me the whole time to get involved. But I'd been hesitant and didn't take him up on it.

'The window of opportunity is closing,' he said. 'I can't keep offering you jobs if you're not gonna take them.'

Knowing I had a baby on the way, and needing a steady income, I accepted a role in his company, which involved going into corporate environments and essentially talking about how great I was.

I made a world final. I won European titles. This was how I got there, with my high-performance mindset.

It was all bollocks, of course, pretending to be some sort of guru. But I would gorge all that kind of content on social media, devouring self-help books, and Enda would take me up on stage, saying David did this or that, and I'd be standing alongside, nodding. Then I'd get back in the car, alone, and tell myself a very different story.

You're a fucking idiot. You're falling apart but you're standing up there, telling them all how great you are. You should be over in Hollywood, winning Oscars, with all this acting you're doing. You're an absolute fucking fraud.

As I'd drive home, I would wonder how I ever ran 44 seconds and performed in front of 60,000 people. I felt so far from that person, and things were getting progressively worse. I had again started gorging on food, getting the 'Two for Tuesday' special at Domino's Pizza, eating both in one sitting. I'd pull over at a petrol station and buy a pile of donuts and muffins, milling through a box of six or twelve in the car.

I had hoped the new job might change how I felt, but it didn't. It only made things worse. I wasn't making good money and the thing that probably kept me in it was that my ego was being stroked, talking about my achievements. But looking back at the past wasn't fixing what was wrong, only offering constant reminders of the athlete and person that I *was*.

I could firefight through the day, with constant arguments in my head that were hidden behind this bright, smiling facade, which I'd wear from Monday to Friday. Saturdays were generally OK, I could relax and be me, but on Sundays the dread would rise again. All I could think of was Monday, which I hated. I was so volatile and fragile that the simplest thing made me fly off the handle. I thought they were just tantrums of frustration, anger, resentment and self-hate. Only later did I learn that they were panic attacks.

My chest would tense up, feeling as if it was closing in, just like the walls around me. I never laid a hand on Charlotte, and I never would, but I certainly laid a hand on myself. I'd punch myself, slap myself, trying to release the valve on that internal rage. I'd punch a wall in the house or beat the crap out of the steering wheel if I was in my car.

Little by little, the voice in my head grew darker, louder and ever more convincing. As I'd make those long drives home from some far-flung town, I wouldn't listen to music or a podcast, just my own thoughts: that chronic, caustic voice that kept up a never-ending stream of insults. I'd pass huge trucks coming the other direction and start to imagine doing the worst.

I could just turn the wheel left and put it in there, and it'll all be done. I could just go away. I could just finish it.

All I wanted was to quieten that voice, to feel the serenity of silence.

What's the easiest way to just disappear? I'd think, then I'd imagine hanging myself or throwing myself off a bridge.

I wasn't thinking of other people, of course. When I would imagine turning my car into an oncoming truck, I never once thought about the impact that would have on the driver, only about myself and the desire I had to shut up that nagging voice. The person I did think of, however, was Charlotte, along with the baby she was carrying. I pictured her in the future, left behind to deal with what I'd done. That image is what stopped me. I'd remind myself that if I did it, if I ended it all, I could never get it back. It was permanent. In the darkest hour, she was the light that stopped me from acting on it.

But for both of us, the risk had become all too real.

One day, she was at work and heard that someone had taken their own life on the bridge over the M50. She felt a rush of terror, which was only compounded when she couldn't get through to me all afternoon. She kept telling herself, *If that was David, someone would have called me.* She drove home after work, pulled into the driveway and when I opened the door she was like, *Thank fucking God.* She never told me this at the time, but that was the extent of where we were. We'd get out of bed in the morning and have a blazing row over something stupid, purely because I wasn't in a good place, and then I'd storm out of the house and wouldn't make contact for the rest of the day. In the meantime, she was going to work thinking, *What the fuck is he going to do today?*

In the house, she'd hear my tormented thoughts emerge in furious outbursts. 'I just don't want to be here!' I'd shout. 'I don't want to fucking be around. It'd be easier if I wasn't fucking here.'

It was horrible, for her and me, but the reality is that there's so many people going through that same thing right now, and probably some people you know.

As dark as it got, there was always some part of me, deep in the back of my brain, which thought: *You can get yourself out of this.* As an athlete, I had dealt with plenty of dark days filled with regret about the past and anxiety about the future. The lesson from those moments stayed with me: *Don't give in to this.*

But it had reached a point where simple things, like going to the shop to get some milk or bread, felt beyond me. Charlotte was also struggling. Several months before, I had met Jim Breen, founder of Cycle Against Suicide, at an event and we had a quick chat about what he was trying to do. I never told him what I was going through or feeling, but a lot of what he said resonated. In the weeks afterwards, he'd been trying to get in touch with me but I never replied. It felt very close to home and I just wasn't in a place to talk or accept that I needed help. Unknowingly to me, Charlotte went back to him and they spoke over the phone.

'How are *you* coping?' he asked.

She broke down in tears.

'It's not good,' she said. 'He's not good, and I don't know what to do.'

When she told me that, years later, I felt so guilty. Everyone was asking her how I was coping with retirement, but no one was asking how *she* was doing. And it was so hard for Charlotte. I wasn't the same person she had fallen in love with. When we got together, she would have had ideas of what our future looked like and there she was, with a volatile wreck for a husband. And as I was going through it, I was too absorbed in my own misery to stop and think how bad it all was for her.

Something had to change. I arranged to meet Enda for a coffee in Donnybrook and I opened up about my situation.

'Enda, I'm done with this job. I'm struggling.' He was eating a muffin at the time and he kept eating it, not knowing what to say. He was unaware, as many were, that I was great at hiding how I truly felt.

There was a guy on the board of his company who soon reached out, telling me he'd struggled with similar issues and he gave me the name of a GP who'd helped him. I went to see that doctor, who ran through various questions. 'You're clearly depressed and suffering with severe anxiety,' he told me, before writing two prescriptions. One was for my skin – I had broken out in psoriasis – and the other was for anti-depressants. Later that day, I went into the pharmacy and started doing laps of it, killing time, weighing up if I wanted to go down the medication route. I decided that I didn't. I went up and only handed in the prescription for the psoriasis cream.

The darkness lingered, like a plume of volcanic ash had enveloped me. Every night, I'd get into bed, exhausted, but I couldn't sleep. I'd worry about money, about Charlotte being pregnant and what sort of state I was in to care for our child. If you don't sleep, you don't recover, so I'd get up feeling worse, then mope around the house, not really doing anything. I avoided all social interactions, not wanting friends or family to ask what I was doing or how I was feeling.

In December 2015, it reached a tipping point. The panic attacks had become more frequent and when another one struck on a Sunday afternoon, I began ranting and raving in the house. Charlotte was heavily pregnant and was in floods of tears as she watched me. The sight of her totally distraught, while carrying our child, forced me to confront a key question.

How am I going to be a father to this baby?

There was only one way I could: I needed help.

It wasn't the first time this had come up, but prior to that I'd been hesitant about it. My mother had been at me for quite a while to go see someone, and in May of that year I'd gone to a sports psychologist for one appointment. I went in, had a chat, and she sent me home with a load of sheets to do 'homework.' Where did they go? Straight in the bin.

But the sight of Charlotte, pregnant and in tears, forced me into a reckoning. I suggested to her that I should go to therapy and she agreed that it'd be a good thing. By then, she knew how to play me. We'd been here before, of course, but maybe then she had been too forthright in telling me to go. So, when I suggested it this time, she understood to just listen, playing a quiet, supportive role without telling me what to do, knowing it would probably only cause me to do the opposite.

We decided I should reach out to someone outside our social circle for a recommendation because everyone in it was too emotionally connected. I started to think about who to turn to, and one man was foremost in my mind.

The previous January, I had been part of a panel discussion around mental health in sport as part of the First Fortnight Festival in Dublin. One of those alongside me was Richie Sadlier, a former international footballer who went on to study psychotherapy. He had also dealt with depression and spoke openly about his struggles, having been forced to retire from football early because of injury.

In that sense, we had a natural kinship. He was a few years older than me, from the same area, and we had gone to the same schools. I'd often seen him in local pubs after his retirement but would never, ever have thought that he was going through what he was. But that was probably how people looked at me then, too.

After the panel discussion, I walked with Richie towards the Ha'penny Bridge and we talked about the transition to life after sport. It was something I often got asked about, but Richie asked different questions to everyone else: more pointed and probing. One of them was, 'Are you sleeping?'

How does he know that I'm not?

But he knew because he had lived it, walking off a cliff's edge when his sporting career ended and into that gaping void. Fast forward to that Sunday afternoon and my latest panic attack, and Richie was the first person I thought of when I decided to seek help.

I sent him a message and he got straight back to me. I asked if he'd be up for a chat.

I had never properly opened up to anyone besides Charlotte, but I knew that had to change. One time, I'd been having a pint with one of my best mates and he knew I was struggling so he tried, cautiously, to broach the topic. 'How's the head?' He was so awkward asking it, and I was so awkward hearing it, that we both swiftly moved on to other topics.

Let's just talk about football.

Richie, however, was so at home talking about mental health and he gave me great advice as we walked around Marlay Park, leaving me with the names of three different therapists.

'You're not gonna feel comfortable with all these people; you have to connect with someone to be able to talk,' he said. 'But try it, and if it doesn't work, try someone else.'

I gave it a go, but didn't feel comfortable with the first therapist, so I decided to try another. The second was based in the city centre and as I rang the buzzer to the practice on Wicklow Street, I started glancing around, wondering if anyone would recognise me. Things have come a long way over the past decade when it comes to mental health conversations in Ireland, but at the time, all I could think of was people spotting me and thinking: *If he's going in there, he must be in a really bad way.*

From the start, I felt at ease around the second counsellor. I was more comfortable in that room, in that chair. There was a connection.

'So, what brought you in here today?' he asked.

'I don't really know.'

Thankfully, these guys are well trained to put you at ease and he carefully steered the conversation along. It wasn't long before I felt relaxed enough to be open and honest. I started by talking about the present, and over the 50 minutes that followed, I got a lot off my chest. I got a bit emotional afterwards, having said things I'd never expressed out loud but which had been knocking around in my mind for many years.

My head felt a little fried as I walked to my car, but I asked myself, *How do I feel?* And the answer was a little better, as if some of the weight had been lifted.

Through talking, I began to make sense of certain things. I started going home and opening up to Charlotte about the highs and lows of athletics, what exactly I struggled with, whereas before I would keep such thoughts bottled up until it would all come out in rage.

I told my mates I was doing counselling and quickly realised that I had vastly overplayed how big of a deal it would be to tell them. Maybe that fear was a product of being an athlete, operating in a world of alpha males where it's about being fitter, faster, stronger and not showing any weakness. I had imagined their reactions being along the lines of, *Fuck, you're that bad?* I thought it would lead to a big debate about mental health but they took it in their stride as we chatted over a pint, with one of them saying, 'Fair play to ya.' They acknowledged it and moved on. It was good, it was normal, and I didn't feel I was looked at any different.

Therapy is a process, just like athletics. If you show up and do the work, then you'll get results. I once asked the counsellor, 'How many sessions do I need? When will I be done?' He smiled. 'If I was an athletics coach and you said to me, "When am I going to run 44 seconds for 400 metres?" How would you expect me to answer? We don't know these things. You keep working, you keep at it. It's a process.'

I did keep working at it through 2016, and it wasn't long before I saw results. As we delved into my past, it was clear

I was a perfectionist. A quick skip back to 2008 showed as much: if I missed a target time in training by a tenth of a second, it would eat away at me for a week.

In the post-athletics world, that was highly destructive. Everything had to be spot on in my life, just as it was in athletics, and I was ruthless with myself if it wasn't. On the track, times were the metric that determined success – a clean, objective measure – and in life I tried to replace that with another measurable, money, thinking if I was earning 80 grand a year then people would see me as a success, that I'd be content.

Having experienced the euphoria of victory on the track, the next phase of my life *had* to be more successful or at least on par. If it wasn't, then I saw myself as a complete failure.

Becoming a dad, I had to accept that I was no longer priority number one, that I now had someone depending on me. I wanted to care for him as well as I could.

Oscar was born on 19 February 2016 and suddenly I had a new focus, which helped everything. Before, I had worried about people's perceptions of what I was doing with my life. One day, I had seen an elderly man cutting his rose bush and all I wanted was to fast forward my life to being seventy or eighty, so I could live like that, without people judging me over what I was achieving.

I felt like I couldn't go for a walk or cut the grass on a midweek afternoon or people might see me as a waster, whereas no one thinks that about a retired person. The elite athlete mentality had been drilled into me for so long that I felt I had to be working towards something. I'd been imprisoned, institutionalised, by my ambition, and that's not a switch you can simply flick off.

'Did you work over the weekend?' my counsellor would ask.

'Yeah.'

'Then why not take a day off during the week?'

It sounds so simple, so obvious, but I had to start realising that doing the mediocre and mundane was OK. Life didn't have to be push, push, push.

When Oscar was born, it was an exciting change, even if it felt a little daunting at the time. I had been in such a bad place that things could only get better, and he was a big reason they did. He was what I started living for.

When Charlotte went back to work, we decided I wouldn't work on Mondays and would stay at home with Oscar, taking him swimming. That was my only focus for the day. I stopped wanting to fast forward my life, stopped worrying so much about people's perceptions.

I started to learn the truth in that old saying: that you wouldn't worry so much about what others think of you if you realised how seldom they do.

CHAPTER 16

THE AFTERMATH

As I sat with my counsellor, peeling back the layers of my past, I came to understand the role running had played in my life, long before I'd ever pulled on an Irish vest.

'Have you thought about getting back into exercise?' he asked.

'No, I hate that.'

But as we talked through it, I realised I had been running since the age of seven, then just abruptly stopped in 2013. When I joined the dots, there had been a clear knock-on effect on how I ate, how I slept and how I felt about myself.

That's where therapy is so impactful, helping you make sense of things: realisations you're much less likely to reach on your own. My relationship with running was a complicated one: up and down, on and off.

It had once been my whole world but, after I retired, I genuinely grew to hate it. I felt obsolete. No one was talking about me as an athlete anymore – the identity that so long defined me – and it was clear that all my self-worth and confidence had come from the sport. I'd put all my eggs in one basket and when that river of confidence I took from training and races just swiftly dried up, it left me with absolutely no idea who I was. The therapist helped me figure that out, teaching me that I wasn't simply defined by what I did.

'What hobbies do you have?' he'd ask. 'What are you interested in?'

Hobbies? I was a runner for the last decade. Why would I waste time on those?

But he stayed on it, trying to coax me in a new direction, asking what areas sparked some interest, which people I looked up to. When I named some, he encouraged me to reach out to them.

Some people are obsessed with networking, but I'm not one of them. I'm always afraid of being a burden and annoying people. But when I started to think about people I admired and who I was comfortable around, it led me back to Seán White.

When I would cross paths with people like him, who operated in the upper echelons of business, I'd always think, *I'm just not on that level.* My CV over the previous decade could be summed up in one line: I ran a lap of the track very fast. But when I was out in the real world, I'd look at people like Seán and think they had it cracked, sussed, that things were easy for them. But when you talk to them, you quickly realise it was always a hustle, *always* a struggle – for *everyone*.

I reached out to a few people I had crossed paths with over the years. I was honest and told them how I was and that I was looking for advice, a bit of mentoring. I was beginning to work for myself, doing more corporate talks, events and working with a few brands.

Seán came back to me a few weeks after our initial chat. 'Where are you? You haven't followed up.' It was the coach mentality I'd been missing for so long, someone holding me to account. I liked that. There was no work involved in what I was doing, it was just having chats with a mentor, but it helped me figure out what I enjoyed, how to start moving forward so I could go somewhere new. *Anywhere.*

For a long time, I'd subconsciously been chasing a sense of achievement, the powerful opioid to which I was addicted. A huge number of professional sportspeople fall into addiction when they retire, whether it's alcohol, drugs, sex or gambling, and I could see why. The thing that stopped me going down a slippery slope like that was that I had to work and find money, ensuring I could be a good father to Oscar. I also had good people around me, as my mates weren't heavy drinkers or into drugs.

But I did get addicted to something else: work. I was unable to say no to jobs, throwing myself into anything that was available, trying to fill the void not just so I could pay the bills, but to feel like I was accomplishing something.

I missed athletics terribly and, to be honest, I still do. That's also something you can't just switch off. I missed the routine, the structure, being in an environment with like-minded people where you're always building towards a championship. I missed the training group, the coach, that feeling of hopping into bed at the end of a long day and knowing you'd done everything you could to get faster. I missed getting up in the morning and having clarity about what I was doing that day. I missed the adrenaline; when you stand behind the blocks and a packed stadium falls silent, you will never feel more alive. I missed the exhilaration when the gun fired, and the power I'd feel as I exploded from the blocks. I missed the fluid rhythm as I'd float down the back straight. I missed that feeling of complete exhaustion that awaited at the finish, knowing I'd pushed my body to its absolute limit. I missed waking up the next day with a personal best or a European medal, knowing it wasn't a dream, that it had actually happened.

No drug in the world could replicate that.

In the summer of 2016, I did an interview with the *Irish Independent* in which I was brutally honest about my journey since retiring from sport and I couldn't believe the number of people who reached out. There were high-profile people in the media, in sport, the kind you'd assume had it all sorted and were coasting along. It struck a chord with so many.

There was one guy of a similar age who played GAA at club level and he told me he didn't realise how much the sport was a part of him until he stopped and was hit by that void, that loneliness. It showed me just how many people struggle with the very same thing and it made me feel better about my situation.

I was far from alone, and there was no shame in going through this.

About four months after my counsellor suggested getting back into exercise, I decided to head along to my local parkrun, a 5K staged every Saturday morning that prides itself on being all about participation, not competition.

I was dreading it beforehand, knowing I'd bump into people I knew. 'David, great to see you!' said the first guy I saw after arriving in Marlay Park, who then told me, 'You should win this.'

As they did the briefing before setting us off, I was introduced as the local Olympian and, sure enough, the competitive ego kicked in: *I better put on a show here.* But I'd never run a 5K in my life, and I wasn't fit. Nonetheless, I took off, hammering the first kilometre before my lack of fitness kicked in. Midway through the run, I heard a strange sound approaching from behind and soon a man ran past, pushing a buggy, with his baby rattling a shaker.

I went to the Olympics and now I'm getting passed by a guy pushing a buggy.

I made it to the finish, huffing and puffing with a big red face, and then went for a coffee with Charlotte to reflect on it. Once I let go of the hit to my ego, I realised I had really enjoyed the experience. I started making it my routine every Saturday.

I had a lot of time on my hands and was enjoying running just for the sake of it, so one day I decided to mix it up and went to the track in Santry, where I bumped into distance runners Maria McCambridge and Gary Crossan. I ended up pacing Maria through her track session, relishing being back on that Tartan surface, where I'd plied my trade for so long. That's what led me to reach out to Dan Kilgallon, a coach for Tallaght Athletics Club who, later on, would guide the careers of the fastest man and woman in Irish history: Israel Olatunde and Rhasidat Adeleke. Dan was a similar age to me, he also had a young family, and he knew what headspace I was in.

'Why don't you just come down to the track and jump in with the lads – they're juniors,' he said. 'We'll just train; who gives a shit?'

And so that's what I did. There was no structure, no programme, but linking in with his teenage crew in Tallaght gave me some routine, something to do. In ways, it was like rehab. Through talking to my counsellor, I began to realise this was something I'd suppressed after hanging up my spikes, trying to deny that running was a fundamental part of who I am.

I didn't run with a watch and I had no plans to race. I was happy to just rekindle my relationship with running. I *wanted* to be an ordinary punter. But after several weeks of that, I started to get into solid shape. I decided to hop into a couple of races at the Leinster Indoor Championships to see if I could break 22 seconds for 200 metres. I ran 22.38 and 21.99. I had bigged it up beforehand, wondering what people would think, whether being seen running such mediocre times would be a cause for pity. But they couldn't have been nicer. 'It's great to see you out there!'

What led me back? I wanted to say goodbye to athletics on my terms, to walk away after a race rather than an injury. But in the back of my head, I knew the 200 metres was the easy option. I had been a professional 400 metres runner and the real challenge was to run that again. If I could toe the line and be willing to run 48 seconds instead of 44, for me that would be a triumph. But part of me worried about going back down that path, wondering if it would reopen old wounds if I got injured, perhaps seeing me spiral back into a depression.

I decided to race a 400 metres where nobody cared who I was, so I picked out a meeting in Pavia, Italy, in early May 2016. It was a low-key meeting, the kind I'd have considered myself above when I was in my prime, but I was a long way past that.

I emailed the meeting director, asking if I could get a lane, explaining who I was and that I'd run 44 seconds once upon a time. 'Sorry,' she wrote back. 'No space available.' I got back to her and told her more of my story, about the injuries, why I was coming back, and it was clear she didn't have a clue who I was. But she obviously went on Google because she soon emailed back: 'Did you win *Celebrity MasterChef*?' After telling her I had, she told me they were putting on a B race over 400 metres and that I could run that.

I paid my own way to Italy, staying in a small hotel with one of the athletes I knew from Loughborough. It was like a return to my youth: lying around, watching terrible TV in a tiny room, talking for hours until it was time to head to the track. I scanned the start lists and the dates of birth of my rivals. I was born in 1983 and was about to turn 33; they were all from the '90s.

I came last in the race, running 48.05, and I couldn't have cared less. I ran up the home straight with a smile on my face, overjoyed at having got through it. As I was getting my breath back, a couple of Italians came over and said, 'It's great to race against you.' That was heartwarming. Because when you retire, it's very easy to think you're instantly forgotten. Forty-eight seconds was a time I'd run when I was in school but here I was, at the other end, doing it again. And I was perfectly OK with that.

The following week, I decided to race again in Belfast and I took a big step forward there, clocking 47.24. Suddenly, the European Championships in Amsterdam became a realistic proposition, given Ireland was sending a team in the men's 4x400m.

Another reason I had come back was because I really wanted Oscar to see me run. He was only a baby, he'd never remember it, but I wanted to have that moment before I waved goodbye to the sport. At the Nationals in Santry in June, the week before my thirty-third birthday, I had it.

The 400 metres final there was essentially a race-off for places on the Irish relay team for the Europeans and I relished being back on the line as the old man of the field, trying to ruffle a few feathers. I finished third, in 46.44, and was selected for Amsterdam in both the individual 400 metres and on the Irish 4x400m team.

If we ran fast enough in the relay, there was a chance of securing Olympic qualification for the Rio Games, meaning my ad-hoc comeback had suddenly started to get serious. RTÉ asked me about going to Rio with their broadcast team but I told them I had run myself into solid shape, that I might actually have a crack at going as a competitor.

The relay in Amsterdam brought another bit of drama. Realistically, the three of us who were picked for the individual 400 metres – Brian Gregan, Craig Lynch and I – didn't have much chance of making the final, and it was pitched to us that maybe we should bypass that and save our legs for the relay, knowing that if we edged ourselves into the top-16 teams in the world, we'd make the Olympics.

I was fully on board, but Kevin Ankrom came back to me and said Gregan wanted to run the individual. He thought Gregan *should* run it, arguing that the race would do him good ahead of the relay. If Lynch or I pulled out, then another squad member, Richard Morrissey, would take our place in the 400 metres. But Thomas Barr was also part of the relay pool and Lynch and I thought, *If we sit it out and if Gregan and Morrissey both run well, where does that leave us?* We decided we should also run the 400 metres. Lynch and I both finished seventh in our heats, while Gregan made the semi-final and finished seventh there. In the relay, we were joined by Barr and we finished fourth in our heat, then fifth in the European final, running 3:04 both times. It left us just shy of qualifying for the Olympics.

We'd given it our best, but it wasn't to be.

Amsterdam was nonetheless a huge thrill. I roomed with Lynch and he was great company all week. He had his daughter over for the championships and it was his first senior international. I could see what it meant to him as we pinned the numbers on our vests the night before the race. I had represented Ireland so many times that, by then, it had all become routine, but seeing Craig's excitement, his pride in that vest, brought me back to what this sport was all about.

Three years later, in September 2019, Craig died in a car accident at the age of just 29. His death rocked Irish athletics to the core, and at his funeral there was a massive turn out for one of the sport's true good guys. I was honoured to be asked, along with his international and club teammates, to form a guard of honour. The colours of Shercock AC mixed with all the Irish tracksuits highlighted how close the Irish athletics community really is.

Seeing his family, and in particular his little girl, brought tears to my eyes – a painful reminder of how precious life truly is.

As I left Amsterdam, the feeling was one of contentment, despite falling short of Olympic qualification. I didn't run great in any of the races, but I had still relished the experience, knowing I'd never get to pull on an Irish vest again. The feeling was slowly starting to come that I was ready to move away from it all.

A few weeks later, I returned to my old stomping ground, the national stadium in Santry, for one last lap at full speed. It was a beautiful summer's evening for the Morton Games, an event which pits many of Ireland's best against a horde of international names. I finished fifth in the 400 metres, running a solid 46.93.

Charlotte was there. So was Oscar, along with some family and friends. I had been going to the Morton Games since I was a kid, but this time felt very different.

Santry looked superb, with the sun setting over the trees in the Demesne and the track starting to glisten under the Friday-night lights. After the race, I walked up the grassy hill that flanks the first bend and sat on the grass there for some time, taking in that familiar scent of a track in high summer, with the memories of countless races flooding back from a quarter-century of racing around it.

The following year, I would enrol in a course in sports psychology in Dún Laoghaire and, during one of my classes, the lecturer put up a slide about the Kübler-Ross cycle of grief. Initially, I didn't see how it correlated to sport but as she described the research around injury and retirement, I started to see exactly how it mirrored what I'd gone through in the previous years: unable to come to terms with what I had lost. Looking back at me sitting on the hill in Santry, it was clear that this was the moment where I had finally arrived at the fifth and final stage: acceptance.

For three years, I had been muddling through denial, anger, bargaining and depression, trying to find that one thing that might fix everything and fill the gaping void. But I had finally come to accept that my career was over, that that was OK, and so was I.

It was time to say a fond farewell to Morton Stadium,

the stage for some of the best days of my career – and some of the happiest moments in my life.

As my mind raced back through them, as if flicking the pages on a photo album, my inner voice started to perk up again. But it struck a very different tone to what I'd become used to. There wasn't panic about the future, regrets about the past. It felt, at last, like I'd untethered that dead weight of anger, allowing it to drift gently out to sea. Instead, the voice posed a rhetorical question.

How fucking lucky was I to get to do all of that?

CHAPTER 17

BEHIND THE LENS

My mum always told me, 'You've got two ears and one mouth – use them in that order.'
These days, I try to remember that when I'm trackside at major championships, trying to coax something more out of athletes than the stock answers I used to give.

During my career, I never thought I'd have a future in the media, but when an opportunity first arose to travel to an event for RTÉ – the 2015 European Indoors in Prague – I jumped at it. I juggled co-commentary and mixed zone work, which led to them asking if I'd go to the European Rowing Championships shortly after. The following year, after falling short of making the Rio Olympics in the relay, I was thrilled that RTÉ were willing to take me along as a reporter.

Athletes often think those in the media have it easy at major championships, but in Rio I got a rude awakening on what life is really like. It was hard work; you're on the whole time, running here, there and everywhere. But it was such a buzz. This was a side to major events I'd never experienced as an athlete, but I got to see and hear all about it as I interviewed coaches, fans, parents, seeing the impact an athlete's performance has on so many others. I did radio work, live co-commentary, piece-to-camera reports from around the venues and the city, without having a clue what I was doing half the time. But that's the best way of learning.

At the Olympics, almost everyone is a bluffer at some point, given it shines a spotlight on so many sports that operate outside the mainstream. One day, when the rowing had been called off, I stood in the Olympic Park talking to Joanne Cantwell live on RTÉ. She asked me how officials had determined that it was unsafe to stage.

'White horses,' I said confidently, even though my rowing knowledge at the time was, shall we say, limited. 'When there's white crests visible on the top of a wave in the lake, that's a sign the winds are too high.'

In my head I thought, *you are some waffler*, but I loved the pressure and adrenaline and having to think on the fly with live TV. It was late nights, early mornings, and when I got home from the Olympics I was wrecked, utterly shattered, but it was so enjoyable that it didn't feel like work.

It sparked something in me: I wanted to do it again and again.

When it comes to post-race interviews, the best advice I got came from Phil Jones, the long-time trackside interviewer for the BBC.

I knew him well, having been interviewed by him many

times during my career, and we were alongside each other in the mixed zone at the 2015 European Indoors in Prague. I was nervous, having never occupied that role before, and asked for advice.

'Don't plan,' he said.

There I was, with all the stats on a notepad, a list of questions written for each athlete, but apparently I'd wasted my time.

'You know the subject,' he said. 'Watch the subject, talk about the subject. It's not about what happened last year or what happens next year, it's the here and now.'

He wasn't suggesting not to do any research, but to avoid going into interviews with anything set in stone; better to watch the race attentively and adjust on the fly depending on what the athlete says. He was spot on.

From an Irish standpoint, Jacqui Hurley was a huge help through my early years on the other side of the camera. Off the back of Rio, we went for a coffee and she said, 'Why don't you pitch RTÉ to do some mojo?' (Mobile journalism.) I put an idea together to go to the World Championships in London the following year. RTÉ didn't have the broadcast rights but I told them I could be in the mixed zone and if anything happened, they'd at least have boots on the ground.

That was Usain Bolt's swansong, fifteen years on from his first global championship in Kingston, where he made that rickety old stadium shake as I stood in the stands, mesmerised by the spectacle.

In London, Bolt had a massive media scrum awaiting

him every time he walked into the mixed zone. If athletes of that stature stopped for every journalist who asked, they'd be there the entire night, so they pick and choose a handful of broadcasters in the first part and when they reach the lower sections – the internet, radio and written press – they'd usually make one or two more stops. The scrum would huddle around, sweaty bodies pressed against each other as we try to get close enough to record them.

Bolt, to my surprise, stopped right in front of me. A few dozen journalists quickly crowded around as I hit record and started chatting. I was delighted with myself, having snagged a great interview with the sport's superstar, then I went back and listened to it, and there was silence. The wire from the phone to my mic hadn't connected properly so it never picked up any audio, and I had nothing to show for it other than a video of one the biggest names in global sport silently moving his lips. I was absolutely raging.

There's success and failure, pride and pain, on both sides of the camera at major championships. In the media, you also have good championships and bad championships, nights when you nail it and nights where it all goes wrong.

In 2019, I went to the World Championships in Doha for RTÉ, the same way I had in London, and it was brilliant. The big story for the Irish was Ciara Mageean reaching the 1500 metres final – the first time in her career she'd done that at global level – and I bagged some great interviews with her. I'd then go into the cubicle of the toilet at the stadium, putting a towel over my head and recording voice-overs to send back to RTÉ. (Yeah, it's not such a glamorous life.) My reports went everywhere on RTÉ outlets and it amplified the impact of Ciara's achievement, making sure the Irish public was aware of it.

Like everyone across Ireland, I was deeply shocked to hear the news that Ciara was diagnosed with cancer. Having interacted with her so many times over the years, I can honestly say she's one of the most open, genuine people you could ever meet.

I always look forward to our conversations because you know, with Ciara, what you get is real. She was also the subject of one of my most embarrassing interviews, one we laughed about many times after.

At the 2018 Europeans in Berlin, she finished fourth in the 1500 metres and seemed OK as we began our post-race interview. But as I learned in my career, it can take several minutes for an all-out effort to wreak its full havoc. Midway through our chat, she stopped to vomit. The camera kept rolling and I asked if she was OK, she said she was grand, and so we continued. Then it happened again, at which point I said, 'We'll go back to the studio.' I felt like an idiot, regretting that I didn't stop the interview and plenty of viewers felt that way too. I beat myself up about it for weeks, and even though I knew Ciara didn't mind, I felt awful.

Post-race, athletes are often vulnerable – physically, mentally, emotionally – and my career was a huge help in developing the cop-on to read how they're feeling. I had far more awful days in the mixed zone than good ones, and I think Irish athletes know and appreciate that I've walked in their shoes. I'm not a pundit who's trying to analyse or critique their performance, I'm a reporter: the medium for them to speak to people at home. I always remind myself: it's *their* opinion that matters, not mine, so my mum's words of advice are always in my mind, to listen far more than I talk.

At times, I get nervous as athletes walk towards me. One of those was at the Paris Olympics when Rhasidat Adeleke finished fourth in the 400 metres. I knew exactly how devastated she'd be and I had a good idea of the scrambled mess of thoughts she'd likely have in her mind.

It was an unorthodox interview set-up. RTÉ's slot was in position forty in Paris but the BBC were in number eighteen, meaning if Rhasidat won a medal, the first interview she'd do would be with the BBC. We couldn't allow that to happen.

Olympic Broadcasting Services (OBS) had a slot beside the BBC and so RTÉ booked that specifically for the 400 metres final, allowing us 90 seconds to catch her when she came by. That position had a mic fixed to the front barrier and I remember looking at it and saying to my producer, 'Rhasidat is really tall, will that pick her up?' I did have a mic in my hand as a back-up, which was a damn good thing because OBS never turned on their mic at all, and it was only because Elaine Buckley of RTÉ pushed my elbow forward during our interview that we picked up any sound at all. The quality was terrible as a result but RTÉ put it out anyway. Meanwhile, I hightailed it back up to position forty before Rhasidat got there, apologising and asking if we could do the interview again. In that moment, she'd have been well within her rights to tell me to get lost, but she was kind enough to do it again, opening up more the second time around.

In situations like that, it always helps to know the athlete: to have built a rapport over many years. Because I know how hard it is to walk off the track, crushed by the result, and how comforting it can be to see a familiar face when you try to put it all into words.

When I returned from Paris, I felt a bit embarrassed to see lots of praise for my work, feeling the reaction was over the top, but I was also proud that I was clearly getting something right in the mixed zone. It was the first championship where I felt very present while talking to the athletes, very relaxed, as if the camera wasn't even there.

When it came to interviews with international athletes, Paris was undoubtedly the highlight of my career. When I was growing up, you'd always have to switch the channel to get interviews with global stars, but in Paris, I decided to get as many A-list names as I could, throwing the mic in front of them and seeing if they'd talk to RTÉ.

Oscar absolutely loves Femke Bol and I was thinking of how many kids like him there were across Ireland who'd love to hear not just from the Irish athletes, but from the sport's superstars. I knew there was a huge audience who'd never normally watch athletics and thought, *Let's see if we can make them fans.* When the men's 100 metres champion, Noah Lyles, said 'the double is alive, baby!' on an RTÉ mic, it was a huge buzz.

I always find Jakob Ingebrigtsen brilliant to talk to. In Paris, he gave me a fantastic interview despite the frustration of finishing fourth in the 1500 metres. A few days later, after he won gold in the 5000 metres, I was caught in another interview when he walked past. By the time I had finished, he'd gone 20 metres by me and was well down the line of broadcasters. So I shouted, 'Jakob! Any chance?' and he walked back up and we had another brilliant chat. His fellow Norwegian Karsten Warholm is another joy to interview; he's always a bit of craic.

Most star names make for decent subjects, though Sydney McLaughlin-Levrone is a struggle. She hardly talked to anyone in Paris and when I interviewed her at the Tokyo Olympics, shortly after she won gold and broke the 400 metres hurdles world record, she barely cracked a smile.

It's rare athletes won't talk to you. Nowadays, most understand that media duties are a key part of their job, their chance to speak to everyone at home. The vast majority are very generous with their time and while some are quieter than others, after a decade of standing behind the lens, I can safely say nobody has really been an arsehole.

What makes my job easier is that athletics, right now, is buoyant among the Irish public. When it comes to recent championships, there's been momentum building through the medals, and a lot of the public are a lot more aware of Ireland's best than they were 10 or 15 years ago, with everyone from taxi drivers to hairdressers more willing to engage and talk about the sport. Social media has also played a big role in building athletes' profiles.

Is athletics in Ireland in a better place than it was 15 years ago? In ways, yes. Athletics Ireland have made improvements, recruited new sponsors, with more money available for athletes today, but there are other areas where nothing much has changed. We're still at a point where our top coaches are, essentially, volunteers. Key services like physio and medical support have greatly improved, the talent pipeline has grown stronger, but I still have concerns around the coaching structures. There are a lot of medals being won, but is that down to the good work being done by Athletics Ireland in various areas, or is it more down to the efforts of volunteer coaches around the country? I think it's more the latter. We still don't have full-time, professional coaches, which leaves us lagging behind other nations in that department.

For me these days, asking questions is still a whole lot easier than answering them. There's one question I still struggle with when it's pitched my way: 'What's your title?'

It pops up every time I give a talk or do a podcast and my honest answer? I don't know. The question of identity is one I've struggled with since finishing my athletics career. I've come to accept that I'm now one of these modern freelancers who has a portfolio of things going on, that I'm doing many things but I am not one, single thing.

And, to me, that's a good thing.

I like that I'm my own boss, that I earn my own money and am not relying on anyone. I like the freedom and variety and the fact it's not the same thing day in, day out, week after week, year after year. There are busy times and quiet times and I've learned to accept those peaks and troughs.

I've been offered certain jobs in recent years and thought long and hard about them, but as my sister said: 'You've got flexibility. There's such a value to that.' She's right. When I'm on, I'm on, and when I'm off, I use that time with the kids.

Oscar's little sister, Olivia, arrived in August 2018 and their younger brother, Louis, came along in March 2021. I want the flexibility to go to a match or a race with them or to bring them out to the field and kick around, not worrying about needing to get back to the laptop.

Oscar does a bit of athletics, though soccer is his big thing, while Olivia did her first official race this year – at the Spraoi Games, a team-based, multi-event programme designed to support children's athletic development in a fun environment. As I signed her up for the Under-8 event, I thought, *Am I now one of those parents?* But she loved it, the natural bounce and spring in her stride a joy to watch. I get nervous watching them compete. Before Oscar did his first Spraoi Games, he had a familiar look on his face: the same one his dad used to have thirty-odd years ago.

I knew exactly what he was feeling and I'd talk him through it. 'The moment the gun goes, the nerves will be gone,' I'd remind him. He can be a chip off the old block, looking left and right on the start line and worrying about his rivals, so I tell him, 'Just imagine there's a brick wall going down the sides of that lane, left and right. All you have to worry about is that lane.' There were many times in my career when I wish I'd followed that advice.

Oscar and Olivia do all sorts: running, throwing, jumping, relays. I'd like them to do well but I suppress my competitive instincts, keeping the focus on enjoyment. I had a professional career in sport, but that doesn't happen for the vast majority so I just want them to participate, to make friends and be active. Hopefully they'll form a lifelong habit, which will serve them in so many ways.

If my kids were good enough to pursue a career in professional sport, I certainly wouldn't push them away from it. My story might not sell it all that well, but it's extremely rewarding, and being able to do a sport as your job is, truly, a privilege. It's taken me many, many years to understand and appreciate that, and if they are ever able to follow my path, then I'd like to think that I have the knowledge and experience to help guide them along the way.

When I look back now on all that my career was – and the handful of things it wasn't – the overwhelming feeling is pride. It took several years to reflect with fondness and let go of the urge to want more, which initially left me with a whole heap of resentment.

That caused me to push athletics away, literally hiding any evidence of my career around the house, not wanting to be reminded. But that's changed these days. My medals are now in Oscar's room, while there's various bits around the walls of our home. I want my kids to see those photos and be inspired to go after their dreams, whatever field they choose.

On my birthday in 2017, nine years on from the Beijing Olympics, Charlotte got me a voucher for a tattoo. 'I want you to go and get the Olympic rings,' she said. I always felt

I didn't deserve them, given how I ran, but by then I'd come around to the idea that that wasn't true. 'You should be really, really proud,' she said. 'There's so many kids that dream of going to the Olympics. You've done that.'

She was right, and sometimes when I catch sight of that tattoo on my left arm, I think, *I have done that*. The one thing I had wanted to do at the end of my career was to look in the mirror and say, *You gave that one hell of a crack*. These days, I can do that. I wanted to win more, of course, but even Olympic champions walk away feeling like that.

Recently, I came across a speech Snoop Dogg had given after receiving his star on the Hollywood Walk of Fame. After thanking various people who helped him achieve what he did, he said, 'Last but not least, I wanna thank me. I wanna thank me for believing in me. I wanna thank me for doing all this hard work. I wanna thank me for having no days off. I wanna thank me for never quitting. I wanna thank me for always being a giver and trying to give more than I receive. I wanna thank me for trying to do more right than wrong. I want to thank me for just being me at all times.'

I loved it.

Some might see it as arrogant or egotistical, but to me that's missing the point. Because through all the struggles before, during and after a career in sport, yes, a huge number of people have to help you, but there also comes a time when you have to help yourself. I'll be forever grateful to the many who helped me, in so many ways, but these days I'm also able to give myself a pat on the back, to say 'well done' for giving it the effort I did.

Did I make mistakes? Of course. Lots of them. But when I look back, I never regret the effort I put in – I gave it my all.

These days, running serves a very different role in my life: it's a source of clarity, my unofficial therapy; a time when I can muddle through my mind and make sense of things. I guess you could now call me a distance runner. I do various races, from 5K to the marathon, and I know I'll never finish up front, but I've accepted that's perfectly alright. As Baz Luhrmann wrote: 'The race is long, and in the end, it's only with yourself.'

People ask if I'd ever do masters races – which are for those who are 35 and older – in the 400 metres. My answer: *Fuck no.*

I've been running that my whole life; now I want something new. My coach, Emmett Dunleavy, keeps me accountable, giving me a plan. There are elements of what I did as a kid and what I did as an elite, a blend of freedom and enjoyment with structure and process. Ultimately, I do it not for rewards or attention, medals or money, but the sheer thrill of pushing myself. Running is a cornerstone of my physical and mental well-being.

When I walked away from athletics for the second time, I didn't make any announcement. Why? Because I only stepped away from the elite side. In that dark period of my life, between 2013 and 2016, I discovered something important: I am, in my heart and soul, a runner.

It's not all I am, as it once was, and it's not all I want to be. But it is a fundamental part of me, one that's been there as long as I can remember, ever since I felt that joy and freedom of floating across the grass on a summer's day in Marlay Park.

Following that feeling, and sticking with it, allowed me to travel the world, from Berlin to Beijing, from Kingston to California, from Rome to Rio. It allowed me to earn a good living, to perform in some of the world's most beautiful stadiums, at some of the world's biggest events.

It also led me to the love of my life, Charlotte, and it's the reason I now have three beautiful kids. Athletics gave me so much, and it still does, far more than it ever took away.

I'll never push it away again. I hope to keep running forever.

Acknowledgements

I'll be honest: I never thought I'd write a biography of my career. Over the last decade, I was asked on numerous occasions, but I always said no – it just didn't feel right. So, why now?

The answer lies in where the sport is today. The recent results, the new wave of talented, articulate athletes, and the way they've lifted athletics into living rooms and pubs across the country has been inspiring. People are talking about the sport I love again – and for that, I'm deeply grateful to our athletes for giving us the headlines, the stories and the spark.

It all started with a random email in late 2024 that gave me butterflies. Did I really want to look back at my career? At first, no. But I followed up on that email from Sarah Liddy at Gill Books. I told her some stories; she laughed and said, 'This is good stuff.' From there, the plan was born.

From the outset, I knew there was only one person I wanted to work with: Cathal Dennehy. Cathal, I owe you so much. Those long weekly – and often daily – sessions were like therapy, peeling back the layers of a career I'd never fully revisited. You turned drafts around so quickly, refining them and always bringing clarity. To my surprise, I came to enjoy the process and even looked forward to it, despite how exhausting it could be. Your professionalism, efficiency and skill are second to none. Thank you for being part of this journey.

ACKNOWLEDGEMENTS

Of course, a book doesn't just appear on shelves. It takes a team. To everyone at Gill Books – thank you for your time, support, honesty and belief in something so personal to me. I'm grateful for the opportunity.

Moments like this make you reflect on just how lucky you are. I've crossed paths with many people – some I clicked with, some I didn't – but each helped shape the road ahead. To where it all started, Dundrum South Dublin Athletics Club – Liz, Eddie, Lucy, and Jim – thank you for believing in me, challenging me and investing your time. That foundation was priceless.

Leaving home for Loughborough was a leap into the unknown, but it became my home for most of my career. I grew as a person and met incredible people, none more important than Nick. Meeting him was a turning point – the stars aligned, belief followed and I'll be forever grateful for his guidance.

To my family – being the youngest of four in a busy household was a gift. Tony, I'll never forget you giving me money from your first pub job. John, I'll always laugh about the mystery of the green moped in the garage. Eileen, watching you win medals inspired me – and yes, I remember the day you kicked me up the garden for hitting you with a ball! Through it all, Mum and Dad were the anchor. You gave us everything we needed, but more importantly, you taught us hard work, dedication and perseverance. If I can raise my kids the way you raised us, I'll be on the right track.

With my own family in Ireland, it was often a lonely road but Keith, Audrey and family, you welcomed me with open arms. From providing support and giving me a warm and wholesome place where I could take refuge from the intense world of athletics, to the much-needed shelter you offered when I was at my lowest ... which we did rename the 'The Wickham Rehabilitation Centre'.

And then there's Charlotte. Writing this book wasn't easy – reliving moments that were sometimes better left in the past. When I told you, 'I'm doing a book', I could see the worry in your eyes. But this isn't just my story – it's ours. While some moments were hard, there were also plenty of good days, reliving the amazing memories we have had over the years. Thank you for your patience, support and willingness to walk back through those years with me.

To Oscar, Olivia, and Louis – only one of you can read this right now, and when I try to share advice, you usually look at me like I've ten heads. But one reason I wrote this book was for you. I hope, someday, you can take something from my experiences. At a time when I felt lost, you gave me purpose. My world revolves around you – walking to school, weekend adventures, family holidays. These are the best days and I want to make the most of them. Remember this: life is never a straight line. Work hard, have goals and never be afraid to ask for help.

Finally, almost 10 years ago I made that call for help. It was by far the most important call I ever made. The person who answered will remain nameless, as that's the way these things go, but without his professional support I'm not sure where I'd be. Thank you!